Argentina and the United States

David M. K. Sheinin

Argentina and the United States: An Alliance Contained

The University of Georgia Press
Athens and London

© 2006 by the University of Georgia Press
Athens, Georgia 30602
All rights reserved

Set in 10/14 Palatino by G&S Typesetters, Inc.
Printed and bound by Maple-Vail
The paper in this book meets the guidelines for
permanence and durability of the Committee on
Production Guidelines for Book Longevity of the
Council on Library Resources.

Printed in the United States of America

10 09 08 07 06 c 5 4 3 2 1
10 09 08 07 06 p 5 4 3 2 1

Library of Congress Cataloging-in-Publication Data

Sheinin, David.
   Argentina and the United States : an alliance
contained / David M. K. Sheinin.
      p.   cm. — (The United States and the Americas)
   Includes bibliographical references and index.
   ISBN-13: 978-0-8203-2808-9 (cloth)
   ISBN-10: 0-8203-2808-1 (cloth)
   ISBN-13: 978-0-8203-2809-6 (pbk.)
   ISBN-10: 0-8203-2809-x (pbk.)
   1. United States—Relations—Argentina.
   2. Argentina—Relations—United States.   I. Title.
II. Series.
   E183.8.A7S53   2006
   327.73082—dc22
                                          2005029969

British Library Cataloging-in-Publication Data available

For Dr. Rose Sheinin

Table of Contents

Acknowledgments

I first read *Banana Wars* as an undergraduate student in Ron Pruessen's cold war America class at the University of Toronto. That book opened my mind to both the field of U.S.–Latin American relations and to the historian's craft. My dog-eared copy is still in a handy spot in my office. It remains a model for my work. Since the publication of *Banana Wars*, Lester Langley has charted a brilliant academic career. When he invited me to write this book, the United States and the Americas series already represented a distinguished collection. I was daunted by the prospect of working with Lester. He more than lived up to my expectations. He has been a dedicated, generous, and intelligent editor of this monograph. His detailed critical comments and good advice have made this a much better book than it might otherwise have been.

I often think of the late Richard V. Salisbury. Rich was a treasured mentor and friend. He taught me about priorities, professional discipline, teaching with verve, and cherishing an academic home. He also taught me how to hit a strong, fade-away overhead volley. I wish he might have seen this book, about which we had many good conversations.

Portions of chapters 2 and 3 are drawn from my earlier study *Searching for Authority: Pan Americanism, Diplomacy and Politics in United States–Argentine Relations, 1910–1930* (New Orleans: University Press of the South, 1998). At times, I use the term *American* to mean *U.S.*

At the National Archives of the United States, the National Archives of Canada, the Public Record Office (Great Britain), the Archivo General de la Nación (Argentina), and the Argentine Foreign Ministry Archive, among some twenty libraries and archives, professional librarians and archivists have contributed enormously to this project. I am especially grateful for the enthusiasm and dedication of Min. Carlos A. Dellepiane, who, for almost twenty years, has done everything possible to facilitate my research in Argentina.

This study was funded in part by grants from the Social Sciences and Humanities Research Council of Canada and Trent University. I thank Nancy Grayson of the University of Georgia Press and Jane M. Curran of Jane M. Curran Editorial Services. At Trent, George MacDougall, David Glassco, Ivana Elbl, Bob Wright, Bryan Palmer, and Joan Sangster have been great friends. I'm fortunate for the lasting support, advice, and friendship of Jeff Lesser, Raanan Rein, Kris Ruggiero, John Bratzel, Tom Leonard, Daniel de Anchorena, Raul García Heras, Sara Fridman, Isaac Traiber, Teresa Traiber, Marc Epprecht, Sandra McGee Deutsch, Joaquin Fermandois, the late Hugh Hamill, Paul B. Goodwin, Pedro Martinez Lillo, María José Henriquez, Jorge Troisi, Bill Hoglund, Rosita Levin, the late Emilio Levin, Ruth Urba, Bjorn Holmgren, and Tom Paterson. This work has benefited from the advice and assistance of Claudio Blanchart, Juan Carlos Areso, Beatriz Gurevich, Estela de Avruj, Roberto Raggi, Rolfi Weinstein, and Raquel Weinstein.

I could not have written this book without the concern, care, and guidance of Dale Graden, Sergio Palma, Liliana de Palma, Jack Shuber, Eleanor Shuber, Carlos Mayo, Dani Fridman, José Luis Rebagliatti, and Marilu Rebagliatti. Carmen Rebagliati, Javier Lafont, and Mariano Lafont have nurtured this project from day one.

I thank Matias Caballero, Joe Sheinin, and Daniela Sheinin. Mica and Gabi Sheinin have picked me up and dusted me off a few times. Mariana Gomez made this book possible in all sorts of ways.

Argentina and the United States

Introduction

In August 1988, Argentine and Bolivian military officers met secretly in Buenos Aires. The occasion was the Fourteenth Bilateral Conference on Military Intelligence. Both countries were under democratic rule. Each had come through violent periods of military dictatorship in the 1970s and early 1980s. Both faced an ongoing threat of military intervention in national affairs. Just over a year earlier, during the 1987 Easter Week uprising, renegade army officers had tried to oust the government of Argentine president Raúl Alfonsín. The coup attempt was crushed by military units loyal to constitutional rule. U.S. president Ronald Reagan had come out immediately in defense of democracy in Argentina and in Latin America, as had editorials in the *New York Times* and the *Washington Post*. Reagan would shun any national military not committed to constitutional rule in the Americas. The United States and Argentina shared a public commitment to democracy. They joined with other governments in the Organization of American States (OAS) in decrying the period of dictatorship that had gripped the region through the early 1980s. Reagan and Alfonsín administration policies promoted the purging of the Argentine armed forces of lingering dictatorship-era hard-liners who continued to defend military rule as a necessary alternative to democracy in the face of a range of ambiguously defined crises.

U.S. and Argentine civil societies reviled dictatorship-era political intervention and state-directed violence in Argentina, Bolivia, and elsewhere in the Americas. In the aftermath of the Easter Week uprising, the Argentine and U.S. governments advanced the notion that the Argentine military was now gripped by an internal struggle pitting forces for a modern professional military against those stuck in a violent past. Most Argentines remained suspicious of that simple bipolarity; they saw their military leaders as too closely linked to the recent dictatorship.

1

Those suspicions proved well founded. The 1988 Bolivian-Argentine military intelligence summit highlighted that the supposed division within the Argentine military between dictatorship-era hard-liners and democracy-era loyalists was uncertain. In discussions with their Bolivian counterparts, senior Argentine officers loyal to Alfonsín drew on the 1960s National Security Doctrine to define Argentine security threats in the 1980s. Developed by the U.S. military during the Vietnam War to explain foreign and domestic threats from international Communism, the National Security Doctrine had proved an inspiration for the senior military officers who staged the March 1976 coup d'état in Argentina and administered the most brutal regime in Argentine history. The military hierarchy that had foiled the 1987 coup attempt continued to define national security threats in a context similar to that which had shaped military strategy a decade earlier. Argentine officers explained to their Bolivian counterparts that Argentina's principal strategic concern remained the "International Communist Movement" directed by the Soviet Union.[1]

Echoing a position that now ran contrary to publicly stated Argentine government policy, Argentine officers declared their backing for apartheid South Africa as "the last bastion" of the West. At the same time, Argentine military officers worked secretly against Argentine government policy in Central America. President Alfonsín had consistently opposed U.S. military intervention in Central America. After his 1980 election, U.S. president Ronald Reagan had cited the Truman Doctrine in a project to roll back the influence of the Soviet Union in different parts of the world. There was no region more important to Reagan than Central America, where Washington took aim at the nascent revolution in Nicaragua and the growing leftist insurgency in El Salvador. U.S. officials worried about a "second Cuba." The U.S. government poured hundreds of millions of dollars in economic and military aid into defeating the El Salvador insurgency, supporting the opposition Contras in Nicaragua, propping up repressive regimes in Guatemala and El Salvador, and launching covert military operations in the region. In 1983, the Contadora group (consisting of diplomats from Panama, Colombia, Mexico, and Venezuela) won the backing of the five Central American governments for a twenty-one-point peace program. Agreed upon goals included democratic institutional reforms, strict limits on Cuban, U.S., and other military advisers in the region, and weapons trade-in programs, among other projects. Cuba backed Contadora and urged Salvadoran insurgents and the Sandinista regime in Nicaragua to support the plan. But Washington, fearing what it called Cuban duplicity and unwilling to cede control of the Central American peace process to a multilateral body that might not be sufficiently hard on cold war enemies, opposed the plan, which withered as a result.

Through the mid-1980s, the Alfonsín administration strongly supported Contadora. Argentine officials took every public diplomatic opportunity to criticize the American military presence in Central America. But in sharp contrast to this position, Argentine intelligence identified Argentina's national interest with U.S. military intervention in Central America—activity that Argentine officers believed was being threatened by Cuban intelligence activity. More important, General Francisco Gassino, who directed the Second Command of the Argentine Armed Forces, blamed the advance of democracy in both Argentina and Central America (a prime Contadora objective) for the revival of "subversion"—a vague dictatorship-period term for an assortment of enemies on the left.[2]

If the Alfonsín government consistently criticized U.S. military activity in Central America, why did the military high command adopt a contrary position? If Argentine government policy was critical of South African racism and supported the economic, political, and cultural isolation of that country, why did senior Argentine military officers lionize the South African regime as a defender of the "West"? Moreover, why did the military continue to evoke National Security Doctrine as a basis for Argentine national security when that doctrine had been repeatedly attacked by Alfonsín administration officials as having contributed to the violence of military rule?

The answer to these questions points to defining features of U.S.-Argentine relations for much of the twentieth century. Often, the sorts of contradictions explored in the questions have emerged in a context of the uneasy transitions to and from military rule. Like the Alfonsín administration, other Argentine governments over much of the past century have come to power under violent circumstances, as an answer to a period of political turmoil or as a result of a nonconstitutional or undemocratic transition of power. As a result, their agendas for governance have tended to stress radical policy reversals and changes. Often, those changes have been transitory and incomplete. On many occasions, they cast Argentina as an antagonist of the United States and American influence in the Americas. Argentine policy was frequently critical of and antagonistic toward the United States. But, on financial, military, and strategic concerns, the history of U.S.-Argentine relations is mostly one of quiet cooperation.

It was not as if Alfonsín did not confront the United States on a number of important issues. A member of the nonaligned movement, Argentina rejected the U.S. justification for its nuclear arms buildup and worked in international fora for superpower weapons reductions. It opposed what it regarded as American complacency on the exponential increase in Argentina's foreign debt. And Alfonsín rejected U.S. nuclear nonproliferation policies that would have curtailed Argentina's freedom to develop an independent atomic program. But as in other periods of U.S.-Argentine relations, bilateral economic, diplomatic, cultural, and military relations remained strong. Areas of conflict were temporary. Or when they proved more lasting, such as bilateral disputes over patent law after 1980, the tensions had little impact on other areas of relations.[3]

This book argues that although frequently punctuated by episodic conflict, the history of U.S.-Argentine relations is one of cooperative interaction based on generally strong and improving commercial and financial ties, shared strategic interests, and strong cultural contacts. This analysis challenges the prevailing scholarly and popular view of U.S.-Argentine hostility from the Age of Jackson in the United States to the Carlos Menem presidency in Argentina and beyond.

The first chapter of this book explains the origins and strengthening of bilateral ties in the nineteenth century. Improved relations came primarily as a product of consistent and expanding economic ties, as well as the tendency of Argentine leaders to see the United States as a model for governance, education, and in other areas. Chapter 2 considers an early, brief period of bilateral conflict. At the First Conference of American States (1889–1890), Argentina countered U.S. efforts to establish Pan-American dominance in the Americas. The conflict was short lived. Between 1890 and 1920, as Argentine interests in Latin America dovetailed increasingly with those of the United States, Argentine leaders came to back American economic and strategic leadership within the nascent Pan-American Union. Shared bilateral economic, ideological, and strategic interests led to cooperation during the First World War and a shared anti-Communist alarm toward the end of the war. Chapter 3 considers the period between the early 1920s and the end of World War II. It reviews the growing U.S. cultural influences in Argentine society, bilateral conflict over the presence of U.S. oil companies in Argentina, endemic foot-and-mouth disease on the *pampas,* economic depression, and growing strategic tensions between the United States and Argentina during the Second World War. Chapter 4 shows ongoing American cultural impact on Argentina in the 1950s. It also documents the rapid rise of U.S.-Argentine nuclear ties, the dramatic reversal of Juan Perón's anti-American rhetoric after 1950, and the emergence of international lending agencies as crucial to bilateral relations. Chapter 5 highlights the shift toward National Security Doctrine as a basis for U.S.-Argentine ties during the 1960s, whereas chapter 6 focuses on the rise in political violence in 1970s Argentina and how the coming of military rule at middecade impacted relations. Chapter 7 charts the rapid influx of American cultural production into Argentina with the collapse of the dictatorship in 1983. Accompanying that influx was the rapid increase in U.S. investment in Argentine technologies and industries that played a major role in the dissemination of American film, music, and television programs. The chapter covers U.S. foreign policy shifts in the 1980s, with an emphasis on Washington's support for democracy in the Americas, the growing problem of the international debt crisis, and the perceived increase in a Communist menace in the Americas. Facing a heightening economic crisis through the course of the decade, the Alfonsín government stressed debt reduction as its foreign policy centerpiece toward Washington. The 1990s represented a triumph for U.S. policy in Argentina. President Carlos Menem saw his government as an ally of Washington in all respects. The epilogue looks forward, past the financial crisis of December 2001 and Argentina's loan default.

1   Trade, Progress, and Nation Building, 1800–1880

Until about 1900, what Argentines and Americans shared was a modest commercial exchange, a relationship limited by distance and differing views of history and nation. At midcentury and beyond, U.S. commercial activity in Argentina, highlighted by the presence of a handful of American railroad entrepreneurs, took ideological, business, and political inspiration from the U.S. expansion west and south, past the Mississippi, into Mexico, and on to the Caribbean basin. Though on a much smaller scale than the advance across the continental United States, American commerce and investment in Argentina can also be tied to the consolidation after 1790 of national political and economic structures and a widespread ideological affirmation of the American Revolution.

While Americans saw their commercial and strategic presence in Argentina as part of a manifest destiny emanating from successful revolution and early nation building, some prominent Argentines saw U.S. success in contrast to what they believed were Argentina's failures to modernize effectively through the 1850s. For some Argentines, the United States had begun to emerge as a representation of what might have been—and what still might be. During the nineteenth century, relations between Argentina and the United States were shaped by two related phenomena—expanding bilateral commerce and contrasting national structures of economic growth and political development. Particularly after 1850, Americans and some Argentines came to equate the United States with progress and Argentina with stagnant agrarian capitalism, dominated by lethargic large landowners. Both the United States and Argentina experienced burgeoning capitalist expansion that produced conditions for rapidly advancing bilateral exchange. But this expansion also brought bilateral commercial tensions. As early as the

7

1860s, American produce competed with some key Argentine agricultural exports in U.S. markets, creating a protectionist political climate in Washington that would continue to prove a sore point in generally good relations during much of the twentieth century.

Independence North and South

Argentine and American independence struggles were distinct. In Argentina, the independence wars—led first from Buenos Aires (1810) and then the Congress of Tucumán in the interior (1816)—produced a more uncertain, less cogent national project than the Revolutionary War in the United States, where military triumph led to a central authority that was strong relative to its Argentine equivalent. In Argentina, General José de San Martín's military victories prompted armed uprisings in Uruguay, Paraguay, and a number of Argentine provinces that produced a fractured polity in the decades before 1860.[1]

In spite of this difference, similarities exist in the two independence movements. In their late-eighteenth- and early-nineteenth-century struggles for independence from colonial rule, revolutionary leaders in both the North American colonies and the viceroyalty of La Plata gave priority to a foreign trade free of colonial strictures. Each stressed the legal protection of property and the political control of commercial profits as central to nation building. In the early years of both the United States and Buenos Aires province, government income from foreign commerce was a vital source of revenue and, in the case of Buenos Aires, a primary reason for its autonomy through midcentury from less wealthy provinces in the interior.[2]

The Argentine and U.S. independence movements were both supported by local capitalists hoping to break colonial rule to expand regional and international markets. The 1765 Stamp Act crisis in British North America, for example, was one of many steps toward revolution that highlighted breaking free of British commercial dominance in the first instance; it also addressed larger political and social questions around democracy, the power of the assemblies, and their control over taxation. In Buenos Aires, at roughly the same time, an expanding merchant elite with unstoppable illicit ties to foreign traders pressured Spain to liberalize colonial commercial rules—and to overlook ongoing breaches in those regulations. Not surprisingly, in both Argentina and the United States, merchant elites that had fought hard for freedom from colonial rule quickly emerged in positions of political strength in the new republics.[3]

The first trade between the American colonies and Spain's River Plate viceroyalty reflected political and economic ferment in both regions. Dynamic New England merchant houses that helped spearhead the revolution were among those whose ships reached Buenos Aires and Montevideo in the late 1700s. As early as the 1770s, New England whalers sailed off the coast of Argentina and established base camps on the Falkland/Malvinas Islands. The creation of the viceroyalty of La Plata in 1776 reconfigured exports; silver mined from Peru would now be sent through Buenos Aires and Montevideo, a shift that would prompt the growing exchange of raw materials and coins for American-made goods. When the Crown established new settlements on the coast of Patagonia in 1778, Spain warned that officials would have to be alert to the danger of British incursions, but also to the threat of occupation from the "insurgent colonies" in North America.[4]

In 1785, the viceroy of La Plata remarked on the presence of a number of "Bostonian" vessels off the Argentine shore. Although described as "whaling ships" by their owners, the viceroy believed that these and other American craft were trading illicitly at Buenos Aires and Montevideo. After 1797, faced with Atlantic trade route disruptions brought on by the Napoleonic Wars, Buenos Aires merchants sought permission from the Crown to recognize what they had been practicing illegally— trade outside the Spanish empire. Spain responded by granting permission for neutral vessels to trade at Buenos Aires, and as early as 1798, U.S. trading ships reached the ports of Montevideo and Buenos Aires under provisions of the Spanish neutrality decree. In the early years of the nineteenth century, as north-south trade grew, Buenos Aires merchants forged strong associations with their counterparts in New York, Philadelphia, Providence, and Boston.[5]

By 1800, U.S. merchants were increasingly intermediaries in the trade of other nations' goods with Argentina. They were also active in the slave trade with Buenos Aires, in the legal and illegal introduction of dozens of products, and in supplying ships. The Buenos Aires merchant Tomás Antonio Rivero was among many Argentine traders who relied heavily on his U.S. counterparts; in 1800, at least three ships purchased in Boston and Providence reached Argentina in Rivero's name. A typical U.S. cargo to Buenos Aires might include slaves, rum, cognac, Baltimore and Philadelphia flours, wine, furniture, fabrics, elements for navigation and drawing, saddles, horseshoes, and carriages—all goods that marked the ranging economic prosperity of the United States in the aftermath of revolution.[6]

Between 1798 and 1810, some 125 U.S. ships docked in Montevideo and Buenos Aires. In 1801 and 1802 alone, 43 American vessels operated in the Río de la Plata. In 1805, of the 22 U.S. ships that arrived in Montevideo, 11 traded in slaves. The emerging merchant class in Buenos Aires contributed significantly to regional economic growth during the early nineteenth century—more so than domestic traders in most other Latin American ports. In Buenos Aires and other parts of Latin America, foreign merchants from Great Britain, the United States, and elsewhere provided overseas trade contacts essential to the economies of nascent states.[7]

By 1835, U.S. exports to Argentina exceeded five hundred thousand dollars annually. This marked barely one-third of the equivalent trade between the Río de la Plata region and Great Britain (a trade disparity that would become still greater later in the century). But the rise in U.S.-Argentine commerce represented significant growth in light of the disruptive impact of international warfare. Though British traders would outpace their U.S. counterparts through the century, the ongoing presence of U.S. merchants in the South Atlantic had rendered commerce the prime bilateral policy concern for both Argentine and American leaders.[8]

The Argentine independence struggle had drawn directly and indirectly on trade with the United States. Beginning in 1811, despite sympathy for the insurgent cause in American society, the United States had adopted a policy of neutrality toward Latin American independence struggles. For all intents and purposes, though, neutrality was a sham. U.S. merchants continued to supply Buenos Aires and other Latin American ports with crucial products. Latin American ships were repaired at New Orleans, Philadelphia, and other American ports. Rebel trade with the United States helped undermine Spanish economic and administrative dominance in the Río de la Plata region. In 1811, the rebel government in Buenos Aires sent agents Diego de Saavedra and Juan de Aguirre to the United States to purchase arms. Received by both President James Madison and Secretary of State James Monroe, the Argentines bought 1,000 each of muskets and bayonets, as well as 363,050 flints.[9]

Trade complemented and helped initiate other forms of early U.S.-Argentine contact. Leaders of both insurrectionary movements tried to export their respective revolution. The first attempt to export the American Revolution (to Canada in 1775) was a failure.[10] Even so, the writings and ideas of Thomas Jefferson, James Madison, and other revolutionary-era thinkers reached the Río de la Plata through North American sailors, artisans, whalers, and merchants who visited or settled in Buenos Aires. By 1804, some 29 of the 475 foreigners living in the port city were from the United States. Some leaders of the Argentine insurgency remarked on their indebtedness to the ideals of the American Revolution. Manuel Belgrano cited Washington's Farewell Address as a source of inspiration. Articles by Benjamin Franklin were published in Buenos Aires in 1803 and 1804. On 29 March 1812, the first issue of the newspaper *Mártir o Libre*, edited by Bernardo de Monteagudo, transcribed an article from the *New England Palladium* (20 September 1811) reporting that Americans were watching the independence struggle in South America and wishing Spanish Americans well.[11]

Despite these and other references in elite and popular circles to the American Revolution, and even though Argentine foreign trade had clearly benefited from the American economic break with its metropolis, the U.S. independence struggle was not a major source of encouragement or incitement for Argentine insurgents. Some leaders of the Argentine independence struggle shared the concerns of the American founding fathers that too much democracy might be dangerous. Many Argentines took this concern much further than did the Americans; Argentine politicians decided early that there would be far more severe limits on popular rule than in the United States. General José de San Martín was among Argentine revolutionary leaders who found the U.S. model for republican rule too democratic and, as such, unworkable. Moreover, there was no equivalent among Argentine independence movement leaders to the strong Radical Whig assumptions that an informed citizenry was essential to the revolutionary cause and a strong republic. The strong aversion to dictatorship among Americans at the time of the Revolution and the widespread American mistrust of military leaders as civilian authorities were also absent in Argentina. Where political and social disorder continued past independence in both countries, the responses of government authorities in each was dramatically different.[12]

Order and Disorder

In the first generation after Argentine independence, the *caudillo*, or dictator, Juan Manuel Rosas consolidated his authority in Buenos Aires province by drawing on his strength and popularity among rural workers; he depended on the backing of the *gauchos*, or Argentine cowboys and ranch hands—a notoriously unruly worker group that was difficult to control. Moreover, Rosas drew strength from the alliances and agreements he negotiated, sometimes personally, with native peoples on the Buenos Aires *pampas*. In the late eighteenth century, Rosas's father had agreed to treaties with native leaders that had allowed the advance southward of Creole settlement in Buenos Aires but had also permitted natives access to trade with nonnatives and to their markets. This helped integrate aboriginal peoples into Buenos Aires frontier life in a manner that conceded their endurance as first nations far longer than was accepted over much of the quickly expanding American frontier. During the independence wars, perpetual warfare took place against native bands on the plains as Creoles drove further south. After a campaign against indigenous peoples between 1825 and 1828, Rosas led peace negotiations that reversed earlier native gains; now plains bands were denied access to nonnative markets as they had been before León Rosas's accords. But Juan Manuel Rosas did not eliminate native power. Beginning in 1833, he forged his national political authority in part on alliances with band chiefs whose loyalties were tied to government annuity payments as a component of newly negotiated peace settlements. Their political loyalties were often to Rosas alone and specifically tied to his political rise.[13]

In the United States, disorder was repressed more decisively as part of early nation building, and in a manner that confirmed the strength of the new central government as well as the mythology of the Revolution. At the time of the Whiskey Rebellion in 1794, for example, the U.S. federal government put down rebels emphatically, setting an example for others who might challenge the authority of central rule. There was no equivalent suppression of regional muscle flexing in Argentina, where, before 1850, local uprisings meant virtually constant civil war. At the same time, fewer Americans than Argentines benefited from disorder. In the United States, state constitutions were far more open to popular pressures than Argentine provincial polities; most states boasted democratic political structures pressed for by popular rural constituencies that included manhood suffrage, the secret ballot, regular elections, and unicameral assemblies. Argentina saw nothing equivalent in the nineteenth century.[14]

For the United States, order fostered a level of early government promotion of economic development that had no complement in Argentina. The historian Jeremy Adelman argues that Argentine merchant elites wanted what their U.S. equivalents also sought before 1840—the primacy of property rights in the judicial system. But where in Argentina political disorder contributed to the authority of the Buenos Aires merchants and the property rights they defended, in the United States the state moved quickly in the early nineteenth century to guarantee property rights, enforce contracts, and provide judicial, transportation, and financial infrastructures. Here the Jeffersonian vision, backed by rural farmers, of a small and thrifty federal government succumbed to the pressures of merchants, land speculators, and early industrialists. Before 1834, government contributed $41.2 million of the $58.6 million spent on canals; in the decade that followed, public agencies contributed an additional $57.3 million of $72.2 million spent— figures without an Argentine reference point. At the same time, judges subordinated juries by declaring an increasing number of legal points to be matters of law. A body more likely to decide against the interests of an encroaching entrepreneur than a judge, the jury became less a corps charged with interpreting the law than one designated by a judge to weigh evidence in contradictory testimonies and to assess damages. Provisions in British common law changed to favor merchants and industrialists. A long series of verdicts protected business owners from lawsuits filed for damages by neighboring property owners and extended eminent domain—where state governments might seize private property in the interests of economic development—to include land for canals, turnpikes, and railroads.[15]

Commercial Expansion

While U.S. and Argentine polities evolved distinctly during the independence and early national periods, both underwent steady economic growth that formed the basis for trade and for related diplomatic ties. Between 1820 and 1830, cotton goods became a key U.S. export to Argentina and other Latin American states. American officials quickly came to regard the River Plate trade as an important source of badly needed specie at a time of severe foreign indebtedness for the United States.[16] In October 1820, John M. Forbes was named U.S. special representative in Buenos Aires. His principal mission through the end of his stay in 1831 reflected an emphasis on trade in U.S. policy toward Argentina. The secretary of state asked him to report on political conditions, to oppose privileged commercial status for any foreign power, and to challenge privateering by ships under the Buenos Aires flag.[17]

In 1823, the United States recognized the United Provinces of La Plata (as Argentina was first called) and other newly formed states in the region. Recognition was followed later that year by what would become known as the Monroe Doctrine, expressed in President James Monroe's annual message to Congress. Argentine political leaders believed that Monroe's enjoinder against future European colonial expansions in the Americas would contribute to the security of their nation against foreign incursions. In August 1826, Argentine president Bernadino Rivadavia met with Forbes to put the new policy to the test. Rivadavia asked whether the United States would protect Argentina in the event of a Portuguese-backed Brazilian attack on Buenos Aires. There was no response.[18] Rivadavia asked again in 1828. Secretary of State Henry Clay disappointed the Argentines. He insisted that strict U.S. neutrality be maintained. On the other hand, the United States sought an inter-American accord that would favor commercial privileges for the United States while excluding Britain and other European powers. Clay hoped to garner commercial opportunity by gaining Latin American support for the U.S. positions on neutral trade rights and port blockades.[19]

Argentine disappointments over the American reluctance to implement the Monroe Doctrine extended to competition over the Falklands/Malvinas. In 1831, the Buenos Aires–appointed military governor of the Falklands/Malvinas, Louis Vernet, seized by force three U.S. vessels fishing in the islands' vicinity. In subsequent negotiations for the release of the vessels, the Andrew Jackson administration characterized Vernet as a pirate. When the British seized the islands in the 1830s, Argentines called unsuccessfully on the Americans to expel the British occupiers. In 1839 and again in 1884, Argentina sought U.S. intervention against the British presence on the islands. On both occasions and subsequently, the Americans left Argentine overtures unanswered. The Monroe Doctrine had not been intended to redress Latin American grievances. Argentine irritation over American refusals to invoke the Monroe Doctrine lasted well into the twentieth century.[20] Despite this position, the United States was willing to confront Brazil and other countries over trade interruptions. Maintaining open trade routes became a centerpiece of U.S. policy in the region. In 1845, for example, American officials called for open trade during a disruptive Argentine blockade of Montevideo and a joint British-French blockade of Buenos

Aires. U.S. policy focused on competition with European powers for commercial advantage.[21]

The inability and unwillingness of the United States to exercise much influence over blockades in the Río de la Plata is best explained by the comparatively low levels of U.S. trade with South America through midcentury. Despite trade-oriented U.S. policies, annual levels of Argentine commerce with the United States remained low by comparison with British-Argentine exchange. Between 1841 and 1850, the United States sold goods worth less than four hundred thousand dollars annually to Argentina. By the 1860s and 1870s, however, American annual exports reached almost two million dollars.[22]

Many factors contributed to the increase in U.S.–South American trade after 1850 and to the emergence of the United States as a strong commercial competitor in Latin America. Beginning in the 1840s, expansionist sentiment in the United States, tied to overseas business interests, led to quickened settlement in the American West, war with Mexico, and renewed interest in Asian markets. More than any other single act, Commodore Matthew C. Perry's "opening" of Japan in 1853 wedded growing U.S. naval influence with political notions of empire and opportunity for commercial exports.

In Argentina, conditions became more conducive to North American trade. Estancia, or large estate capitalism, grew during the period of Rosas's rule and created local, national, and international markets for Argentine goods. The high profitability and efficiency of the large estates at midcentury drove an expanding bilateral commerce in which the trade balance favored Argentina for the latter half of the century. Between 1830 and 1870 the main item exported from Buenos Aires to the United States was hides. Wool exports to the United States began in the late 1830s, maintaining a relatively constant value between 1840 and the American Civil War. The war prompted a sharp increase in the demand for Argentine wool, which persisted through the end of the century.[23] Though these ventures were less dramatic than the opening of Japan in 1854, U.S. naval mapping expeditions uncovered the potential for railway building and other trade-related enterprises in Argentina, Chile, and Brazil.

Although centralized rule and the political boundaries of modern Argentina would not be finalized until the 1860s and 1870s, as early as 1852 Argentine leaders took important steps to reverse decades of instability and related impediments to foreign ties. The Entre Rios *caudillo* Justo José de Urquiza helped end the almost constant warfare and commercial competition that, since independence, had pitted Buenos Aires province against alliances of other provinces. Urquiza oversaw the promulgation of a new constitution in 1853 that included a bill of rights and other political structures modeled on those in the United States. Though not implemented for a decade, the constitution provided for an elected president and a two-tiered Congress. It mandated Congress to undertake economic programs and find foreign financing for these works. Even though the nation Urquiza governed—the Argentine Confederation—did not speak for the port and province of Buenos Aires, it successfully negotiated two agreements with the United States. The Treaty for the Free Navigation of the Rivers Paraná and Uruguay (10 July 1853) and the Treaty of Friendship, Navigation, and Commerce (27 July 1853) corresponded with Urquiza's determination to expand Río de la Plata trade and end the era of naval blockades.[24]

Alberdi, Sarmiento, and the Ideal of American Civilization

The constitution served as a basis for the geographical consolidation of the nation in the decade that followed and was inspired in part by political leader Juan Bautista Alberdi's writings on linkages between immigration and modernization in the United States. Breaking with Rosas's model of dictatorial order in government, the constitution stressed the protection of individual liberties, particularly for those interested in immigrating to work in Argentina. The constitution was also meant to promote the building of a civil society that would allow people to work, educate themselves, and move freely across the national territory. For Alberdi, Argentina lacked what Americans regarded as a "citizenry." Moreover, immigration would be essential to establishing a nation. If Alberdi can be seen as the architect of nation building through immigration in a U.S. model, then Domingo F. Sarmiento can be thought of as the leader who acted on the idea, particularly during his presidency from 1868 to 1874. Both men wanted Anglo-Saxons to come to Argentina and, with an eye on the United States, envisioned a society of small independent farmers. Far more so than in the United States, Argentine leaders tried to remake their nation through European immigration.[25]

The 1853 constitution emphasized individual material well-being. Alberdi believed—and the constitution confirmed—that the leadership of the nation should be concerned in the first instance with economic development. The country's moral, cultural, and institutional structures would unfold as an adjunct to its economic mission. U.S. political and economic progress in the nineteenth century inspired state-sponsored, nonsectarian public schools, specifically as a means of attracting northern European immigrants. Alberdi conceived of a republican structure that would maintain class structures and a strong centralized state as an antidote to too much popular democracy. Sarmiento's 1847 visits to Europe and the United States infused him with a more favorable attitude toward popular democracy that included a conception of public schooling as an engine for democracy. In 1856, at the time the Buenos Aires legislature was debating what to do with public lands, Sarmiento proposed the dismantling of what he thought was a backward system of large landholding by following a U.S. lead. Agricultural zones would be brought into production with new settlements and markets nearby. Settlers would be sought from among northern European immigrants because they would be able to change the *pampas* into farmland.[26]

This vision proved a pipe dream. But both the constitution and the Treaty of Friendship helped promote U.S. investment and commerce, as did the capitalism boom in ranching that may well have been undercut by Sarmiento's land settlement project. The latter guaranteed conditional most-favored-nation status for the United States in diplomacy, commerce, and navigation—privileges that had already been won by Britain and France. U.S.-Argentine relations were transformed. In 1856,

U.S. shipments to Argentina were valued at one million dollars for the first time. Although without the urgency of American interest in the Caribbean basin, the U.S. government initiated policies to support the expansion of trade with Argentina. The State Department appointed a commercial agent at Rosario in 1858. In 1872, a bilateral postal accord was negotiated. The two governments pursued plans for improved telegraph communications and increased shipping. In the mid-1880s, following earlier congressional inquiries into trade in Mexico and Central America, a congressional committee identified the need for U.S. attention to a variety of problems in U.S.-Argentine trade including modified banking regulations and competition with Great Britain.[27]

After 1850, U.S. traders, railroad builders, and other entrepreneurs reached Argentina in growing, if still limited, numbers. The political and economic opening that allowed for that presence owed much to the debate primed after 1840 by Alberdi and Sarmiento on what direction national development should take. Alberdi and Sarmiento focused on and were shaped by what they saw as the keys to U.S. progress—links between egalitarian democracy, civic values, and strong economic growth in many sectors. The postrevolutionary exemplar of an American nation built on yeoman farmers, not a landed agricultural gentry, on democratic government structures, not rigid class hierarchies, and on the rule of law, not power politics, was in large part an ideological construction of Thomas Jefferson and other early U.S. leaders. Even so, there had been no Argentine equivalent to "American subsistence culture's explosive expansion" before 1810, integrating tens of new local markets, the quick movement of Americans through farming regions in the east, and the boom in the family farm. Moreover, no Argentine development paralleled the post-1815 U.S. boom, where economic growth spread south and west from major ports, depending in part on government-fostered transportation systems and an accelerating division of labor over the frontier.[28]

Both before and during his presidency, Sarmiento fostered railroad expansion as a key to frontier conquest and a means to expand the economy on a U.S. prototype. He also celebrated the U.S. model of public school education as a motor for civilization. But with the rapid expansion of the Argentine agricultural economy in the 1870s and 1880s, Sarmiento's vision of an Argentine political culture that followed a U.S. lead became more elusive. There were historical similarities between the two nations. Just as the United States closed its frontier with dramatic wars against native peoples and a technological explosion in transportation, so too did Argentina lead a successful conquest of indigenous bands and create a network of railroads that promoted economic growth. But unlike in the United States, Argentine political and economic strength remained concentrated largely in one region and one economic sector, the landowning elites of Buenos Aires province, with political authority exercised through the new national capital of Buenos Aires. While small farmers emerged in some parts of the country, there was no pattern of immigrant farmers assuming a strong political stake and influence in the nation. There were no Argentine equivalents to Chicago, St. Louis, San Francisco, or other great western cities emerging in a context of economic expansion and immigration west and contributing to an ongoing regionalization of economic and political power.[29]

In their zeal for the U.S. example of capitalism and democracy, Alberdi and Sarmiento missed three vital points. First, what Americans celebrated was more complex than what the Argentines imagined as an equation that tied together education, civic virtue, democracy, immigration, and economic growth. Poverty persisted in a nation whose ideal of progress did not include want. The nation of small farmers envisioned by Thomas Jefferson materialized only in part and without displacing landed and other elites. Democracy remained incomplete and, in some circumstances, very limited. Second, the American ideals of nation building were scarcely viable in Argentina in the absence of a broad range of historical conditions that had made them possible in the United States. One such factor was the growth and improvement in living standards in many cities and regions of the United States between 1800 and 1860. In Argentina, although people lived relatively comfortably in the littoral areas touched by expanding national and international commerce in the late eighteenth and early nineteenth centuries, living standards remained unchanged in most of the Argentine provinces through the early part of the twentieth century.[30] Culturally, politically, and economically, the interior was apart from Buenos Aires and outside the modernizing imaginations of Alberdi, Sarmiento, and others. Third, and most important, like some historians of Argentina who came later, Sarmiento in particular equated one model with growth, the other with backwardness. This was simply not the case.

Argentines shared more with Americans on the place of frontier in nation building than Alberdi or Sarmiento accepted; moreover, both men missed where the two nations differed. In both the United States and Argentina, the frontier played a key ideological, economic, and political role in shaping national development. But like nation building more broadly, the civilizing role of nonindigenous societies was more ambiguous in nineteenth-century Argentina than in the United States. Americans had incorporated a civilizing mission into their ideologies of nation building. Wilderness and native peoples were equated. The tendency of native peoples to avoid a conquest of nature contributed to what nonnative Americans believed was their barbarism. In Argentina, the protracted nineteenth-century wars that juxtaposed city versus rural areas muddied the position of native peoples in the Argentine imagination. Rosas was among a number of Argentine *caudillos* who structured their political power after 1820 around tacit alliances with native peoples. By 1830, the U.S. frontier as a source of violent conflict with native peoples was far from major urban centers, which allowed for the evolution of a renewal myth. In Argentina, wars against native bands continued through the 1860s only miles from the city of Buenos Aires, making the creation of such myths less safe and less probable. Moreover, Argentines never developed a historical memory or set of mythologies that clearly juxtaposed white cowboys against "savage" indigenous peoples. Through the twentieth century, urban middle-class Argentines viewed the *gaucho* as Sarmiento had seen him—as suspiciously close to aboriginal peoples, as barbaric.[31]

Sarmiento's hostility toward the *gauchos* as a barbaric representation in Argentine culture underlines both similarities and differences in Argentina and the United States. Cowboys were far less important to U.S. nation building than were *gauchos* to the Argentine political economy. In both countries, romantic myths developed celebrating the cowboy/*gaucho* as embodying a pure essence of liberty and nation (despite the fact that in Argentina this was tempered by suspicion). And in both countries, mythologies contrasted with a reality where ranch workers were badly paid, often overworked, and without the civic freedoms enshrined in legend. But in Argentina, popular imagery of the *gaucho* came after Sarmiento's denunciation of the ranch worker as a core element in Argentine barbarism; Rosas's dictatorship had found political backing and ideological underpinnings in *gaucho* political culture. Moreover, the importance of *estancia* capitalism in Argentina was such that as workers, *gauchos* were at the core of Argentine nation building. In the United States, despite a high degree of racial mixing on the frontier, where perhaps as many as 20 percent of cowboys were of African or Hispanic descent, a lore developed of cowboys as a racial wedge against native peoples. In Argentina, even among those who celebrated the myth of the *gaucho*, no racial counterpoint to native peoples infused the image of the Argentine cowboy.

Sarmiento strongly supported what he understood as a Protestant work ethic in the United States and the associated American notion that public primary education held an important key to modernization. Public schools marked a vision for an ordered and progressive society facing threats of social and economic unrest. Sarmiento's policy on native peoples also reflected U.S. actions. He was influenced during his first visit to the United States in 1847 by the intellectual and political linkages between the Indian Removal Act (1830) and ideas of civilization and progress. Much later, as president, Sarmiento sent delegations from his Army and Navy Department to the United States to meet with officers of the federal Indian Bureau and seek advice on civilizing aboriginal Argentines. His ideas on the purported biological inferiority of native peoples derived from American thinking on the same theme. They led to Sarmiento's conclusion that the U.S. westward expansion was the inevitable result of people exercising the right of free movement and that indigenous survival would be impossible in the face of that movement. In 1876, General Julio A. Roca, who would ultimately lead the Conquest of the Desert against Plains Indians, publicly cited

Sidney Johnson's campaign against Rocky Mountain native bands in 1857, ordered by President James Buchanan, as a basis for his argument for an all-out war against Argentine native peoples. Sarmiento had opened a debate in Argentina after 1850 on aboriginal removal, a possible war of conquest, problems of civilization, and education as a tool for democratic good.[32]

To be sure, while Alberdi and Sarmiento concentrated on differences between Argentina and the United States, most Argentine *estancieros*, who dominated the economic life of the nation, paid scant attention to the U.S. political and economic trajectory. For the landowning elites of Buenos Aires province and other sections of the Argentine *pampa humeda* (humid plains), the U.S. model not only held little interest but also served as a contrast to what they wanted for Argentine development. By midcentury, Argentine *estancieros* and other capitalists had built an already burgeoning export-driven capitalism in the Argentine littoral that depended on their dominance of a distinctly undemocratic government and judicial system, as well as their ongoing control of large tracts of the best agricultural land. They wanted none of the U.S. models or Jeffersonian ideals that they believed would undermine their economic success.

That Sarmiento in particular failed to bring American-style growth and political change to Argentina during his presidency underlined not the weakness of the Argentine polity, as Sarmiento himself believed, but the strength of Argentine *estancia*-driven capitalism as a competitor to and trading partner with the United States. Sarmiento could not claim to have engineered a radical transformation of Argentine society toward a U.S. model for growth and development. But his vision and that of Alberdi led directly to the arrival of U.S. railroad entrepreneurs after 1850. Their arrival complemented both the pro-American development sentiment of Sarmiento and Alberdi and the economic necessities produced by expanding commercial agriculture under the direction of *estancieros* who did not share Sarmiento's enthusiasm for the United States. In his final message to Congress as president, Sarmiento commented on his achievements, which included an influx of eighty thousand immigrants in 1873 (compared to only thirty-nine thousand in 1868), a vast increase in the amount of mail handled (from four million items in 1868 to seven million in 1873), and a jump in public school education (from one thousand children in 1868 to four thousand in 1873). As important, by 1873, railroads traversed Argentina's agricultural zone, and expansion was ongoing.[33]

If expanding agriculture and ranching had provided the economic opening for U.S. railway building in Argentina, Alberdi and Sarmiento had established the cultural and ideological openings for U.S. entrepreneurs. At the same time, American expansion west had defined a fifteen-hundred-mile boundary along the Pacific coast at midcentury, and Americans had initiated the first thorough regional land surveys of the trans-Mississippi West. As Sarmiento and Alberdi were thinking through the ingredients for U.S. stability and progress as they might be applied to Argentina, the U.S. Congress turned its attention south, commissioning a series of expeditions to survey South America. Americans looked far south, to the temperate regions of South America, for some of the same reasons they looked west; they considered Argentina, southern Brazil, and Chile as potentially progressive zones that might be both investment and trade markets.

Distinct from the Caribbean basin region—straining, in the American imagination, under the weight of nonwhite populations—the far south of South America presented geography not unlike the American West. While the U.S. Army had led the exploration of the trans-Mississippi West, the U.S. Navy sent surveying parties to South America. The Herndon-Gibbon mission surveyed the Amazon basin in 1851–52. The Page mission explored the Plata-Paraná-Paraguay river systems from 1853 to 1855 and in 1859–60. And from 1850 to 1854, Lieutenant James M. Gilliss and Lieutenant Archibald MacRae went overland to map the interior of Chile and Argentina, looking for potential trans-Andean railroad routes. In the United States, the South American survey expeditions followed from Jefferson's ideas on inland expansion and the consolidation of the republic; after the Louisiana Purchase in 1803 extending U.S. control to include the Mississippi, commercial traffic to the far south became a logical extension of the move west. In Argentina, the surveys were a welcome expansion of ties to the United

States for those like Alberdi who associated North America with progress. The American survey of the La Plata estuary and beyond followed
sharply on the 1852 opening of that river system by the Argentine Confederation and Paraguay to international navigation.[34]

Railroad Entrepreneurs

Jorge P. E. Tornquist, William Wheelwright, and other American entrepreneurs reached Buenos Aires shortly after the survey teams began
their work. They came in the wake of political stabilization in Argentina, with the enthusiastic support of Alberdi and other pro-U.S. political leaders and in the hope that bilateral economic links could be further enhanced. Tornquist was an American trader whose son founded
Argentina's most important nineteenth-century banking house, Ernesto
Tornquist & Compañía. Wheelwright was a railroad contractor who
oversaw the construction of the Córdoba-Rosario railway during the
1850s and 1860s. He modeled his vision of transportation and economic
growth in South America on the American West. This included an approach to railroad building that contrasted with the British equivalent;
U.S. engines and cars had coarser features, but the engine designs made
possible higher speeds, sharper curves, and the negotiation of rough
track. Wheelwright reached Argentina in the mid-1850s intent on
bringing American-style railroads to the *pampas*. In 1855, entrepreneur
Allan Campbell gave the Argentine Confederation an estimate for a
250-mile railroad from Rosario to Córdoba. As part of the plan, Campbell stressed the role the railroad would have in expanding commerce
in the region, stimulating immigration, and priming new economic
ventures. The cost per mile would be $20,250, and the line's viability
would be tied to the economic growth it would generate. Campbell's
bid configured the project around the American land grant system; the
railway company would be granted 1.5 miles on either side of the track,
as well as a trunk route to the north.[35]

By the early 1860s, Wheelwright had taken charge of what became
known as the Central Argentine Railroad. His negotiations with the

Argentine government had much in common with similar bargaining in the United States. Mail would be carried without charge on the rail line. Soldiers would travel at half price. In return, the span of the initial land grant increased to three miles on each side of the track, with Alberdi's enjoinders on immigration and modernization on the minds of the Argentine negotiators. The grants came on condition that the company would settle immigrants on the land while building churches and schools. Wheelwright proposed to build towns at eight- to ten-mile intervals along the track as a stimulus to progress, and he understood that his agreement with the government, which conceived of development around a new population of small farmers, directly threatened large land ownership. It was not until 1866 that Wheelwright was able to initiate construction. The project was immediately threatened by the declining importance of Rosario in the wake of Argentine unification and the outbreak of the Paraguayan War, which led to violent disruptions through the regions to be served by the railroad. Despite delays, the Central Argentine Railroad opened in 1870, just a year after the Golden Spike ceremony linked the Union and Central Pacific Railroads in the United States. Argentina had become the first country outside North America to introduce land grant railroads.[36]

Between 1865 and 1870, at the same time that he supervised railroad construction, Wheelwright boosted settlement on the land grant. As was done in the United States, he began by advertising and writing in local newspapers on farming and other opportunities in the region. He became a joint editor of the Rosario newspaper *La Patria*, which subsequently changed its name to *El Ferrocarril*. But in 1870, shortly before the line was completed, the land grant was moved to the newly incorporated Central Argentine Land Company. Organized to streamline administration and foster new investment, the new company helped weaken the project because the railroad no longer had a contractual responsibility to populate and modernize. When Wheelwright died in 1873, his vision of peopling the plains and stimulating economic growth collapsed. In the end, Argentine railroads did not follow the U.S. model. They took on no responsibility for bringing in immigrants, for priming economic growth, or for helping in the creation of a class of small farmers. Unlike their equivalents in the United States, they helped build no new regions of economic growth outside the littoral region and no equivalents to Chicago or other Midwestern American cities.[37]

Trade Growth, Tariffs, and the Philadelphia Exposition

As the economies of both nations expanded in conjunction with rising trade after 1860, U.S. policymakers continued to focus on commercial opportunities in their diplomacy toward Argentina. But after 1860, tariffs complicated U.S. policy. For decades, members of the agriculture-based southern states had opposed tariff barriers on imports, fearing inordinate price increases on incoming manufactured goods. During the Civil War, with southern opinions no longer voiced in Washington, Congress initiated a series of upward tariff revisions in conjunction with legislative initiatives intended to benefit industrial expansion. By the end of the war, protective duties averaged 47 percent, compared with 18.8 percent at the outset of the conflict. In 1867, faced with a postwar decline in wool demand and a continued expansion of the sheep industry, the Republican-dominated Congress responded to pressures from American wool producers by passing the Wool and Woolens Act. This ended decades of relatively open U.S.-Argentine commerce and halted the rapid growth in wool imports from Argentina and Australia during the Civil War at a time when the Argentine export economy relied heavily on such exports. Between 1860 and 1895 the number of sheep in Argentina increased from 14 million to 91 million, yet the U.S. tariff of 1867 eliminated prospects for future North American sales. At the time of the legislation, the United States bought 18,500 tons of Argentine wool annually. By 1882 that figure had dropped to 1,000 tons. These statistics are especially striking when compared to equivalent values for furs, skins, animal hair, and hides, none of which experienced a parallel fluctuation.[38]

While Argentina allowed the free entry of such American commodities as timber and agricultural apparatus, the sales representative of the essential export component of the burgeoning American economy, the United States barred some of Argentina's most important products. That Argentina was unable to resolve what its leaders believed was a trade inequity showed the growing international influence of the United States. Argentines would find it equally difficult to counter American tariff barriers after 1890 when, in response to rising European protectionism, the United States implemented the highest duty rates in the nation's history. Yet despite commercial duties, trade between the two states rose sharply. From 1891 to 1895 some $9.5 million worth of goods were traded. That commerce remained at the core of bilateral relations despite the introduction of a strict tariff regime confirmed that the bipolarity of nation-building models that Alberdi and Sarmiento had described was an inadequate explanation for development in the two nations. Trade remained strong because of rapid economic expansion in each state.

At the end of his presidential term, Sarmiento could boast many accomplishments that had had their inspiration in what he viewed as progress in the United States. But he was unable to bring an American model to Argentina and saw that effort as a failure. The implications of the "failure," though, meant less than what Sarmiento assumed about progress, political change, and democracy. To be sure, key differences did exist between the two countries. The United States did develop to an extent far greater than Argentina as a nation powerfully influenced by small farmers whose political influence was notable. The gap between Buenos Aires and the rest of Argentina remained politically, culturally, and materially more significant than the urban-rural gap in the United States. Even so, there were important parallels in the two nations. Although agriculture and ranching played a less significant role in the United States than in Argentina and although in the United States that role was more regionally based, in both countries they had a vast impact on economic development and foreign trade. Indeed, because Argentina and the United States both emerged as agricultural and livestock producers in the late nineteenth century, their potential for trade was much less important than that between the United States and other Latin American countries, or between Argentina and some European nations. In both countries, massive immigration shaped popular culture and the political economy. The nativist reaction to immigration in each country was often based on race and was critical of both radical politics and what were seen as culturally threatening foreign influences. After 1880, Americans would increase their search for markets and investment opportunities in Argentina.

Argentines continued to find in U.S. progress both political and cultural models for change in Argentina, as well as the possibility for new trade ties. When Americans decided to celebrate their 1876 centennial with a massive exposition in Philadelphia, Argentine political leaders were enthralled. At the first of several important international fairs before 1930 that were meant to show to the world American industrial, agricultural, and cultural achievements, Argentines were eager participants. The Argentine government took part in the 1869 Paris Exposition and organized an international exhibit in Córdoba in 1872. That year, shortly after President Ulysses S. Grant named a commission to coordinate the Philadelphia exhibition, planning for an Argentine pavilion got underway, as did the work of several Argentine provincial commissions charged with collecting products to send to the United States.[39]

Some opposition arose among Argentines to government expenditures on Philadelphia; economic depression, widespread yellow fever, the Paraguayan War, and rebellion in Entre Rios province made it seem to some that there were more important priorities for public spending. To generate support for an Argentine pavilion at the Philadelphia Exposition, the government sponsored a highly publicized preliminary exhibition of Argentina's fair samples in December 1875 at Parque Tres de Febrero in Buenos Aires. It was an enormous success. Argentine Exposition Commission chair Ernesto Oldendorff cast Philadelphia as an opportunity to demonstrate Argentina's potential and wealth to the world; this would be a key chance for Argentines to show their strength and progress on an American stage. In January 1876, after thousands had viewed the preliminary show in Buenos Aires, 1,770 exhibit items were shipped to Philadelphia for display. They included a wide range of mineral samples, woods, various manufactured goods, cereals, flours, and books. Cloth from Catamarca was valued at fifteen hundred

dollars. There were newspapers and provincial statistics on modernization, with reference to education, mapping, and textbook distribution. The fossils of an extinct horse sent for presentation not only contributed evidence for Darwin's theory of evolution but also advertised
the advanced level of Argentine natural science. Dozens of Argentine
samples won prizes in competition at Philadelphia, including wines
from Cuyo and La Rioja, tobacco, hats, photographs, sugar, the *Annals
of the Argentine Rural Society*, and Argentina's most important export
item, wool. In their participation at Philadelphia, and in their prizewin-
ning results, Argentines confidently rejected Sarmiento's juxtaposition
of U.S. progress and Argentine disorder. In American fora and more
generally, Argentines planned to compete with the United States, and
to win.[40]

2 Pan-Americanism, World War, and the Bolshevik Menace, 1880–1923

In the last half of the nineteenth century, Argentine elites consolidated their national political structure by tying the interests of commercial and finance capital to those of the state. This was done to a degree far greater than in the United States. In the constitution of 1853 popular politics and the protection of individual freedoms were subordinated to the authority of merchants and bankers in the running of government. By the 1880s, private bankers determined credit rules, held public debt, and determined national economic policies. In the United States, during a severe financial crisis in the first decade of the twentieth century, New York banker J. P. Morgan gathered the capital necessary to offset financial exigency for the federal government. But in contrast to the Argentine case, where private merchant bankers regularly held this kind of authority, the 1907 crisis in the United States was anomalous for the unusual strength of a private banker in determining the nation's financial course.[1] In Argentina no financier held Morgan's sway. But over the long term, a number of private bankers and business leaders were able to influence government policy more directly and more powerfully than in the United States. This curtailed political, social, and legal reforms and contributed to the emergence of authoritarian political structures. By the 1920s, this threat to democracy was expressed in repeated federal military and political interventions in the Argentine provinces and by the repression of organized labor.

The formation of a state structure that limited popular sovereignty and entrenched extraordinary powers in the hands of a small commercial and financial elite had two important consequences for U.S.-

Argentine relations between 1880 and 1923. First, as U.S. business predominance in South America grew, the Argentine government was quick to subscribe to U.S.-led Pan-Americanism—the principal policy set that advanced Washington's objectives for open trade and investment in the Americas—as advantageous for Argentine economic growth. Indeed, the period from 1880 to 1923 marks the rise of U.S.-led Pan-Americanism in the Americas and the emergence of Argentina's staunch backing for that project. Second, Argentina's pro-U.S. Pan-Americanism was quiet. The public face of a more critical Argentine policy toward the United States ran contrary to Argentine Pan-Americanism in support of Washington. Beginning with the First Pan-American Conference in 1889–90, continuing with trust-busting attacks on U.S. meat packers in Argentina by politicians and journalists, and culminating in the anti-interventionist, anti-American nationalism of leading *radicales* Hipólito Yrigoyen and Honório Pueyrredón in the 1920s, Argentine policy toward the United States was contradictory. The Argentine government reconciled the contradiction—a consistent backing for strong business ties with the United States and intermittent, but vocal, criticisms of the United States from government and other sources—by limiting the impact of the latter in both the long and short terms.

In addition to the growing importance of U.S.-led Pan-Americanism to U.S.-Argentine relations, this chapter considers four related issues: the growing predominance of U.S. business interests in Argentina, racism in international relations, the impact of World War I on bilateral ties, and U.S. fears of a Bolshevik menace in Argentina. In the first years of the twentieth century, fueled by a confidence generated through Argentina's dramatic export-led growth, Argentine leaders became sympathetic to U.S. foreign policy objectives in Latin America and even sought to compete with the United States strategically and economically. Twenty years later, U.S. leaders saw an Argentina dangerously subject to social upheaval and political disorder. Ironically, just as Argentines had worked hard to distinguish themselves from other Latin Americans, Americans came to see Argentina as just one more Latin American nation.

The Origins of Argentina's Quiet Pan-Americanism

Starting with the Drago Doctrine, many scholars have overestimated the anti-American current in Argentine diplomacy. Though taken as a criticism of U.S. intervention in the Americas, Argentine foreign minister Luis María Drago's 1902 stand was never meant as a challenge to the United States. Drafted as a letter to Great Britain protesting the latter's coercion of Venezuela over defaulted loan repayments, the Drago Doctrine held that no foreign power should intervene in the affairs of a nation in the Americas over loan defaults. Had these views been recognized by the international community as international law, the Drago Doctrine might have come to impede U.S. expansion in the Caribbean basin. But when he made his remarks, Drago was building on a thirty-year-old tradition in Argentine diplomacy that was critical of European, not American, filibustering. In fact, Drago insisted that such interventions were contrary to the tenets of the Monroe Doctrine, which he invoked as a basis for his statements. The Argentine minister in Washington, Martín García Merou, declared Drago's statement the first acknowledgment and acceptance of the Monroe Doctrine "as a principle of American public law by a nation of South America."[2]

Continued economic growth in Argentina tied to an associated expansion in foreign trade was at the root of Argentina's quiet pro-U.S. Pan-Americanism. Argentines came to see as advantageous the U.S. interest in Pan-Americanism as a means to stabilize hemispheric conditions for international trade and finance. Driven by agriculture, Argentina experienced rapid growth in exports after 1870. Large-scale meat exports to Europe began with the introduction of refrigerated transport ships. By the 1890s, Argentina dominated the frozen beef trade across the Atlantic. Immigration fueled business growth. Construction in Buenos Aires rivaled progress in the most cosmopolitan European centers. Having undergone industrialization much earlier than Argentina, the United States was well positioned to send capital and finished goods when Argentines sought both in large amounts after 1890. U.S. companies gained a stronghold in the dynamic Argentine meat-packing industry. Swift & Company and other Chicago-based packers, for example, acquired several Argentine packinghouses between 1907 and 1909.[3]

Although British exports to Argentina represented more than the combined sales of France, Germany, and the United States during the first years of the twentieth century, U.S. sales grew faster. From 1891 to 1895 some $9.5 million worth of goods were traded between the United States and Argentina. Between 1910 and 1914 the two nations exchanged $80 million in commodities. Juxtaposing the periods 1894 to 1898 and 1899 to 1903, annual American sales to Argentina rose by 100 percent, compared with increases of only 50 percent for the United Kingdom and 26 percent for Germany. Moreover, in the first years of the twentieth century, in Argentina and elsewhere in South America, the United States began to overcome such disadvantages as limited steamship transport, an absence of American banking facilities, and poor sensitivity to market conditions. In 1906, the U.S. State Department insisted that "South America should offer the most favorable field, of all quarters of the globe, for the exploitation of American trade." Americans led Great Britain in sales of steel rails ($2,841,430), as well as automobiles, cycles, and cars other than railway cars ($981,535).[4] By 1910, the United States led all competitors in sales of agricultural machinery, sewing machines, wood, scientific instruments, and a handful of other goods.[5]

Modern Pan-Americanism began in 1889–90 in Washington, at the First Pan-American Conference. The meeting set a number of precedents for how the United States would try to ensure stable conditions of trade and finance in the hemisphere. Delegates passed motions favoring the adoption of the metric system, the creation of an inter-American bank, and the establishment of an international monetary fund. They agreed to work for the implementation of international regulations for patents, port dues, and sanitation. But when the United States tried to win support for its most ambitious conference project, a customs union for the Americas, Argentine delegates were among a number who balked.[6] Influenced by the anti-American criticisms of the Cuban essayist José Martí, the diplomat and future Argentine president Roque Saenz Peña rebuked the United States for trying to isolate Latin America from traditional European trading partners.[7]

Argentine qualms over U.S. expansionism in Latin America persisted into the twentieth century as the United States began to intervene politically and militarily in the Caribbean basin. But others found merit in U.S. foreign policy and action. In 1905, for example, Argentine minister to the United States Epifanio Portela expressed his government's approval for President Theodore Roosevelt's Corollary to the Monroe Doctrine, which authorized the United States to respond with military force to what U.S. officials perceived as disorder in Latin America. Manifesting his sympathy for the race-based underpinnings of the corollary, Portela described it as a civilizing force that showed a new and important interest by the United States in the Americas.[8] Over the next two decades Argentina became one of the staunchest supporters of a U.S.-led Pan-Americanism that continued to stress close inter-American financial ties, the dismantling of trade barriers, and inviting conditions for U.S. companies doing business in Latin America. Some Argentine officials criticized the United States. But where bilateral trade and diplomatic problems surfaced, they did so in a context of long-term cooperative understanding between the two countries.

By the Third Pan-American Conference (1906), Argentina had come a long way from the customs union rejection. The Foreign Relations Ministry instructed Argentine delegates to cultivate U.S. friendship, to state opposition to any future European colonization in the New World, and to praise the Monroe Doctrine as having defended Latin America for almost a century. In contrast to 1889–90, conference delegates were to advance ideas for better commercial relations in the hemisphere and to sponsor commercial treaties. Argentina would support U.S. goals of the simplification and unification of tariff, consular, and patent laws in the hemisphere from 1906 through the Second World War.[9] Through the First World War, U.S. leaders incorporated South American political and business leaders into the implementation of Pan-American policy through the Pan-American Union. At the first Pan-American meeting, Latin Americans had found the U.S. approach heavy handed. But between 1914 and 1925, at the first two Pan-American Financial Conferences and in the work of the International High Commission, Americans integrated the views of leading bankers and business leaders from Argentina, Chile, Brazil, and elsewhere in an effort to standardize monetary and finance policy in the Americas.

Race and International Affairs

After 1910, there were growing similarities in how U.S. and Argentine elites understood race hierarchies and international affairs. A *hispanista* cultural renaissance in Argentina helped generate widespread anti-American sentiment at the time of the Spanish-American-Cuban War. White urban Argentines came to consider Spaniards (and themselves) as racially and ethnically superior to Argentina's Latin American neighbors as well as to Italians and other immigrants. At the same time, Argentines praised the United States for its modernity, military prowess, and social order, virtues they found lacking in Argentina and other American republics.[10] In early 1898, the *Buenos Aires Herald* voiced the opinions of many in the middle and upper classes. Editorials asserted that neither Spain nor Cuban "revolutionists" had shown any capacity for governing Cuba; Argentines found little hope for what they would have viewed as a "modern" or "civilized" solution for government of the island. But the newspaper also found no reason to trust Cuban reports of Spanish atrocities. This meant that there was no basis in international law for U.S. intervention against Spain on behalf of Cuba, and no relevance of the USS *Maine* explosion to the question of intervention.[11]

Argentina remained neutral during the war, but a decade later Argentine policy had become more favorable toward the U.S. military presence in the Caribbean basin. In 1912, when Afro-Cubans rose in rebellion against the U.S.-dominated Cuban republic, Argentine diplomats and political leaders sided with U.S. forces sent to suppress the rising.[12] The Argentine chargé d'affaires in Havana, Jorge Reyes, backed U.S. military action citing the need to offset a potential attack by a European power for similar reasons—the protection of political stability and private property. Reyes described insurgents as "negradas," racist language that ascribed violent behavior to African Cubans.[13]

In 1915, the veteran diplomat and foreign minister Carlos Becú combined race-based thinking with strategic foreign policy planning when he translated putative Argentine racial superiority into a model for tactical control in the hemisphere. As what Becú considered a white republic, the United States would be responsible for the Caribbean and Central America. For similar reasons, Argentina, Brazil, and Chile might apply a "Monroeism of their own" to South America.[14] The race-based logic was not always consistent. Argentina, Chile, and Uruguay (not Brazil) were the nations best adapted for white inhabitants by reason of "climate and geography."[15]

The imagined race-based partitioning of Latin America into U.S. and Argentine spheres of influence never materialized. Even so, Argentina continued to back military, diplomatic, and economic components of U.S. expansionism in Latin America. Late in 1914, the Americans began organizing the First Pan-American Financial Conference. U.S. treasury secretary William Gibbs McAdoo and others planned this meeting of finance ministers to normalize commercial and financial relations in the hemisphere on the assumption that the United States could successfully compete against and overtake traditional European rivals under such conditions.[16] The five-day conference began in Washington on 24 May 1915, with nineteen countries participating. Argentina backed U.S. goals as beneficial to Argentine trade. In the normalization of trade relations, the ground was laid for future agreement on patent legislation, postal rates, and uniformity in terms of trade throughout Latin America. Delegates made plans for a second financial conference and formed a permanent body to oversee the dismantling of impediments to commerce and finance: the International High Commission would be composed of the finance minister and eight specialists from each member country.[17]

The Advance of U.S. Business in Argentina

If Argentines identified with American policy objectives and followed a U.S. Pan-American lead, American leaders identified Argentina as distinct from its Latin American neighbors, much as Argentine elites saw their country. Americans accepted the underpinnings of Carlos Becú's reasoning on race and civilization; Argentina was essentially a nation of Europeans whose potential progress and modernization derived from that ethnic and racial heritage. In 1909, the newly arrived U.S. minister in Buenos Aires, Charles H. Sherrill, marveled at Argentine advancements. The Buenos Aires opera house was "much finer and in distinctly better taste than ours in New York," and the new subway system was a sure indicator of progress.[18] Viewed by U.S. visitors through the prism of a modernizing Buenos Aires downtown core, Argentina was worlds away from the Cuba of the Platt Amendment. This vision was borne out by American commercial and financial triumphs. During World War I, Argentina became a model success story for dollar diplomacy. Buoyed by wartime disruptions of the Argentine economy and Atlantic shipping lanes, U.S. exporters and investors did a booming business in the Río de la Plata, displacing British and German competitors in many sectors.

Yet despite these successes, and while Argentina was clearly something apart from the Dominican Republic or Haiti, it remained essentially "Latin American" in American minds. The tango, which first reached New York and other U.S. cities in the second decade of the 1900s, was the first glimpse that many Americans had of Argentina. A sexually charged dance that had its origins in working-class Buenos Aires brothels, the tango scandalized some in the United States as it exhilarated others, exoticizing Argentina as Latin. First taught to the wealthy by *porteño* dance masters, the tango was quickly popularized for middle- and working-class New Yorkers through stage performances, published step manuals, and dance halls. The tango as depiction of Argentina as exotically Latin reached a peak with Hollywood's *Four Horsemen of the Apocalypse* (1921), starring Rudolf Valentino as the violently romantic Latin/Argentine paired with Beatrice Domínguez's dark Latin beauty.[19]

Argentina as Latin America is also reflected in U.S. policy. The two Argentinas were essential to American planning on economic relations. U.S. business, investment, and finance did well in Argentina as a function of what distinguished Argentina from smaller Latin American countries, a burgeoning and diverse economy. But Americans also benefited from persistent economic weaknesses, including the Argentine need to borrow heavily from international sources. Because U.S. policy was focused primarily on economic opportunities, policy for Argentina tended to be that for the region as a whole, often negotiated by and large under the umbrella of the Pan-Americanism. In addition, confidence in Argentine governance fell away during World War I, first because of President Hipólito Yrigoyen's unwillingness to declare war on Germany and, shortly after, because of U.S. fears of an unmanageable Bolshevik menace. By late 1918, Americans had come to see the Argentine government as unreliable, unstable, and a risk to U.S. interests—in other words, a Latin American government.

But the U.S.-Argentine economic connection proved durable. In the first years of the twentieth century, large and small American firms did a booming business in Argentina. By 1913, U.S. companies had invested $40 million. While this represented only 1.2 percent of all foreign holdings, U.S. capital was concentrated in sectors where it had a disproportionately strong influence. In 1909, Americans entered the Argentine petroleum industry with the founding of the Compañía Nacional de Petróleos (renamed the West India Oil Company in 1911), which produced kerosene, gas oils, coke, and fuel oil. Also in 1909, J. P. Morgan offered the Argentine government a loan of $50 million. The Argentines eventually contracted with a European consortium for the needed funds, but Morgan, the First National Bank, and the National City Bank underwrote almost $10 million of the loan, an unprecedented figure in South America for New York houses. The United States built economic ties with Argentina faster than its European competitors. Americans became leaders in the export to Argentina of industrial machinery, petroleum, agricultural equipment, and lumber. For the fiscal year ending on 30 June 1910, the United States exported $40.4 million in goods to the Argentines, making Argentina the ninth largest customer for U.S. goods and the largest South American purchaser.[20]

U.S. government assistance for American business bore quick results. The State Department waged diplomatic battles on behalf of Glidden

Varnish and the Southern Cotton Oil Company, among many firms. A far more important example of U.S. business-government contacts fostered during the Taft presidency was the Argentine Navy battleship contracts awarded to American firms in 1910. That sale confirmed the distinction between Argentina and the countries of the Caribbean basin, the strong success of American heavy industrial exports to South America, and the business Pan-Americanism that the United States had fostered after 1889. A contract for the construction of the battleship *Moreno* at the New York Shipbuilding Company's Camden, New Jersey, yards and the *Rivadavia* at the Fore River Shipbuilding Company shipyards in Quincy, Massachusetts, became the most profitable foreign sale of military equipment in U.S. history.[21] It also showed that U.S. industry could compete favorably for the richest international contracts, as well as the growing linkages in U.S. foreign policy between international finance, diplomatic pressure, strategic concerns, and foreign commerce.

The contract for two battleships merged Pan-American diplomacy in Argentina with thirty years of U.S. industrial expansion tied to naval modernization. Following on the publication of Captain Alfred T. Mahan's *The Influence of Sea Power upon History* (1890) linking national greatness with naval power, leading U.S. businessmen spoke out in favor of a military buildup and a big navy. In 1905, after the Russo-Japanese War, the United States announced plans for 20,000-ton "super battleships." A year later, Brazil stated it would buy the largest battleship in the world, touching off an arms race between Argentina, Brazil, and Chile (the ABC countries).[22] Brazil took delivery of the warships *Minas Gerais* and *Sao Paulo* in 1910, establishing clear naval superiority in Latin America. The power shift was exacerbated further when Brazil indicated it would shortly receive a third Dreadnought, the *Rio de Janeiro*, from the British firm Armstrong, Whitworth & Company.

In 1908, Argentines countered with plans for two ships of their own. The Argentine Navy set up office in London to receive bids, and not long after, Charles M. Schwab of Bethlehem Steel and Admiral Francis T. Bowles of Fore River followed to try to win the Argentine contract. Fifteen companies placed bids, including Blohm and Voss; Armstrong, Whitworth & Company; and Vickers, Sons, & Maxim. In January 1910, the Argentine government announced that U.S. firms had won the second round of bidding.[23] Not only had Fore River underbid its competitors, but it had also been the only company to meet the Argentines' structural and speed specifications. The impressive credentials of the U.S. companies, though, were only part of the story of how the contract was assigned. The State Department worked hard on several fronts to help assure the deals. It instructed the U.S. ambassador in England to ensure that American corporations had equal treatment in the bidding. But in addition, Assistant Secretary of State Alvey A. Adee asked the American legation in Buenos Aires to lobby the Argentines. He reminded them of favorable U.S. duties on hides, the importance of private American bank loans to the Argentine government, and the limitless trade opportunities the Argentines might anticipate should an American bid succeed.[24]

In June 1909, when the Buenos Aires press reported on defects in U.S.-built armor-plate, the State Department ordered the U.S. chargé d'affaires in Buenos Aires, Charles S. Wilson, to take "immediate and energetic steps to refute and contradict such press reports."[25] Wilson also tried to persuade the Argentines regarding the battleship purchase by citing a recently issued $10 million bank loan to the Argentine government from Drexel-Morgan. The United States attached "great importance" to the sale, according to Wilson, especially with regard to "increasing and promoting closer relations, as has lately been demonstrated by American participation in the recent Argentine loan." The Argentine foreign minister resented the arm-twisting and made that known to the State Department, but to no avail.[26] Secretary Philander Knox and President William Howard Taft understood the importance of the sales in both industrial and strategic terms. In July 1909, Knox wrote to the secretary of the navy that "the standard adopted in the present order would establish a precedent for the future, and might have its influence on orders hereafter placed by other South American governments." Taft instructed the newly appointed U.S. minister in Argentina to pursue the contract energetically. He did. On his own initiative, Charles Sherrill promised the Argentine president and foreign minister that if American companies won the contract, the United States would guarantee Argentine security against any Brazilian naval aggression.[27]

Some Argentines criticized the purchase from the start as financial folly. In June 1914, in the midst of a sluggish economic cycle, Argentine politicians hotly debated whether to sell the U.S. battleships before they had been delivered. Congressional deputies Julio Costa, Julio A. Roca Jr., and Luis M. Drago led a "pacifist" group that favored the sale. Those opposing the sale included the current foreign minister, José Luis Murature, and the former foreign minister, Estanislao S. Zeballos.[28]

But for President Taft, the sale marked a foreign policy pinnacle, representing the best of how "dollar diplomacy" integrated commerce and diplomatic relations. In 1910 he told a Pittsburgh audience:

> As a confirmation of the friendly relations which now exist between this country and all of South America, Argentina has placed the contract for two battle ships and certain additional naval armaments, amounting in money value in all to about $23,000,000, and there is reason to believe that we shall have further contracts of a similar sort placed in the United States by other South American governments. . . . The theory that the field of diplomacy does not include in any degree commerce and the increase of trade relations is one to which Mr. Knox and this administration do not subscribe. . . . There is nothing inconsistent in the promotion of peaceful relations and the promotion of trade relations, and if the protection which the United States shall assure to her citizens in the assertion of just rights under investment made in foreign countries shall promote the amount of such investment and stimulate and enlarge the business relations it is a result to be commended.[29]

The 1914 ABC Conference

Over the next two years, foreign contracts won by Americans came to more than $100 million.[30] Taft's successor in the White House, Woodrow Wilson, also helped foster a cooperative climate for business and diplomacy in South America. Commerce Secretary William C. Redfield and Treasury Secretary William Gibbs McAdoo backed business-oriented Pan-Americanism, and under Wilson, U.S. business activity in the Southern Cone of South America continued to grow. Wilson moved also to consolidate U.S. military and strategic primacy in the Caribbean basin and to reverse the threat to American business of escalating violence in Mexico. In 1913, Wilson came up with a new variant on the Roosevelt Corollary to the Monroe Doctrine, with a different set of implications on U.S.-Argentine ties than the battleship sale. The corollary had conditioned U.S. nonintervention in Latin America on political stability. With specific reference to the Mexican dictator General Victoriano Huerta, Wilson now insisted on democratic rule as a precondition for U.S. diplomatic recognition.[31]

Through late 1913, the United States contemplated military intervention to end the Huerta dictatorship, opting in the interim to participate in a massive arms supply to revolutionary forces. On 21 April 1914, U.S. Marines occupied Vera Cruz hoping to push Huerta from office by seizing customs house revenues. The United States developed plans for an occupation of Mexico, including a march on Mexico City. But Wilson shied away from escalating the conflict, opting instead to bargain from strength. With economic and political stability still the primary American goal in Mexico, the United States asked Argentina, Brazil, and Chile to mediate a settlement. The Americans hoped that the threat of a march on Mexico City and the multilateral diplomacy of the ABC countries might win what Wilson had not been able to accomplish on his own, Huerta's fall.[32]

Prominent Argentines had bristled at the implications of a nonrecognition policy based on the American president's thumbs up or thumbs down on a country's form of government. The normally pro-American Buenos Aires daily *La Prensa* had criticized Wilson, as had ex-foreign minister Estanislao S. Zeballos, who worried that Americans would be unable to differentiate between the smaller, less stable republics and what he viewed as more advanced states like Argentina.[33] But like Chile and Brazil, Argentina agreed to participate in the mediation that took place in May and June 1914 in Niagara Falls, Ontario. All three countries sent their Washington-based diplomats to mediate the U.S.-Mexican conflict—Rómulo S. Naón for Argentina, Eduardo Suarez Múgica for Chile, and Dominicio da Gama for Brazil. The United States sent Supreme Court Justice Joseph E. Lamar and former Department of

Justice solicitor Frederick W. Lehmann as ex officio delegates. Unofficial status would contribute to a false illusion that the ABC countries were presiding over an effective mediation. Newspapers from around the United States cast doubt early on the efficacy of the mediation.[34]

The press was right to question the mediation, but journalists missed a multilayered U.S. strategy at Niagara Falls. Once the conference began, Huerta's strength waned fast in the face of the revolutionary onslaught. For the United States, the value of the mediation lay in removing Huerta. With Huerta's fortunes on the wane, American leaders were more inclined to try to find their own solution to restoring stability in Mexico. While holding up the fiction of international mediation, the United States turned to its own diplomacy in Mexico to unseat Huerta. Discussions began on 20 May 1914 with the suggestion that Huerta step down. Seven days later, in the face of no progress on mediation, the Argentine delegation warned the United States that the Niagara Falls meeting risked failure. But the mediators lost touch with political and military change in Mexico. The Americans had all but abandoned their interest in a mediated settlement. With Huerta in retreat, they now backed the ABC negotiations as a diversion from their quiet support for Huerta's rival, Constitutionalist leader Venustiano Carranza, who had been banned from the mediation.[35]

Five years later, the U.S. counsel to the Niagara Falls conference confirmed publicly what the ABC nations had not understood in June 1914, when the mediation concluded without a settlement. William F. Buckley testified before a congressional committee that the Americans had entered the mediation in support of a provisional government that was neutral in the conflict between Huerta and the Constitutionalists. Without alerting the ABC negotiators, the United States had quietly shifted its backing to Carranza. In response to an admonishment from Buckley at the time, the secretary of state had simply responded that "[w]hen you can't keep a promise you can't keep it, and that is all there is to it."[36] The ABC Conference settled nothing. While the South Americans had thought themselves at the center of an important mediation, the United States had followed an independent diplomatic tack with the Mexican revolutionaries.

World War I

With the outbreak of World War I, the Argentine economy went into a tailspin, but U.S. investors actually increased their investments. They won concessions for high-power telegraph communication between New York and Buenos Aires and proposed a range of major projects including the construction of an extensive grain elevator network and fast steamship service between North and South America.[37] In September 1914, the U.S. chargé d'affaires in Buenos Aires, George Lorillard, called on Americans to seize the chances war presented: "Never was there a more favorable opportunity than the present for American financiers and merchants to enter this field. Manufactured articles of all sorts as well as coal can find an open market here at the present time and Americans can thereby gain a commercial foothold which they will never again lose."[38] In October 1916, the U.S. ambassador in Argentina, Frederic Jessup Stimson, expressed similar hopes, reviving Carlos Becú's notions of race and geography. Stimson told an audience in Massachusetts that Argentina, Chile, and the United States were the only great countries entirely within the temperate zone. Tropical nations, Stimson went on, were unsuited to "the same colonization by northern races or, what is still more important, the same system of labor that we find in countries of the temperate zone."[39]

The United States worked to influence neutral Argentine wartime policy, for strategic and economic ends. Led first by the British, Allied pressures to shape Argentine neutrality during the war were unrelenting. After the United States entered the war, Argentina's formal neutrality was transformed into tacit economic support for the Allied cause. Before that, the pro-American Naón evinced a neutral stance similar to that of the United States. He evoked a Wilsonian zeal in defining the mission of a neutral country in maintaining "the progress of the world" and the conservation of "its moral and material energies as a nucleus for the reestablishment of the disturbed equilibrium in a future which we all earnestly hope will be immediate."[40]

Yet despite this backing for the United States, Argentines envisioned a leadership role for themselves among Latin America neutrals. In

July 1916, President Saenz Peña cornered Stimson at a dinner party and spoke with the ambassador for an hour on his vision of a future common leadership of Latin America by Argentina and the United States, though on questions of trade and finance he insisted that Argentina would be prepared to "follow the lead of the United States."[41] President Hipólito Yrigoyen followed Saenz Peña's example trying to combine Argentine diplomatic leadership with economic deference to the United States. Through the war Argentina proved a staunch supporter of the Allies, supplying food and raw materials. In 1913, Argentina exported nearly $56 million in goods to Germany. Four years later it sent nothing. Exports to the United Kingdom, France, and the United States rose sharply over the same period. The American share of Argentina's exports swelled from only $22 million in 1913 to $155 million in 1917.[42] To Germany, its allies, and other neutrals, Argentina's neutrality was hardly credible.

But the United States wanted more. After April 1917, the Americans pressured Argentina to join the United States in a declaration of war. Yrigoyen refused. Argentina planned to support the Allies economically and to lead a Latin American group of neutrals, while leaving open the possibility of a quick rapprochement with Germany after the war. Yrigoyen also saw neutrality as a chance to compete with the United States for diplomatic and strategic leadership in Latin America. At the time of the U.S. declaration of war, Yrigoyen began planning for a meeting of neutral countries in Latin America. He asked the State Department for support. Secretary of State Robert Lansing turned him down, instead directing U.S. diplomats in Latin America to discourage heads of state from attending the conference. As a result, plans for the conference of neutrals came to naught. Late in 1917, Yrigoyen tried again for a conference, and for a second time Lansing was able to marshal enough support to block the Argentine effort.[43]

Still, Argentine commercial support for the Allies came in conjunction with dramatic U.S. economic inroads in Argentina. Between 1914 and 1917, the United States surpassed both Great Britain and Germany in the quantity of goods traded with Argentina. The United States won vast markets for railway cars, steel rails, electrical machinery, and leather goods, gaining a virtual monopoly on Argentine imports of lumber, agricultural machinery, and sewing machines. Sales jumped for American cars and their parts (from $1,333,873 in 1914 to $5,805,556 in 1918), coal and coke (from $113,584 to $1,459,582), knit goods (from $30,907 to $2,926,772), and automobile tires (from $8,153 to $1,649,840). In cars alone, U.S. sales to Argentina accounted for 19.3 percent of Argentine imports in 1913 and 73.1 percent in 1915. In return, Argentina helped fuel the U.S. war effort. According to the Allied Maritime Transport Council, the American leather industry would have been "seriously crippled" without its annual supply of quebracho for tanning and would have "suffer[ed] materially" had the Argentine supply of skins and hides come to an end. U.S. military demand prompted a 1,400 percent jump in wool imports from Argentina, from $5 million in 1914 to $75 million four years later. In these and other areas, American gains came at the expense of Germany.[44]

Argentine reliance on U.S. goods became extreme in 1917 and 1918. At the same time, the United States wanted more control over the terms of bilateral trade. After the American entry into the war, Naón appealed repeatedly to the War Trade Board (WTB) Bureau of Exports for the release of goods. In the last week of July 1918 alone, the Argentine government requested that the WTB clear shipments of 6 tons of antimony, 15 tons of lead sheets, and 320 tons of steel locomotive and railroad car tires, among many other goods for the Argentine state railroad.[45] Some Americans supported Argentine calls in 1917 for a U.S.-Argentine commercial agreement that would cover both countries' wartime needs. Consul General W. Henry Robertson suggested a straight exchange of coal for hides, wool, quebracho, and cereals. Acting State Department foreign trade adviser Marion Letcher agreed with the proposal for more friendly ties with Argentina, fearing that the ongoing American denial of goods would throw Argentina "into the arms of Germany." But the United States suspected Argentina of pro-German sentiments, particularly after the Argentines implemented a grain export prohibition in the wake of food shortages.[46] Citing the likelihood of a European grain shortage, Food Administration director Herbert Hoover advocated that the Argentine wheat surplus be traded for coal, agricultural machinery, and other goods.[47] Shipping Board chairman Edward J. Hurley reached a similar conclusion two months later, but in January 1918, when Argentina and the Allies reached a new commercial arrangement, the United States insisted that there be no provision for coal. Argentina agreed to sell 2.5 million tons of grain to the Allies and to provide $200 million in loans to the French and British to pay for the shipments.[48]

In the last months of the war, the United States enjoyed new commercial inroads. On 15 March 1918, W. R. Grace & Company became the Argentine government's agent-in-trade with the United States. The Beaver Export Corporation signed a contract with the Argentine State Railways for the supply of $1.5 million in materials.[49] Yrigoyen designated Rómulo Naón as Argentine financial high commissioner to the United States; until 1917, Argentina's only Financial High Commission had been in London. One of Naón's first tasks was to find out how $60 million in credits had been lost. Argentina had offered the funds to the United States to pay for Argentine exports over the calendar year. But within three months, the credit had been spent.[50] There was nothing the Argentines could do: Argentina needed U.S. exports for its faltering wartime economy and relied on American purchases of its foodstuffs and other products. With markets in Europe much reduced and with no shipping space available (save what the United States could offer), Argentina counted on the Americans for the marketing of its goods abroad.

Red Scare

Despite U.S. business successes in Argentina during the war, Americans continued to view Argentina as a problem, first for perceived ties to Germany and then, after the Bolshevik Revolution, as a hotbed for Communist agitation. American leaders translated their concern for Argentine political stability into a new dimension in bilateral ties, military espionage. U.S. fears over Argentine Bolshevism reflected changes at home, including criminal syndicalism legislation, a crackdown on radical organizations, and the infamous "Palmer raids." The Military

Intelligence Division (MID) of the U.S. Army and the Navy's Office of Naval Intelligence (ONI) changed their intelligence gathering mandates in 1917 and 1918 to reflect the new enemy. At first, the ONI and MID distinguished poorly between Germany and the new Communist danger. U.S. suspicions of the 1918 Treaty of Brest-Litovsk initially primed the confusion. Subsequently, fears of a German commercial comeback contributed to a clouded reading of a Bolshevik/German enemy.[51]

Germany began the war ahead of the United States in secretive transmissions, having developed a complex system of intelligence dispatches sent through Uruguay to Brazil for transfer to European-bound ships. In April 1918, Germans stepped up their propaganda in Argentina and Chile: "All the papers possible are to be bribed," reported the MID, "whether they be Argentine or Ally. The object is to prepare a favorable atmosphere for Germany, and avoid the loss of the only two commercial fields left in South America—Chile and Argentina."[52] American intelligence operatives worried about the forty thousand Germans living in Argentina, compared to only four thousand Americans. In late 1918, U.S. businesses held property worth $200 million in Buenos Aires. In spite of the American commercial advance, German companies still held $500 million in Buenos Aires property.[53] Americans also worried about German economic advantage in other parts of Argentina. So prevalent were German firms and managers in the export of hides and wool from Comodoro Rivadavia that when Argentine president Hipólito Yrigoyen visited the city early in 1918, a workers' committee specifically protested against German employers for their treatment of workers. In solidarity with the workers, Yrigoyen reminded Germans that they were in the Argentine Republic.[54]

Two weeks after the armistice, the ONI noted that "German education and 'kultur' have influenced a very large number of Argentines, and this is a group intellectually strong."[55] Even though the war was over, Germany still seemed to Americans to be unrelenting in its Argentine activities. Washington held Germany partially responsible for declining Argentine orders for U.S. manufactured goods (though ongoing Argentine economic problems were more likely to blame). In December 1918, the U.S. postal censor identified what it called a "complicated system of intermediaries and cloaks" that helped explain rising German-Argentine commerce.[56]

As it became clear that Germany would not reverse U.S. wartime gains, fear of Germany subsided, and the United States focused more exclusively on Bolshevism. Some saw American radicals, and even Progressives, as a source for Argentine leftism. Ambassador Stimson cited the prolabor U.S. Seamen's Act (1915) as the culprit for Bolshevik tendencies among many sailors in Buenos Aires.[57] While federal and state authorities in the United States were shutting down the union-organizing activities of the Industrial Workers of the World (IWW), American officials were uncovering what they believed were equivalent and related dangers in Argentina and Chile. On 18 April 1918, for example, the U.S. postal censor intercepted a letter from an Argentine ranch worker to imprisoned IWW leader "Big Bill" Haywood that raised the threat of worker unrest. In 1919, a member of the Buenos Aires Port Workers' Union sent a telegram that fell into the hands of the U.S. War Department. The document declared solidarity with the IWW and ended with the enjoinder "Down with the capitalist goalers, long live world proletariat."[58]

The MID believed that Communists were crawling all over Buenos Aires. Its operatives infiltrated left-wing organizations and reported on an estimated thirty-five hundred "Maximalists and Bolshevists" in Argentina. The MID identified the working-class Boca district of Buenos Aires as a hotbed of leftist activity and repeated Argentine suspicions of a tie between Communists and Jewish-Russian immigrants.[59] This link was most poignantly established in the MID's erroneous belief that Jewish Bolshevists had been partially responsible for the 1919 Tragic Week (Semana Trágica) violence that had, in fact, left dozens of Argentine Jews dead in street violence.[60]

The American Loss of Confidence in Argentina

These American perceptions and accusations had an impact on U.S.-Argentine relations. As policymakers began to differentiate between

German and Bolshevik threats, they became convinced that the Yrigoyen government lacked the strength to hold back Communism. Based on their understanding of a Bolshevik threat to Argentine political stability, U.S. intelligence officers and State Department diplomats began to mistrust the Argentine government.[61] For the first time, they began to see Argentine leaders as a risk to stability. The United States repeatedly criticized Yrigoyen personally, as well as the Argentine government's failure to maintain stability. The ONI described Yrigoyen as favoring labor, because he feared assassination and hoped to win votes at the expense of the Socialist Party. Naval intelligence found the president to be selfishly placing his political interests above those of his country: the "only thing that would ever rouse Irigoyen to action would be the knowledge that his Administration was in actual danger of being overthrown."[62]

Ironically, Washington found value in Yrigoyen's antidemocratic defense of his authority. Americans praised Yrigoyen's heavy-handed federal interventions in the province of Buenos Aires. The ONI described Buenos Aires as long-suffering under a corrupt provincial government. In 1917, federal authorities moved against these elected officials by appointing an interventor to take charge of the provincial government.[63]

American criticism of Yrigoyen began after the Argentine president's first signs of ambivalence toward labor activism during the war. In January 1919, in the face of strike-related street violence in Buenos Aires, military and police units intervened, independent of Yrigoyen and his ministers, who seemed paralyzed with fear.[64] Alarmed, the United States pressured Yrigoyen to take a firmer hand against labor agitators. The British Embassy proposed a joint Anglo-American ultimatum to the Argentine government. If the United States and Great Britain were to "continue sending ships to the Argentine steps [would have to] be taken to enable commercial transactions to develop in accordance with existing contracts." The Argentine government would have to do a better job of cracking down on leftist strike agitation on the docks and at industrial facilities. The British accused Yrigoyen of having friendships among the "foreign" strike leaders. Acting secretary of state Frank

L. Polk rejected the British ultimatum, and the State Department urged a milder statement of purpose, suggesting the "serious effect" that strikes were having on trade.[65] But by late March, the State Department suggested an embargo of U.S. shipments to Argentina as a response to Yrigoyen's failure to control worker unrest. For over a month, the U.S. Shipping Board refused to send ships to Buenos Aires, calling for a guarantee that cargoes would be unloaded.[66]

The State Department rejected an open challenge to Yrigoyen, turning instead to forces capable of taking on the left—the police, the military, paramilitary groups, and conservative factions of the Radical Party. The acceptance that force was needed in labor suppression marked a precedent in U.S.-Argentine relations. One group to which the United States turned was the Liga Patriótica Argentina (LPA). Organized in 1919 by military and police officers, the LPA consisted of shock troops that fought striking workers in the streets. In the 1920s, the LPA played an expanded political role, assuming some of the fascist postures of Primo de Rivera and Mussolini.[67] U.S. diplomats and policymakers identified the league as a patriotic and reliable political force. In May 1919, not long after LPA members had brawled with striking dockworkers in the port of Buenos Aires, Consul General Robertson wrote that the "Army, Navy, and police element in the League is particularly strong, since the troops and police have never forgiven the federal administration for the insults and inactivity to which they have been subjected repeatedly during the operations of the strikers. . . . The League has been created solely, and is being used solely for the maintenance of law and order."[68]

Americans also backed the Argentine military's sometimes violent response to striking workers. The MID assessment of the Tragic Week violence was that the working class had run amok "due to past [Argentine government] leniency and to natural lack of self-restraint and love of lawlessness (for which this population, the working portion, is noted nowadays)." A month after the armistice, the MID explained the persistence of labor violence through 1917 and 1918 as the product of several factors, only one of which was the high cost of living and the demands for higher pay. Other factors included the presence of some

"100,000 working class Russians" in Argentina and the activities of anarchists and "professional agitators," financed by the Germans, to "hinder rail transportation of the crops and the packing of meat destined for the Allies." In January 1919, during the Tragic Week, Argentine general Luis J. Dellepiane led soldiers in attacking workers in the streets of Buenos Aires. For the U.S. military attaché in Buenos Aires, Colonel Alfred T. Smith, Dellepiane had acted appropriately in a time of crisis.[69]

The U.S. Pan-American Triumph

If the first years of the 1920s left unresolved the American concerns about Argentine political stability, the U.S. economic advance persisted unabated, still under the umbrella of the Pan-American Union and in a climate of Argentine economic growth interspersed with crises of varying proportions. Increasingly, U.S. policy toward Argentina was formed in a Pan-American context, rather than a specifically Argentine diplomatic context. In the early 1920s, the United States chose two meetings at which to advance plans for the normalization of business conditions in the hemisphere, the Second Pan-American Financial Conference (1919–20) and the Fifth Pan-American Conference (1923).

As Americans planned for economic gains in South America through the Pan-American Union, Argentina's postwar economic uncertainty persisted despite the promise of a bumper grain harvest in 1920. Falling overseas prices for Argentine exports exacerbated an already unfavorable trade balance with the United States. In mid-1920, the Argentine government released the country's gold reserves in New York to pay for the imbalance. As a result, the value of the Argentine peso fell sharply and continued to drop through the mid-1920s. Argentina responded with loan requests to American bankers. In 1921, U.S. commerce secretary Herbert Hoover approached New York bankers on behalf of Argentina. In response, a syndicate that included Blaire & Company, White Weld & Company, and the Chase Securities Corporation issued a $50 million loan to the Argentine government. Argentina's economic uncertainty continued. And the nation's foreign debt rose from $90 million in 1922 to $290 million in 1928.[70]

The United States orchestrated its business diplomacy in Argentina and elsewhere in the Americas through the Pan-American Union. At the Second Pan-American Financial Conference in 1920, Argentina was one of several nations hoping for an American decision on new financial credits. But Washington led the conference in a different direction by setting aside the financing of railroad improvements in Argentina and other development-related projects in Latin America. Delegates continued the work of the First Pan-American Financial Conference by passing motions on improved maritime and railroad transportation, the standardization of bills of lading and trademarks, and the operation of foreign bank branches in South America. These initiatives were of no use in resolving Argentina's immediate financial crisis.[71]

Three years later, the author José Ingenieros followed in the tradition of José Martí by warning Argentines about U.S. commercial dominance through Pan-Americanism. But Argentine delegates arrived at the Fifth Pan-American Conference in Santiago de Chile without any sort of independent plan.[72] The Argentine Foreign Relations Ministry instructed its delegates not to challenge the United States and to recommend no more than adjustments in conference language detail.[73] Secretary of Agriculture Henry C. Wallace wrote the American position on the elimination of cattle diseases, the Navy Department set policy on arms limitations, and Secretary of State Charles Evans Hughes negotiated with Latin American diplomats to make certain that only eighteen preapproved subjects would be deliberated.[74] U.S. conference delegate Leo S. Rowe won Argentine ambassador Tomás LeBreton's promise that Argentina would counter an expected Uruguayan conference proposal for a League of Latin American Nations.[75]

At Santiago, the United States dominated proceedings. Delegates approved new rules of trade that included provisions for uniform merchandise nomenclature and guidelines for trademark protection.[76] The Gondra Treaty on the avoidance and prevention of armed conflict also suggested the still increasing significance of Pan-Americanism to Washington's plans for the Americas. The pact outlined a dispute arbitration process in the event of armed conflict between Pan-American Union (PAU) members.[77] Although the United States supported the fast implementation of Pan-American agreements on commercial dispute resolution, the Gondra Treaty was a different story. Unlike agreements on trademarks and merchandise nomenclature, which had the backing of the United States for quick exercise, American support for Gondra was lukewarm. The United States wanted structured arbitration for conflicts, but not in an agreement that could limit U.S. intervention in the region. The Gondra Pact, therefore, remained impractical for the United States and unexecuted. U.S. diplomatic and economic influence in South America was never higher.

3   Sanitary Embargo, Cultural Connections, and Wartime Neutrality, 1924–1946

Traditionally, historians have considered the period from 1924 to 1946 one of escalating misunderstanding and conflict between the United States and Argentina. It began with the political fallout from the Fordney-McCumber Tariff (1922) that imposed heavy duties on many Argentine exports. Argentine leaders accused the United States of restricting fair and free competition. Then came the spread of foot-and-mouth disease in Argentina, the U.S. ban on Argentine beef in 1926, and Argentine denunciations that the United States was now relying on trumped-up charges of unhealthy cattle to block beef imports from South America. Problems continued in 1928 at the Sixth Conference of American States in Havana. At that meeting Argentine representative Honório Pueyrredón spoke out against U.S. intervention in Nicaragua and elsewhere in the Americas. In 1936, U.S. president Franklin Delano Roosevelt traveled to Argentina for a meeting the United States had called to promote a new inter-American security agreement. Although Roosevelt received a warm welcome from Argentines, the meeting ended without the agreement the United States had sought. Argentina was among the nations most suspicious of what looked like an American effort to revive the Monroe Doctrine. Many U.S. diplomats and policymakers began to view Argentine leaders as uncooperative and irascible. The period ended with the Second World War and the rise of Juan D. Perón in Argentina. During the war, Argentines viewed the United States as hostile and limiting of Argentine strategic and commercial ambitions. American leaders became mistrustful of what they viewed as fascist tendencies in Argentina's government and pro-Nazi positions.

This chapter challenges those historical assumptions. It argues that while there was episodic conflict between the two countries, the years 1924 to 1946 represent a period of generally sound relations. Argentines excoriated the United States for military intervention in the Caribbean basin, for the activity of American trusts in Argentina, and for limitations placed by Washington on the importation of Argentine beef. But anti-Americanism grew in conjunction with a powerful attraction among Argentines for Hollywood films and other areas of American culture. Pueyrredón's 1928 outburst proved anomalous in the context of Argentina's supportive positions for U.S. policy in the Americas. And while the Great Depression slowed the growth of U.S.-Argentine economic ties, those relations remained strong during the 1930s. During World War II, despite tensions, Argentina played a wartime role not unlike what it had played during the First World War. Although remaining neutral for most of the war, Argentina was a strong supporter of the Allied cause through the foodstuffs and other goods it shipped to the United States and Britain.

Anti-intervention

Federal political and military interventions against the provinces were the most hotly debated Argentine political problem of the 1920s, an issue contributing to a growing awareness of U.S. intervention in Latin America, the other major source of Argentine animosity toward Washington in the 1920s. Argentine opposition to U.S. military intervention in the Caribbean basin reached a peak in the late 1920s and generated strong popular backing but shallow support among Argentine political leaders. Argentine cattle rancher and ambassador to the United States Honório Pueyrredón led the charge against the United States at the Sixth Conference of American States in Havana, criticizing U.S. military and political intervention in the Americas. His subordinate, Felipe Espil, a future ambassador to the United States, attached less significance to U.S. intervention than to Argentina's traditional backing for U.S.-led Pan-Americanism regarding business. In the end, Espil's vision prevailed among an Argentine political leadership willing to challenge the United States on animal disease, tariff policy, and intervention—but unwilling to allow any of that to alter strong bilateral economic ties.[1]

In Havana, the 1928 Sixth Pan-American Conference began as U.S. military activity in Nicaragua intensified in the hunt for rebel leader César Augusto Sandino. The United States had intervened repeatedly in Nicaragua since the first decade of the century. In 1912, U.S. Marines had joined Adolfo Díaz's successful insurgency. When Díaz won the presidency, one hundred Marines remained in Nicaragua to prop up the shaky regime. The United States all but ran Nicaraguan affairs through 1925, keeping the pro-U.S. Conservative Party in government. In 1926, the administration of President Calvin Coolidge sent Marines back to Nicaragua on the basis of reports of Bolshevik activity in that country. Washington's intelligence held little more credence than similar reports from Argentina a few years before. Many Americans were doubtful of this rationale for U.S. military activity. Some in Congress, including Senator George Norris, criticized the intervention. By 1928, the U.S. Marines had become mired in their search for Sandino.

Through the mid-1920s, Latin American condemnations of the U.S. Marine presence in Central America mounted. In Argentina, the Liga Pro Unión Americana distributed literature on the "unjustified and unspeakable Yankee invasion of Nicaragua," and socialist leader Alfredo L. Palacios worried out loud that "when the bankers were British, the Monroe Doctrine defended us. But who will defend us today from the grandchildren of Monroe?" Palacios charged that the Pan-American Union was a "faithful instrument" of imperialism.[2] American goals at Havana varied little from earlier U.S. Pan-American objectives. Americans determined a conference agenda that stressed trade normalization and sought to proscribe, where possible, antagonism of the sort Palacios had directed toward the Monroe Doctrine.[3]

U.S. diplomats reached Havana prepared for a fight. The State Department anticipated a multilateral effort to bring an anti-intervention resolution to the floor. It instructed American officials to undermine the effort. Ironically, the Americans believed they could count on Argentina to help oppose anti-interventionist sentiment. Pueyrredón's challenge to the United States was widely reported. Press accounts documented a heated diplomatic clash between Argentines and Americans over U.S. interventionism.[4] It was less well reported that the Argentine Foreign Relations Ministry immediately disavowed Pueyrredón's remarks and that the Argentine position toward the United States was generally supportive at Havana. On the normalization of trade and financial relations, the Foreign Relations Ministry backed U.S. positions.[5] The Havana conference marked a crest of U.S. Pan-American influence and capped two decades of the steady expansion of U.S. business in Latin America. In 1928 and 1929, the International Telephone and Telegraph Corporation and the American and Foreign Power Company sent nearly $160 million to Argentina. By 1930, U.S. direct investment in Argentina, some $335 million, was third in Latin America to U.S. investments in Cuba and Mexico.[6]

Five years after the conference in Havana, the strategic and economic position of the United States had changed in relation to both Argentina and the Pan-American movement. In 1933, at the Seventh Pan-American Conference in Montevideo, in keeping with President Franklin Roosevelt's Good Neighbor Policy, Secretary of State Cordell Hull reversed the U.S. stand on intervention at Havana; military intervention would no longer be a foreign policy option. Latin American diplomats and politicians—Argentine foreign minister Carlos Saavedra Lamas among them—congratulated themselves on having evoked the reversal. To be sure, Latin American pressures played a part in the concession to the sovereignty of Latin American states, but the Great Depression was the prime factor in the U.S. retreat from its 1920s Pan-Americanism.[7]

In September 1930, the Argentine military staged its first coup d'état of the century, overthrowing the weak second administration of Hipólito Yrigoyen. U.S. ambassador Robert Woods Bliss quickly recommended U.S. recognition of the de facto regime; American businessmen in Argentina supported the coup. U.S. recognition quickly followed, as did suspicions in Argentina that Standard Oil was behind the coup d'état as a means of advancing the company's prospects for new concessions. American officials justified their recognition of a military regime because, according to the State Department, the coup would not threaten Argentine democracy. Faced with the policy precedent of non-recognition in the case of Central American military dictatorships, Under Secretary of State Robert Cotton set Argentina apart: "I think that the sooner we realize that our Central American policy does not extend to South America, the better." In fact, the implications of the U.S. response to the 1930 coup underscored the opposite. Americans no longer held to a policy that distinguished clearly between Argentina and the other Latin American republics on the strength and efficacy of democratic rule. For the United States, there was no threat to Argentine democracy because that democracy, under siege for a decade from the radical left, was already in shambles, having ceased to guarantee political stability. The military government in Argentina quickly offered that it would cooperate enthusiastically with the U.S.-led Pan-American program for economic stabilization, reaffirming Argentina's backing for U.S.-led Pan-Americanism.[8]

Argentine Cultural Affinities / Argentine Suspicions

While European cultural and social influences in Argentina remained stronger than their U.S. equivalents, Argentines have long underestimated their own interest in the United States, which, in turn, stood in stark contrast to Argentine dismay over U.S. military intervention in Central America. Through the 1920s and 1930s, for example, the writings of Argentina's most prominent twentieth-century author, Jorge Luis Borges, reflected his reading of Ralph Waldo Emerson, Herman Melville, and Edgar Allan Poe. The latter's influence is evident in the emergence of Borges's mathematically determined plot lines and the logical inversions in his detective fiction. Borges translated William Faulkner and, in the pages of Victoria Ocampo's literary magazine *Sur*, reviewed Charlie Chaplin's *The Gold Rush* and *City Lights*. Hollywood movies flooded Buenos Aires. American story characters and cartoons became daily reading for Argentines—"El pibe" (Jackie Coogan) and Laurel and Hardy in *Billiken* magazine; Percy L. Crosby's Cachito (Skippy) in *Noticias Gráficas;* "El chiquito Abner" and Blondie in *La*

Razón; and Popeye, "el ratón Mickey," and Betty Boop in *Crítica*. American themes crept into Argentine popular writing and drawing. Hector L. Torino's cartoon *Don Mamerto, Detective* parodied the hard-boiled American gumshoe. The ideal of the American automobile as modern was revealed in J. E. Suárez's cartoon *Pepe Faroles*. In *El Diario,* a 1938 cartoon by the socialist artist Manuel Kantor showed Joe Louis standing triumphant over Hitler ("Supremacia Aria").[9]

U.S. advances in science and education were at the core of dozens of studies, including Carolina Tobar García's *Educación de los deficientes mentales en los Estados Unidos* (1933). In *Seis Ensayos* (1928), with attention to Sinclair Lewis, Willa Cather, and Ring Lardner, Pedro Henriquez Ureña analyzed the American novel as a sophisticated reflection of social progress. Also in 1928, Roberto Kurtz published two widely read books on the United States, *La Argentina ante Estados Unidos* and *La Verdad sobre Estados Unidos*. An engineer employed by the Argentine government in a massive highway construction project, Kurtz was immersed in the Argentine consumer culture of the 1920s, primed by the importation of American automobiles and other goods. Named a representative to the First Pan-American Highway Conference in Buenos Aires (1925), Kurtz joined other delegates at preconference meetings in the United States in 1924. On travels that took him from Lexington, Kentucky, to Duluth, Minnesota, Kurtz described in glowing terms dozens of features he believed defined American life, including freedom for women, an American "democratic spirit," and university excellence.

Without papering them over—but without much evidence behind his counterarguments—Kurtz took on Argentine negative impressions of the United States. He emphasized the law-and-order features of U.S. intervention in the Caribbean basin and the promise of nationhood for Cuba in the Platt Amendment. He remarked on the realization of Thomas Jefferson's vision of assimilated Native Americans, describing the supposed successes of the Haskell Institute and other residential schools in the education of "los pieles rojas." Though conceding that the hatred of black Americans by some whites was real, he characterized the "problema negro" more as a national bother than a national trauma. Argentines, he pointed out, believed in error that lynching was mandated by legislation. On many fronts, he found that Americans ran their society more effectively than did Argentines. Kurtz took aim at patronage politics in Argentina. Unlike its Argentine equivalent, he wrote, the U.S. civil service was not in the first instance a source of employment for thousands of people. The professions were governed by rule-making societies like the American Bar Association and the American Society of Civil Engineers that ensured high-quality work. Most important, according to Kurtz, Americans had a higher conception of liberty, education, and civic duty than did Argentines.

But as Argentines bought American cars and other consumer goods, and as they modeled their lives and pastimes to some extent on how they believed Americans lived, they also became increasingly critical of the United States. The most widespread criticism came in response to a perceived threat over U.S. oil and beef interests. Commercial oil production in Argentina began in earnest when deposits were found in Patagonia in 1907. Almost immediately, political debate over oil was framed around a nationalist defense of Argentina and against reliance on British coal and the American oil trust, Standard Oil. After 1920, U.S. firms raced to win oil concessions in Argentina. An American company, the Bolivia-Argentine Exploration Corporation, launched a plan to send inexpensive Bolivian oil to Argentina to drive the state-owned oil company out of business. Some Argentines suspected that Bolivia-Argentine was a Jersey Standard shell company. Such was the uproar in Argentina that in 1921 U.S. secretary of state Bainbridge Colby quizzed Bolivia-Argentine president Spruille Braden about possible ties to Jersey Standard. Braden claimed there was no link, but suspicions in Argentina persisted.[10]

Argentines were equally concerned about U.S. predominance in meatpacking. All areas of the Argentine cattle industry grew quickly between 1900 and 1920. Between 1914 and 1918 alone, the cattle population of Buenos Aires province rose by 33 percent from nine million to twelve million. In 1909, responding to the purchase of the Argentine La Blanca meatpacking plant by the National Packing Company—a combination made up of the American firms Swift, Armour, and Morris—congressional deputies Carlos and Manuel Carlés introduced legislation to prohibit the activity of "trusts" in the packing industry. Though the bill was defeated, during the debate politicians, journalists, and others spoke passionately on what they believed was the danger of U.S. trusts to Argentine control of the meat sector. Primed in part by ranchers and meat packers with business connections to the British companies that competed with American firms—but also by trust-busting activity in the United States—criticisms of American trusts persisted. An antitrust bill was finally passed by the House in 1921 and by the Senate in 1922.[11]

Lingering suspicions of purportedly sinister meatpacking interests contributed to an angry Argentine response to the U.S. decision in 1926 to ban the importation of Argentine chilled and frozen meat. Washington's judgment was, in fact, motivated by reports of foot-and-mouth disease endemicity in Argentina.[12] Argentine ranchers, unlike cattle raisers in the United States and Great Britain, had no guarantee of government compensation for foot-and-mouth-related losses. As a result, at a time when American ranchers were quick to report the disease, their Argentine equivalents were more wary. *Frigoríficos* (meatpacking companies), governments (national and local), and agricultural societies hoped to avoid antagonizing ranchers, who were jumpy over losses they might sustain if foot-and-mouth were discovered in the countryside; they became accomplices to the movement of diseased herds to slaughter. The U.S. Department of Agriculture (USDA) sanitary ban had no immediate impact on Argentina's foreign trade. In 1926, Argentina shipped 4,075,000 pounds of fresh meats to the United States, valued at $534,250, compared to total export figures of 657,467 tons—almost all of which went to Great Britain. Of greater concern to Argentines than the current trade were prospects for future exports to the United States and a sense that U.S. business and government were out to undermine Argentine economic independence. Argentines saw the U.S. ban as a trade-related punishment. The U.S. Tariff Act of 1922 (the Fordney-McCumber Tariff) had subjected most Argentine exports to heavy protective duties. At the time of the beef ban, the Argentine government was also fighting Washington over U.S. rules on the importation of grapes, alfalfa, and corn.[13]

Influenced in part by similar criticisms from self-interested British diplomats, Argentine anger over the USDA ban expressed a larger dissatisfaction over the triangular trade between Great Britain, the

United States, and Argentina. After the First World War, the triangle came to be determined increasingly by the dominance of American financial institutions, U.S. mastery of key Argentine commercial markets (automobiles and agricultural machinery, for example), a relative decline in British exports to Argentina, and persistent Argentine reliance on British markets, especially for beef. Argentine animosity was influenced by the self-described leading propagandist for British interests in Argentina, British minister Sir Malcolm Robertson—whom Americans credited with having coined a phrase popularized by the Rural Society after the sanitary ban, "Buy from those who buy from us."[14] Some Radical Party leaders found injustice and economic imbalances in the triangle; whereas the British were contributing to the Argentine trade balance by maintaining strong markets for beef, Robertson and Argentine leaders held, the United States restricted the entry of Argentine produce while garnering new marketing opportunities in Argentina.[15]

Even as Argentines continued to vilify the U.S. position, foot-and-mouth spread. In 1927, USDA veterinarian Severin Fladness found terrible inspection facilities in Argentina. Conditions at meatpacking plants remained poor. The British veterinarian John Lamb Frood described a general confusion that prevailed when diseased cattle entered municipal markets in Argentina; contact was common among infected, suspected, and healthy animals.[16] The Argentine Ministry of Agriculture enforced sanitary laws badly. Congress never inquired into or pressed for a resolution of the factors contributing to animal disease. In part, this reflects the disinterest in foot-and-mouth of successive political administrations and congressional leaders in a context of long-term political stalemates during successive congressional terms. At the time of the sanitary ban, the Argentine Senate was consumed with the problem of federal interventions against provincial governments.[17]

Hollywood and Waldo Frank

Argentines may have disputed U.S. policy in Central America and on the risks of infected cattle, but they looked to the United States for direction in other areas of public life. Argentine efforts at urban beautification and wilderness preservation were both influenced by American precedents. In 1923, the City of Buenos Aires created the Comisión Estética Edilicia to consider and make recommendations on the future of the city. The commission's report, "Proyecto Orgánico para la Urbanización del Municipio" (1925), drew heavily on the American City Beautiful model that combined French classicism in town planning with an emphasis on American landscapes. The commission's emphases on the construction of inexpensive housing, the creation of a construction code, and the formulation of an urban plan also drew on current U.S. urban design.[18] A nascent parks movement in Argentina reacted to significant ecological devastation in many regions before 1930. Between 1906 and 1915 there was widespread deforestation in Santiago del Estero. In Mendoza, olive trees cultivated for two hundred years had disappeared. In San Juan, scientists believed that excessive tree harvesting had had an impact on the climate. Responding to the crisis, Argentine governments established the country's first national parks. Though Nahuel Huapi National Park in Argentina was inaugurated for its natural beauty and Lanin National Park for its picturesque landscapes, like several U.S. parks in the early twentieth century, the Los Glaciares National Park was established to accommodate tourism, to give travelers access to glaciers in southern Argentina.[19]

The area of greatest cultural interchange between the United States and Argentina before 1950 was in the production and marketing of motion pictures. Between 1920 and 1950, the history of Argentine filmmaking and distribution followed the course of U.S.-Argentine relations more generally in several respects. The U.S. cultural assault continued almost unabated. American films were marketed in Argentina as successfully as cars and tractors. By 1925, more than 90 percent of feature films shown in Argentina were U.S. made. In 1941, Walt Disney led a team of artists to South America to do research for a full-length cartoon that would feature Donald Duck and other Disney characters in Latin America. In Argentina, they worked with the famous folk artist Florencio Molina Campos, whose recognizable drawing style was evident in the film *Saludos Amigos* (1942).

During the Great Depression, in keeping with political and economic retrenchment in the United States more generally, Hollywood sent many fewer films to Argentina. Argentine industry underwent a boom in many sectors after 1930, partly as a result of the slowdown in U.S. exports. As part of this expansion, through 1942 the film industry experienced a "golden age" in both the quantity and quality of films produced. Argentine filmmakers continued to rely on advances in American technology. With the U.S. entry into the Second World War, the fortunes of the Argentine film industry continued to follow those of U.S.-Argentine relations. Beginning in 1942, U.S. economic pressures on successive Argentine governments, whose policies the Americans opposed, had strong negative impacts on many areas of Argentine life, including the film industry. A decline in movie production can be tied directly to a U.S. embargo on film for moviemaking. After 1946, with the election of President Juan Perón, the film industry underwent a partial recovery. Perón's nationalist policies fostered Argentine production at the expense of Hollywood films, but his tight regulation of film content meant that Argentine moviemaking would not recapture the originality and substance of the 1930s until the 1960s.[20]

Hollywood's marketing strategy in Argentina through the early 1930s focused on distribution subsidiaries that sent rental profits directly back to American producers; as had happened in the United States, independent distribution companies in Argentina were eliminated in the face of competition from Hollywood studios. By 1930, after Australia, Argentina had become the biggest importer of U.S.-made films. The quick expansion of Argentine film production in the 1930s occurred partly because Hollywood could not hold its cinema audiences in Argentina and elsewhere in Latin America. The Great Depression prompted a scaled-down production schedule in Hollywood, but in addition, early efforts to market Spanish-language talkies in Latin America produced lackluster results.[21]

The most prominent Argentine film actor of the 1930s was tango superstar Carlos Gardel. For many Argentines, Gardel embodied in personality and song essential Argentine cultural qualities. Inspired in part by Al Jolson's success in talking films, Gardel became interested in a movie career in the late 1920s at a time when he was already a celebrity. Late in 1930, in the hope of making a feature-length film, Gardel made contact with the Paramount studio in France. Paramount believed that Gardel could be made over into an English-language star, but the singer's language skills were weak. In 1934, Gardel sang very briefly in English for NBC but gave up quickly. Even so, Paramount was keen on exposing him to U.S. audiences. The studio gave him a short segment in the 1935 film *The Big Broadcast of 1936*. In March 1935, on a tour promoting his films in South America, Gardel was killed in a plane accident. The historian Simon Collier speculates that had Gardel lived, he might have been as successful in Hollywood as was Maurice Chevalier.[22]

In the early 1940s, the Argentine film sector went into a long period of decline that came, in large measure, as a result of U.S. economic pressures. Because of Argentine neutrality during World War II, the United States thought it appropriate to take restrictive action. Beginning in 1942, the United States began to force the issue with an export embargo of hundreds of products that included raw film stock. Without access to film in other markets, Argentine filmmaking ground to a halt. From fifty-six films in 1942, production fell to only twenty-three in 1945. The U.S. government accused both the Argentine government and the national film industry of having pro-Axis sympathies. In conjunction with the embargo and the decline of Argentina's film industry, American producers stepped in to fill the Latin American vacuum. By 1943, twenty-five films with Latin American themes were in production in Hollywood. U.S. producers brought Carmen Miranda and other South American film stars to Hollywood to "latinize" production and to fill the void left in the Americas by the declining Argentine output.

In literary circles, U.S. influence proved more durable. One of the most important figures in U.S.-Argentine cultural ties during the 1930s and 1940s was the American author Waldo Frank. A prominent social historian and novelist, Frank was influenced not only by the American transcendentalists Ralph Emerson and Walt Whitman, but also by psychoanalysis and American progressivism. That proved a combination especially appealing to Argentine intellectuals. What makes Frank unique in this context is that his impact on Argentine literary culture was notable, but no more so than the effect Argentine society had on his writing. Frank's work and career mark a kind of genuine interchange between the two countries that was unusual. Disillusioned with the American intellectual climate after the First World War, as were many authors, Frank turned to Latin America for inspiration. A six-month trip through the hemisphere included Argentina and helped confirm Frank's rejection of what he believed was a pervasive materialism and conformity in the United States, in favor of higher ideals and values celebrated in Latin America. These included the importance of folk cultures and the closeness of communities to spiritual values and to the land. Frank believed that people in the Americas would define a new hemispheric set of cultures dominated by the ideals he found in Latin America. Frank set about popularizing Latin American literature and cultures in the United States.[23]

A well-known author, Frank was frequently criticized at home for what some read as an overly flowery and dramatic style. In Latin America, on the other hand, readers recognized Frank's long descriptions and passionate analysis as similar to the styles of Rubén Darío, José Enrique Rodó, and other prominent essayists. This surprised Latin Americans, many of whom were used to thinking of American writers as brutish and cold. According to the Chilean journalist Ernesto Montenegro, "we find him at his best when . . . he abandons himself to his keen poetic intuition."[24] When Frank reached Argentina in 1929, he found to his surprise that his works were already well known and that he was considered a great writer. The Buenos Aires dailies *La Nación* and *La Prensa* asked him to be a regular contributor, while Victoria Ocampo and other important literary figures who would found the important *Sur* literary review in 1931 celebrated Frank's refreshing rejection of the pragmatism and materialism they associated with the United States. Some found a different sort of American colonialism in Frank's writing. The Argentine Juan José Sebreli argued much later that Frank had highlighted and romanticized supposedly mystical qualities of events and cultures that were no more mystical than historical developments in the

United States. Even so, the Argentine literary community continued to lionize Frank through the 1930s.[25]

Back in the United States, Frank set about drawing Latin American literature to the attention of the American public. His audience was limited. Almost no publishers or fellow writers were interested in disseminating the works of Latin American writers. Even so, Frank persevered in placing special emphasis on the work of Argentine writers whom he regarded as the best in the Americas. He was fascinated with the short story as a genre in Argentina and wrote that Argentines were destined to excel as "a literary people . . . even as Mexico and Peru are essentially plastic nations."[26] Late in 1930, when he became the editorial adviser for a new Latin America series from Farrar and Rinehart, Frank began by editing a collection of Argentine short stories.

In 1934, Frank rewrote Ricardo Guiraldes's 1926 novel *Don Segundo Sombra,* a lyrical description of life in the Argentine *pampas.* The novel appeared a year later under the title *Don Segundo Sombra: Shadows in the Pampas.* In his introduction, Frank tried to draw a parallel between the novel and the forms of American frontier novels. He found similarities between *Don Segundo* and Mark Twain's *Huckleberry Finn* but showed his limited understanding of Argentine rural society: Frank contrasted the "noble," supposedly nonaboriginal *gaucho* of Spanish, Catholic heritage with what Huck reflected of a wild, base frontier tradition in the United States that had undermined English tradition. In fact, for what they reflected of a cultural and ethnic mixing of indigenous peoples, Europeans, and blacks, as well as in the concern over "savagery" they generated among urban elites in both countries, the Argentine and U.S. frontiers were remarkably similar.[27]

In 1942, the U.S. government financed a new South American trip for Frank in the hope that he might help bring Argentina into the war on the side of the Allies. Relying on an author to help effect policy was an unusual departure for Washington. In one of his tour lectures, "Hacía la derrota del hombre," Frank urged Latin American young people not to join fascist gangs and accused fascism of humiliating mankind. In his speech "Llegado a Buenos Aires," Frank called on Latin Americans to abandon their Second World War neutrality, to join the fight against the Axis, and to bear in mind that the political choice was a stark one, for death or for birth.[28] Days later, five men identifying themselves as police officers beat Frank on the head with side arms they were carrying, while shouting pro-Nazi, anti-Semitic epithets.[29] Frank's beating was front-page news in both Argentina and the United States. An article Frank wrote for *Collier's* in September 1942 not only underlined his dismay over political and cultural repression in Argentina but also focused public attention on the ugly side of what Frank had celebrated, Argentine "primitivism." One photograph that accompanied the essay showed a bandaged Frank lying in an Argentine hospital bed recovering from the beating.[30] Ironically for Frank, it was the press reports of the violence he had suffered—not his own chronicle of the trip, *South American Journey*, or his other efforts to popularize Latin America in the United States—that had the greatest impact on American public opinion.[31] Coverage of the attack in the *New York Times* and dozens of other newspapers helped generate a popular sense in the United States that Argentina was inherently repressive and pro-Nazi, a popular view that would linger in one form or another through most of the cold war period.

Road to War

Though Argentina was drawn much closer to the United States culturally in the first decades of the century, after the coup d'état of 1930 many Argentines pressed for a renewal of strong ties with Great Britain. In the aftermath of the foot-and-mouth controversy, and in the face of uncertain trade conditions in the early years of the Great Depression, many believed that Argentina's future economic growth lay in a new trade agreement with London. That accord would stress guaranteed British beef and grains markets for Argentina, in return for tariff concessions for British goods. As in the 1920s, many Argentines believed incorrectly that Argentine and American trade interests were complementary.[32] When the Ottawa Accords of 1932 locked Argentina out of a series of new trade agreements between Britain and its Dominions, the Argentine government stepped up efforts to reach a pact with Great Britain. Argentina's chief negotiator, Vice President Julio A. Roca, had little to offer. The British reminded Roca that their exports to Argentina amounted to only 4 percent of the British total, whereas Argentina sold to Great Britain 37 percent of everything it shipped overseas. Argentina had been attacked for decades as a sellout to British imperialism, and the bilateral agreement finally negotiated in 1933 guaranteed access to Great Britain for Argentine beef. But the Roca-Runciman Pact did not achieve trade preference for Argentina on par with the Dominions. As a result, the Argentines turned back to the United States for the negotiation of a bilateral trade agreement.[33]

Argentina recovered from the worst ravages of the Great Depression far more quickly than the United States or Great Britain. By 1934, Argentine industrial production was stronger in many sectors than it ever had been. Argentines and Americans negotiated for a new trade pact on and off through 1936. As in the case of British-Argentine negotiations, Argentine efforts fell short of an agreement that would have guaranteed market shares for Argentine products satisfactory to ranchers, packers, and grain producers. Primed in part by the Argentine foot-and-mouth threat, but also by growing protectionist sentiment, the American beef lobby was flooding members of the U.S. House of Representatives with letters opposing any relaxation in the sanitary ban. Members of Congress lobbied the Bureau of Animal Industry.[34]

While trade talks stumbled, Argentines and Americans cooperated effectively, if haltingly, to bring the Chaco War to a close. Tensions between Bolivia and Paraguay through the late 1920s over the large, disputed Chaco territory led to the Bolivian invasion of Paraguay in 1931 and a particularly violent land conflict. Argentine foreign minister Carlos Saavedra Lamas was a key architect of the negotiated model for an eventual peace and the diplomat most active in securing the settlement. His efforts were recognized with the Nobel Peace Prize, for which he had sought Hull's backing at the time of his nomination. What makes the peace negotiations particularly striking in the context of U.S.-Argentine relations is the relative absence of contention between the two countries over almost ten years of negotiation. Because the problem at hand was relatively unimportant to each country's national interests, diplomats were able to work more amenably with one another. The Americans were prepared to concede the vital importance of Argentina's role as a predominant regional power in settling the conflict. Hull was generally content to have the Argentines take the lead. Saavedra Lamas, on the other hand, did not face the array of pressures with which Argentine leaders normally grappled in working with Washington.[35]

Goodwill emanating from the Chaco talks led directly to planning for an Inter-American Conference for Maintenance of Peace, which in turn would form the initial basis for the U.S.-led inter-American security system developed after World War II. Anticipating renewed German influence in the Americas, Hull and Roosevelt hoped to shore up backing for U.S. leadership in the hemisphere. They planned the meeting of American states for late 1936, and the Argentine government offered to play host. When he arrived in Buenos Aires for the conference, Roosevelt received an enthusiastic welcome from tens of thousands of people in the Plaza de Mayo.[36]

The meeting ended in U.S.-Argentine discord, presaging problems between the two countries during the Second World War. Hull's vision of hemispheric security was U.S.-dominated and revived memories of the Monroe Doctrine in the minds of some Latin Americans. To confront potential external military threats, Hull called for a mandatory consultation process among the American states, a permanent committee of foreign ministers to grapple with a coordinated multinational response, and the acceptance by Latin American countries of U.S. positions on neutrality. Saavedra Lamas rightly suspected a U.S. intention to dominate the new security mechanisms. He suggested instead a more internationalist approach to the problem Hull and Roosevelt had formulated that included cooperation with the League of Nations, inter-American consultation through normal diplomatic channels only, and a renewed commitment to nonintervention. In heated floor debates, Saavedra Lamas not only blocked the U.S. plan for hemispheric security but at the same time reaffirmed the important place of Pan-American diplomacy in bilateral relations. He alienated Hull, who tended thereafter to view Argentines as obstructionist and hostile to American interests.[37]

Hull's suspicion of Argentina came at a bad moment for bilateral relations. Inaugurated in February 1938, Argentine president Roberto Ortiz faced an almost nonstop series of political and economic crises that made it impossible for his government to hold back the growing influence of the military on Argentine politics. Moreover, Hull's antipathy toward Argentina consistently outweighed the sentiment of those in the State Department who urged him to take into account Ortiz's tenuous hold on power. After 1938, the sharpening polarization behind political support for and opposition to the Ortiz administration stressed a growing divide in Argentine society over whether the government should tend toward Great Britain or Germany.

Ortiz had emerged as a democratic candidate backed by political conservatives and anti-personalist supporters of the Unión Cívica Radical. He won the presidency in a corrupt election but set about trying to end fraud as an antidote to authoritarianism. As Ortiz pressed for a return to open electoral politics following the more restrictive, military-dominated political structure of the 1930s, Argentines understood that such a move would favor the Unión Cívica Radical, proscribed from full political participation since the 1930 coup d'état. Because the Radicals openly favored strong ties with the British, those who backed favorable relations with Germany, particularly within the military, tried to undermine Ortiz. Once the Second World War was underway, the pro-Allied foreign minister, José María Cantilo, joined Ortiz in expressing support for the Allies. But their position within Argentina's foreign policymaking structure became untenable. In the Foreign Relations Ministry, within the military, and in government more generally—in a context of the growing association in the minds of many Argentines between the Allies and U.S. Pan-American policies for strategic preeminence in the hemisphere—there was growing disdain for the Allies.[38]

Nazis, Neutrality, and War

As in August 1914, the outbreak of war in Europe in September 1939 prompted a sudden financial and economic crisis. Argentina was deeply in debt and facing agricultural surpluses no longer marketable in war-torn Europe, and the country labored under the unresolved problem of a trade pact with the United States that had lingered through the end of the 1930s. Many Argentines were ambivalent about the war, believing that any Argentine support for the Allies should be contingent on guaranteed contracts for Argentine exports.[39] Through mid-1940, when Ortiz had to leave office because of poor health, the Argentine government worked hard for the elusive pact with the United States, both as a solution to Argentina's worsening economy and as a means of salvaging Ortiz's democratizing political project. Negotiations stalled repeatedly over the issue of guaranteed U.S. markets for Argentine goods. The Americans were suspicious of the role played by Argentine Central Bank president Raúl Prebisch, whom the U.S. ambassador to Argentina, Norman Armour, viewed as anti-American. In fact, Prebisch had been the architect of an Argentine negotiating strategy that tried a formula of currency exchange controls to balance the trade between the two countries.[40]

At the same time, the U.S. ambassador in Buenos Aires seemed to understand Ortiz's precarious position and urged his superiors to support Argentina economically. But Washington demurred, partly because of the strength of U.S. farm and ranch lobbies against the importation of Argentine meat, corn, and other foodstuffs. Even so, to a far greater extent than previous governments, Ortiz did all he could to position Argentina as friendly toward the United States in the face of mounting hostility from his political opponents. Shortly after the start of the war, Washington moved to shore up already strong support in the Americas by organizing the First Consultative Meeting of Foreign Ministers in Panama. The Argentine government proved a strong backer of the United States at the meeting, approving a measure to establish a three-hundred-mile neutrality zone around the hemisphere. At the end of 1939 the neutrality zone was tested. After a firefight with the British warships *Achilles*, *Exeter*, and *Ajax*, the German pocket battleship *Graf Von Spee* limped into Montevideo badly damaged. Argentine authorities joined Uruguay and other Latin American countries in protesting the violation of the neutrality of Uruguayan territorial waters. Argentina then argued for a Pan-American declaration prohibiting belligerent ships from entering Latin American waters.

Dramatically, Argentina's trade position began to improve. In the first quarter of 1940 Argentine exports to the United States jumped a stunning 58 percent over the same period for 1939, from $16,743,836 to $26,493,454. Although wool shipments rose by 243 percent, accounting for a fair part of the increase, there were impressive export surges in a number of commodities including canned meat, hides and skins, minerals, and dairy products.[41] Despite this, Argentina was in economic trouble. In June, Prebisch secretly contacted the U.S. embassy in Buenos Aires asking for help. He confessed that several large Argentine power plants were now forced to use domestic corn for fuel, and he urged the Americans to send a representative incognito to Buenos Aires to help the government find a way out of its difficulties. Prebisch wanted Washington to finance Argentine imports from the United States through the Export-Import Bank. He also asked for a new loan to help Argentina meet payments on its external debt and for guaranteed U.S. purchases of Argentina's exportable surpluses. Prebisch tried to tug at U.S. diplomatic sensibilities by stating that such assistance would have "a very beneficial psychological effect upon the Argentine people who are disturbed by intelligent Nazi-Fascist propaganda." "The Argentine government," he went on, "is now probably better disposed towards the United States and sees more nearly eye to eye with the United States with respect to the European situation than any other American Republic."[42] Armour understood that Argentine-U.S. ties regarding the war and most other issues would be shaped by trade. He saw two stark options for the United States in Argentina. Either Americans would provide Latin American countries with a far-reaching and decisive set of economic alternatives to prospects that Germany was offering, or Washington would have to watch as Germany won the upper hand in Argentina.[43]

Through the first four months of 1940, persistent domestic crises prompted Argentina to take the lead in finding a way to develop a united Pan-American position on the war. A quickly worsening foreign debt load and political unrest in a handful of provinces leading to federal interventions left the Ortiz administration shaken and divided. Partly as an effort to reassert control in an increasingly uncertain political climate, Ortiz encouraged Cantilo to advance the position that the American republics set neutrality aside in favor of nonbelligerency. On 19 April, Cantilo suggested the change to Armour. Neutrality, the foreign minister argued, was too meek a stand for the American republics. He meant nonbelligerency as a means for individual and joint action among the American republics to confront the belligerents on a range of military and economic matters. The historian Joseph Tulchin reasons that Cantilo timed the announcement of the nonbelligerency proposal to coincide with the worst of a series of crises unfolding in his now-shaky government. When the federal government intervened against the province of Buenos Aires in March, two cabinet ministers resigned. The Americans knew Ortiz was weak. The president was looking for a way to shore up his political position and sent Cantilo to Armour to do just that.[44] But in addition, the Argentine Navy, the Army, the Foreign Relations Ministry, and other branches of government saw U.S. neutrality as a tacit but strong link with the Allies. Ortiz's government wanted to push Washington to a truly neutral position and, in so doing, to dislodge the Americans from their leadership in the Americas on the neutrality question.[45]

Argentine strategists also tied neutrality and continental defense to trade. Neutrality, as Americans had shaped it for the hemisphere, missed an important set of points around security and power. The United States had done far too little since the beginning of the war to take on a fair share of the cost of continental rearmament, in light of U.S. wealth. In addition, Argentine leaders expected the United States to complement neutrality or nonbelligerency with an aggressive set of trade and financial guarantees to Argentina.[46] The nonbelligerency initiative had the desired effect, but only very briefly. Signals of interest in nonbelligerency from Washington and some Latin American countries were complemented in May with some popular support in Argentina for Ortiz's pro-Allied group, in response to the German invasion of the Netherlands. But the State Department, unwilling to give Argentina a diplomatic or strategic edge in the hemisphere and overwhelmed with news from Europe of Nazi advances, let Argentina's non-belligerency proposal die. Ortiz continued to lose political and economic ground at home. With the German occupation of Scandinavia, Belgium, the Netherlands, and France, with the British naval blockade of Europe, and despite Argentina's relatively strong trade figures with the United States, Argentina's grain exports were decimated by wartime disruptions.[47]

Working with Raúl Prebisch, Finance Minister Federico Pinedo devised the Plan de Reactivación Económica or Plan Pinedo. Its goals were to keep inflation down, employment up, and labor unrest at a minimum. Pinedo channeled funds into agricultural financing, tried to stimulate manufacturing, and promoted a South American free-trade zone. Late in 1940, Prebisch held out the plan for U.S. officials to study and to point out objections they might have. The plan sought increased markets for Argentine manufactured goods in the United States and devised a number of mechanisms toward this end. One such device would be to pressure importers to do their share in helping to boost exports in other areas. The Ford Motor Company branch office in Argentina, for example, might have to export Argentine dairy products to earn exchange for car imports beyond a limited importation quota. The State Department understood the potential restrictions on bilateral trade but approved the plan all the same. Even so, Ortiz's government fell before the Plan Pinedo could be implemented.[48]

On the eve of Ortiz's fall, many Argentines believed his government was too close to the United States. To counteract street protests and other opposition, Ortiz backed a bill proscribing unneutral conduct. The ensuing political debate highlighted a generalized sense in Congress that the government should be pressing the Americans much harder for a favorable trade agreement. Ortiz tried. Long-standing bilateral negotiations had stalled in January 1940. Through a series of informal contacts with U.S. diplomats, the Argentines tried to make Washington understand that without a trade pact, the government would be lost, and Argentina might well fall into the Nazi camp. Norman Armour appreciated the risk to Ortiz and urged his government to reactivate trade discussions. As in the case of the nonbelligerency proposal, the Americans reacted too slowly. Moreover, the Argentine suggestion implied a rethinking of the hemispheric approach to the war that did not coincide with U.S. strategic planning.

At the time, Washington was trying to generate support in Latin America for its wartime agenda by direct, bilateral discussions with individual nations. The United States sought military backing from each nation for a U.S.-led defense of the hemisphere, in the event of an attack from outside. In return for a military commitment from individual states, the State Department held out Export-Import Bank credits, the only area of economic cooperation and assistance that it controlled. Argentina's positions on both nonbelligerency and new financing and marketing commitments from the United States did not fit Washington's larger objective of tying economic points to military issues. Moreover, the U.S. government could not fathom the importance of both Argentine proposals for the survival of Ortiz. Finally, in December 1940, thanks in part to an earlier visit to Buenos Aires from Export-Import Bank president Warren Lee Pierson, the two countries reached a Stabilization Agreement that promised Export-Import Bank credits of sixty million and fifty million dollars from the U.S. Treasury Department toward stabilizing the bilateral exchange rate. According to Tulchin, the agreement was "too little, too late."[49]

Ironically, the Argentine nonbelligerency proposal generated a rebuke from Germany as well. In May, the German government accused Argentina of favoring the Allies. Like the United States, Germany was concerned that the Argentine initiative on nonbelligerency was, in fact, an attempt to assert Argentine diplomatic leadership in South America. Except, according to the German foreign minister, the Argentines were trying to trade neutrality for "an active belligerency against Germany."[50] In the meantime, Ortiz's fleeting hope that the nonbelligerency proposal, if rubber-stamped by Washington, could propel Argentina into a leadership role in South America had the opposite effect. Primed in part by German military successes in Europe, but also by early signals that Brazil, Chile, and Uruguay were favorably disposed to Argentine ideas, Washington stepped up its efforts to craft a U.S.-led hemispheric defense agreement. Argentine leaders sought Brazilian assistance in convincing Washington of the merits of nonbelligerency. Argentine foreign minister Cantilo sent the proposal to his Brazilian equivalent, Osvaldo Aranha, at the same time that he sent it to the United States. He hoped Aranha would prove an ally on the issue, but in the end Aranha accepted U.S. arguments against a shift in inter-American neutrality.[51]

Rebuffed by Washington and facing an unsolvable economic crisis at home, the Ortiz government lost political ground quickly. In July 1940, Ortiz, physically exhausted and ill, left the running of his administration to his vice president, Ramón Castillo. Foreign Minister Cantilo resigned in August. By the time Enrique Ruiz Guiñazú had become foreign minister in June 1941, Argentine popular opinion and government policy had hardened toward the United States. Argentine authorities left the loan agreements with Washington unapproved, criticized U.S. intentions to establish military bases in Uruguay, and made no effort to revive now-lapsed bilateral high-ranking military staff conversations. American scholars have frequently attributed the hardening Argentine position toward the United States as a reflection of pro-Nazi sentiment both within government and among Argentines more generally. In fact, for Argentines circumstances were similar to those that governed policy and American attitudes during World War I. Many Argentines believed that their government should stake out an international position clearly at odds with the Nazis and closer to the United States, but many more believed relations with the United States now were much as they had been during the First World War. While Argentina traded actively with the United States under unfavorable conditions, the Americans pressed unreasonably for a diplomatic and military leadership over the Argentines. At the same time, Washington demanded that Argentina rupture its neutral cordiality with Germany, a country on which the Argentines pinned strong current and future trade hopes.[52]

With the American entry into World War II, Washington became increasingly preoccupied with Nazis in Argentina. Growing concern through the war that Argentine authorities, particularly the generals, were close to Germany culminated in an irrational series of assumptions about Nazis in Argentina. Not all U.S. officials subscribed to simplistic arguments that Argentina was "pro-Nazi." That line was ac-cepted too readily by the State Department, which led directly into a false assessment of Perón as a fascist, presaging the cold war ideologi-cal blinders that would help dispense any nuance in how Americans understood governments in many parts of Latin America. According to the historian Ronald C. Newton, what some in the United States saw as a Nazi menace in Argentina was nonsense.[53]

Perhaps, but the U.S. government and the American media devel-oped an obsession with this perceived threat. To be sure, Nazis did their best to generate support and establish a strong base in Argentina. In the 1930s, German organizers arrived to proselytize in German-speaking communities. Others spread the word more broadly in Argentina, while some German diplomats made the case to political leaders and then worked hard to help ensure Argentine neutrality during the war. Between 1942 and 1944, Argentina became Germany's primary intelli-gence and covert warfare base in the Americas. Moreover, there were pro-Nazi Argentine military officers, most of whom were anti-Semitic.

But as in the First World War, Argentina maintained an increasingly pro-Allied neutrality, though the policy did not ease U.S. suspicions. Americans squandered diplomatic opportunities to capitalize on the genuine interest many Argentines held for Hollywood and a host of other aspects of American culture. In 1941, a limited poll of Argentines conducted by the British embassy in Buenos Aires found no substantial antipathy toward Americans in spite of popular Argentine perceptions that the United States had persistently blocked opportunities for Ar-gentina's advancement through international trade. The question of markets for Argentine meat topped the list of issues Argentines be-lieved were at the core of bilateral ties with the United States. Most Ar-gentines indicated that few of their fellow citizens believed in "Yankee imperialism" as a dangerous force in the hemisphere.[54]

None of this made much difference in the State Department. To some extent, an escalation of U.S.-Argentine tensions in 1942 can be linked to long-standing political struggles in Washington, particularly between Secretary of State Cordell Hull and Under Secretary Sumner Welles, who had policymaking responsibility for Argentina. The historian

Randall B. Woods argues that Welles took a position closer to the Argentine line, forming part of a group that stressed what it believed was the efficacy of the Good Neighbor Policy and the value of strong inter-American relations. Hull, on the other hand, was less concerned with Latin America. His internationalist perspective called for Latin American nations to follow a U.S. lead in the interest of strategic and economic benefits for the hemisphere.[55]

In January 1942, Washington officials organized the Third Meeting of Foreign Ministers in Río de Janeiro to complete the work that Franklin Roosevelt had started in Buenos Aires in 1936. Welles worked with Brazilian and Chilean delegates to help win Ruiz Guiñazú's support for a draft accord on how to confront Germany and to establish an inter-American security agreement. But acting Argentine president Ramón Castillo rejected it. Welles made clear at Río that should Argentina refuse to break ties with Germany, it could expect no further military assistance from Washington. Castillo now faced a catch-22. To receive U.S. military aid, Argentina would have to break ties with Germany. At the same time, an increasingly powerful military, which rejected a break with any of the belligerents, demanded new U.S. military aid in advance of any new signed accords with the Americans.

Despite this conundrum, Argentina and the United States finally signed a new reciprocal trade agreement in July 1942 (the first since 1853). The pact was an important index of the state of U.S.-Argentine ties, despite animosity in Washington for Argentine authorities. In 1940, the United States emerged as Argentina's principal supplier of imports. Argentina bought more from the United States that year than it had in any year through the Great Depression. In 1941, the Argentine government finally liberalized its exchange control regulations, further stimulating trade with the United States and helping to make an agreement possible. U.S. imports of Argentine products, including hides, quebracho extract, and wool, were primed by the war. They amounted to $166,618,000 in 1941, twice the import value for 1940 and the highest level of imports from Argentina since 1930. Whether the State Department recognized it or not, Argentina's trade with the United States made it an important friend on the eve of the attack on Pearl Harbor.[56]

Through 1943, the Roosevelt administration continued to press Argentina for a break with the Nazis. The Americans wrongly insisted on seeing Argentine neutrality as sympathy for Nazism. In fact, as they had during the First World War, Argentine leaders charted a policy directed against the predominance of the world power that they believed most threatened their economic independence, the United States. Some still hoped that at the end of the war, Argentina might aspire again to regional economic, strategic, and diplomatic leadership, at the expense of the Americans.

As in the First World War, the British had a more sensible approach than the Americans to Argentina's wartime position—an approach that better reflected Argentina's contribution and potential contribution to the war effort. By early 1942, Argentina was already fulfilling a wartime role similar to that it had undertaken after 1914, supplying the Allies with crucial foodstuffs and raw materials. The British believed that Argentine neutrality would, in fact, enhance its ability to continue to ship goods to the Allies. While the British joined the Americans in condemning Argentine wartime stands that favored Germany, they accepted Argentine neutrality and generally felt that the Americans were harsh in their insistence that Argentina join the Allied war effort. Cordell Hull and others in Washington simply had no appreciation for the domestic and international pressures on Argentine authorities that made marching in lockstep with Washington impossible.[57]

As the United States became increasingly hostile, Castillo faced pressure from the Argentine military to turn to Germany for weapons, particularly in light of traditional rival Brazil's growing power and its close ties with the Americans. Cut off from U.S. lend-lease matériel, Castillo entered into discussions with Germany for arms purchases. The Americans could not understand the situation. In the meantime, while Washington vilified Castillo as pro-Nazi, Argentine military authorities saw the Argentine government as weak and not up to the task of maintaining order, progress, and a strong military apparatus. When officers staged a successful coup in 1943, the United States feared an open alliance with the Nazis. In fact, hoping for a modernized military, the new junta hoped at first for better relations with the United States. The new, pro-Allied foreign minister, Admiral Segundo N. Storni, spoke publicly of Argentina's commitment to Pan-American military cooperation and told U.S. ambassador Norman Armour that Argentina would break ties with the Axis. But Hull wanted quick results that the Argentine government could not provide. In a letter to Storni, he blasted Argentina's neutrality. The note was made public in Argentina and prompted Storni's resignation. Fallout from what Argentines regarded as a hardening anti-Argentine position in Washington strengthened the position of the nationalist Grupo de Oficiales Unidos (GOU), a secret officers' club unsympathetic to the Allies that pressed successfully for the promotion of one of their own, General Edelmiro Farrell, to the vice presidency.[58]

In part, bilateral tensions at this stage of the war can be attributed to Argentina's changing economic fortunes. Though crop production had entered a long-term slide, through 1942 the economic situation began to change dramatically, leading to the formidable surpluses in export earnings that would help prime social reform and other significant government spending projects after 1945. Construction in the cities thrived, unemployment dipped, salaries and bank savings rose, and Argentina experienced a new round of industrialization. Wartime export-led growth now made neutrality more popular, not less. As Argentines continued to see the Americans as those most concerned with ending Argentine neutrality, the persistence of some popular anti-U.S. sentiment had little to do with pro-German sympathies and everything to do with what was seen as an American threat to Argentine economic stability and growth.[59] The British were beside themselves over U.S. foreign policies. They appreciated Argentina's shipments of meat and found Hull's hard-line position irrational. When the secretary of state suggested to Churchill that the British cancel their meat contract with the Argentines, Churchill angrily insisted to Roosevelt that this was impossible. By early 1944, unrelenting U.S. diplomatic pressure was now complemented by a virtual economic blockade against Argentina. Washington heatedly attributed a Bolivian coup d'état to Argentine machinations. Even so, on 26 March 1944, despite strong opposition within the GOU, Argentina broke relations with the Axis powers, still hoping for better ties with Washington.[60]

Braden-Perón

When Hull stepped down as secretary in November 1944, some saw an opportunity for better bilateral relations. American business leaders called for an economic rapprochement with the Argentines so that they might fully take advantage of postwar opportunities. The military wanted better ties with their Argentine counterparts and a revival of inter-American defense planning. Within the State Department Nelson Rockefeller objected to Hull's hard line. In Argentina, Colonel Juan Perón emerged as the most powerful figure in the military government. In 1945 he spoke openly of the need for revived economic negotiations with the United States and lobbied for a postwar commercial treaty with the British. It was Argentina that called for a Pan-American Union meeting in 1945 to reexamine the possibility of inter-American cooperation. U.S. delegates reached the Chapultepec Conference in February 1945 concerned about shoring up support in Latin America for a new United Nations. But a number of Latin American governments warned that in return for such backing, they expected large-scale American economic support after the war. They also called for Argentina's integration into the new body and pressured Washington to find a way to end its conflict with Buenos Aires. After preliminary discussions at Chapultepec, Argentina declared war on Germany at the end of March. The United States recognized the Argentine government, and Argentina was included as a founding member of the United Nations.[61]

The political and bureaucratic climate in Washington had changed. With Hull gone, Latin American specialists in the State Department, backed by Secretary of State Edward Stettinius, outlined a pragmatist position toward Argentina. To win Argentine backing for U.S. leadership in the hemisphere, the most effective policy would combine economic agreement with a more cooperative diplomacy. This dovetailed with a sentiment among some in the Senate that isolating Argentina simply encouraged the growth of Communism. At the same time, though, there were editorial criticisms in a number of newspapers for the "rapprochement" with Argentina. These criticisms coincided with the presence of some lingering pro-Hull functionaries in the State Department.

That persistence of anti-Argentine sentiment led to the appointment of Spruille Braden as ambassador to Argentina. Braden reached Buenos Aires in May 1945 and quickly set about making an unprecedented mark on Argentine politics and society, a mark that would have a lasting impact on bilateral relations. He pressed hard and publicly for the government to expel Nazi agents and to confiscate Nazi property. Perón countered that Argentina was continuing in its essential wartime role, sending foodstuffs to Europe. As a Perón-Braden antagonism grew through mid-1945, the political and bureaucratic uncertainty in Washington created by Roosevelt's death in April created an opening for the U.S. ambassador. Rockefeller opposed Braden's hard line, as did the British government, which pressured Washington to recall him. But both Rockefeller and Stettinius saw their power decline. Meanwhile, Braden had the backing of unbending Hull-era bureaucrats, political liberals, organized labor, and a national news media now convinced that Argentina was a Nazi outpost. *Time* magazine featured a grinning Braden on its front cover holding a small, handheld fogging machine. Behind him was a leafy branch in the shape of South America. In the area on the leaves where Argentina would be, tiny swastikas appeared like vermin.[62]

Braden was named assistant secretary of state in August. Though no longer taunting Perón in Buenos Aires, back in Washington he proved more disruptive still to stable bilateral relations. Braden played a major role in the development of a new, aggressive hard-line Argentina policy in Washington that would last through the end of the decade. He did all he could to thwart British-Argentine economic ties and won the classification of Argentina as an "ex-enemy." Under that designation, Argentina could receive no U.S. aid and would be excluded from taking part in new discussions on hemispheric defense. Again, the British found the American position on Argentina incomprehensible except as an irrational effort to denigrate the Argentines. In mid-1945, increasingly apprehensive over the personal power Perón wielded in government, the Argentine military removed him from power. But on 17 October, a popular uprising led by Perón's partner, Eva Duarte, marked the start of Perón's campaign for the presidency in the 1946 election.

Braden was determined to block Perón's ascent. In February 1946, only days before the Argentine election, he released the "Blue Book," a supposed compilation of Argentine links to the Nazis during the war. Intended to undermine Perón's campaign, the book had the opposite effect. Perón rightly labeled Braden's publication the grossest form of U.S. intervention in Argentine affairs. Argentines agreed, and Perón won the presidency.[63]

The turmoil in U.S.-Argentine diplomatic ties persisted through 1946. The State Department sent George S. Messersmith to Buenos Aires as ambassador. Messersmith clashed with Braden in arguing for an end to the outrageous treatment of Perón. It was not until January 1947 that Secretary of State George Marshall forced both men to resign. While relations became less openly acrimonious, the legacy of U.S. antagonism through the war was a continued policy of economic aggression through the early cold war period. The U.S. Economic Cooperation Administration oversaw the implementation of the Marshall Plan in Europe. It deliberately isolated Argentina from related economic activity through the end of the 1940s. Beginning in 1947, Great Britain reversed its earlier criticism of U.S. economic pressures against Argentina. Through that year, Argentina relied on the convertibility to dollars and other currencies of the sterling it earned selling grain and beef to Britain. In 1947, the British made sterling earned in Britain unconvertible, which reduced significantly Argentina's ability to purchase goods in the United States. Perón tried repeatedly to have Washington recognize this as discriminatory and made a number of overtures to the State Department to improve relations. But at the same time, Perón continued to unnerve even the more moderate Washington policymakers with his so-called "third position" foreign policy; Perón hoped to stake out a cold war diplomatic and strategic stand apart from both the Americans and the Soviets. Moreover, he planned to lead a Latin American Third Position bloc, which ran directly counter to Washington's early cold war plans for the region.[64]

In early 1944, State Department intelligence explained the crisis in U.S.-Argentine relations as a function of Argentine nationalism: "Argentineans have long been notorious . . . for their condescending and arrogant nationalism. . . . This belief in Argentine superiority has led consequently to a belief in the right to leadership in Latin America." The department's Office of Intelligence Research suggested that nonrecognition was an unsatisfactory diplomatic tactic for the United States against undemocratic governments in Argentina: "Non-recognition is exposed to the odium of unavowed intervention." The report recommended that the U.S. government should either repair its relations with the Argentine government or take a still harder line against it. The United States chose the latter option. At the same time, none of the other Allied countries shared Washington's stark portrait of Argentine extremism.[65]

U.S. hostility during wartime had done more than to usher in a nationalist government under Juan Perón. Years of American hostility and bullying over Nazism and neutrality had created a popular base of anti-Americanism on which Perón was able to build his domestic agenda after 1945 in what the historians Lila Caimari and Mariano Ben Plotkin call a Peronization of Argentine society.[66] Through the late 1940s, Perón's political language appealed to a revived anti-imperialism that, even when directed at Great Britain, drew on the hostility Argentines felt toward Washington. There was no mistaking the source of international oppression in 1949, for example, when a Peronist senator urged a doctrine of economic independence for the nation, where capital could no longer be a product of national or international oppression or enslavement. After Perón's election in 1946, one of his first policy initiatives was to eliminate the external debt, which the government achieved by 1952. Perón's language in highlighting the foreign debt as a source of national weakness was replete with symbolism that emanated from the conflict with the United States and a sense among many Argentines that the Americans were beating them down through economic bullying. For example, although Perón's most celebrated nationalization of foreign capital was of British-owned railways, his language rarely stressed British dominance but rather an "anti-imperial struggle" that focused increasingly on the United States. In the first years of his government, as Perón began to transform May Day celebrations into a key cultural vehicle for his movement, recent U.S.

hostility emerged as a key target for the ire of Argentine workers. A May Day article in the 1952 Peronist organ *Democracia* admonished Argentines to remember that the enemy was not only Braden but "all the Bradens" operating inside and outside the country. A year later, the same publication was even more explicit. It asked its readers, who is our enemy? The answer was "The United States of America."[67]

When they thought of them at all, Americans tended to see Argentines very much as Spruille Braden and State Department intelligence had cast them: irrational nationalists with Nazi sympathies. But ironically, despite tensions with the United States and despite Peronist politics, Argentines held on to their subtle and varied understanding of the United States. Despite much sympathy for the Peronist line, Argentines continued to be attracted to the United States and to look to the United States as a trendsetter in many areas. In the midst of the wartime crisis in relations, for example, Argentines never abandoned their passion for American consumer goods or Hollywood gossip. In 1941, the women's magazine *Para Tí* featured advertisements for Elizabeth Arden, Nivea, RCA Victor, Squibb, Brasso, Quaker Oats, and Helena Rubinstein. Another ad boasted that nine out of ten film stars used Lux soap. Betty Grable, whose photograph and signature appeared in the ad, commented, "I use it for my facial and my beauty bath."[68] In March 1944, thousands of Argentines leafing through the popular and widely read magazine *Leoplán* saw a photo of Joan Crawford happily combing daughter Christina's hair. An October 1944 issue made no mention of tensions between the United States and Argentina. But it did feature an item on Ann Miller's world record for tap dancing speed and one lasciviously captioned "Rita Hayworth's knees."

In June 1946, only months after Perón's election, Argentines read cheery articles written especially for *Leoplán* about the Pulitzer Prize–winning author Louis Bromfield and James Fenimore Cooper. They also saw cheesecake shots of studio starlets Leslie Brooks and Jane Carter and read the latest Hollywood updates on Jimmy Stewart and Ginger Rogers. In August, the actress Evelyn Keyes was shown in a full-page photograph as a "naive vamp," while readers could ogle Leslie Brooks's legs, "the most beautiful in Hollywood." Despite a decade of open hostility from the U.S. government, most Argentines would not set aside what they liked about Americans.[69]

Through the late 1930s and 1940s, Argentines were divided in their wartime sympathies. Some in the military, high political circles, and other sectors favored ties with Germany. A larger number worked to support the Allies. Some were pro-Nazi. But many more simply saw no reason to compromise Argentina's relations with Germany or any other country to follow a U.S. lead. U.S. leaders were unable to grasp this nuance. Secretary of State Cordell Hull led the charge in wrongly defining the Argentine position as intransigent, arrogant, and pro-Nazi. Though there were dissenters in Washington, this mistaken vision of Argentina shaped American policymaking and popular opinion in the United States through the late 1940s. Indeed, through most of the cold war, many Americans continued wrongly to associate Argentina with Nazism. Beginning in 1941, the United States tried to force Argentine compliance with U.S. leadership in the hemisphere through a series of economic pressures focused around denying Argentina crucial export markets overseas and shipping space to move those exports. Argentines, on the other hand, saw the Americans as a mix of positive and negative. Americans believed that Argentines were uncompromisingly anti-imperialist and that this explained their hostility toward the United States. In fact, Argentine suspicion of the United States came principally as a consequence of ongoing American diplomatic and economic pressures.

4 Cold War and the End of Argentine Democracy, 1947–1961

In U.S.–Latin American relations, 1947 to 1961 delimits a period of growing tensions around the related problems of nationalist and revolutionary movements in Latin America, Soviet expansionism in the third world, and U.S. preoccupations with a cold war Communist menace gaining new footholds in Latin America. The Río Pact of 1947 and the Organization of American States Charter of 1948 set in place what President Franklin D. Roosevelt had been unable to achieve during his 1936 visit to Buenos Aires—the basis for a new, U.S.-dominated inter-American security and defense system. Between 1952 and 1961, the United States provided $835 million in economic assistance to Latin America, much of it in military aid to such repressive dictatorships as that of Fulgencio Batista in Cuba. Secretary of State John Foster Dulles was among many prominent U.S. policymakers who viewed Latin America as a tinderbox. Rapid population expansion, massive poverty, and malnutrition all pointed to the danger of a Communist revolution in the region.

For American cold warriors, the first major threat came with the election of Jacobo Arbenz to the presidency of Guatemala. A leftist whose left-of-center coalition government included some Communists and advocated land reform and the expropriation of the U.S.-owned United Fruit Company's vast landholdings, Arbenz appeared to Americans to threaten the stability of the region. In 1953, the administration of U.S. president Dwight D. Eisenhower gave the go-ahead for a Central Intelligence Agency (CIA) initiative to overthrow the Guatemalan government, the first such CIA intervention in the domestic affairs of a Latin American nation. Early the following year, with CIA assistance, Guatemalan military officer Carlos Castillo Armas staged a successful coup d'état.

Many Latin Americans reacted angrily to the very public role of the U.S. government in the coup. That anger manifested itself repeatedly in the 1950s, most famously perhaps in 1958 when, during a goodwill tour of Latin America, Vice President Richard Nixon was repeatedly harangued by angry mobs. In Caracas, Nixon's motorcade was brought to a halt by thousands of Venezuelans who threw rocks at the vice president's car. But even as Nixon was being stoned, a more ominous danger was unfolding in Cuba. For five years Fidel Castro had been working to overthrow the U.S.-backed Batista dictatorship. By the time of Nixon's 1958 tour, Castro's forces had established a firm power base in mountainous eastern Cuba. Early in 1959 Castro's forces took Havana. As the revolutionary government's policies shifted increasingly to the left, the Eisenhower administration decided on measures similar to the response to Arbenz in Guatemala. In March 1960, the president instructed the CIA to train Cuban exiles for a possible invasion. Shortly after, the United States severely curtailed purchases of Cuban sugar. In April 1961, on the advice of the CIA, the recently elected president, John F. Kennedy, ordered the Bay of Pigs invasion. In contrast to events around the ouster of Arbenz, Castro's forces easily trounced the invaders. Washington saw Cuba as a new and perilous Soviet beachhead in the Americas.

In bilateral affairs, the period from 1947 to 1961 was more hopeful for both Americans and Argentines than the course of U.S.–Latin American relations more generally. The period begins with the early part of Juan D. Perón's first presidency and an escalation of bilateral tensions. It ends with Arturo Frondizi's presidency and a stage of relative optimism in relations, despite ongoing economic tensions.

Cold war priorities clearly influenced U.S.-Argentine relations in Juan Perón's first presidency (1946–55), but not always predictably. Before 1950, bilateral ties were tense. Some blame Perón's purported fascism, his antagonism toward the United States, and a reckless economic nationalism that alarmed foreign investors. Others point to ongoing U.S. economic aggression against Argentina in the aftermath of the

Second World War. In fact, a combination of both sets of factors strained bilateral ties through the early 1950s. Perón did try to reconcile with Washington and hoped to reach a quiet understanding with the Americans that might lead to better relations. At the same time, while working behind the scenes to shore up relations with Washington, Perón was unwilling to tone down political rhetoric that Washington found anathema to sound bilateral ties. It was not until Perón explicitly abandoned some elements of his economic nationalism after 1950 that the two countries were able to partially repair their troubled ties. Improved relations were sparked in part by a U.S. Export-Import Bank loan in 1950 and a new Argentine law in 1953 that reopened the country to foreign investment. They were given a further boost with a series of contracts between the Argentine government and Standard Oil and with the collapse of Perón's *tercera posición* (third position) diplomacy. Change came quickly with heavy new U.S. investments in Argentina in the 1950s and strong Argentine support for U.S. cold war policies in Latin America and beyond. But despite these signs of fundamentally good relations, in addition to Argentine backing for U.S. inter-American security strategies, Argentina and the United States could not set aside long-standing tensions over trade and finance issues.[1]

Argentine leaders continued to take domestic economic and political positions that they felt represented strong, often imprudent, support for ongoing U.S. demands that Argentina stabilize its economy and open it to foreign trade and investment. But in comparison to credits offered to Brazil and to countries in other parts of the world, U.S. financial assistance to Argentina was weak. For Washington, this simply marked a combination of Argentina's relative insignificance as a strategic and investment priority and a persistent sense that Argentine authorities could do more on their own to spark economic growth, limit social uncertainty, and resolve disputes between U.S. companies and the Argentine government. For Argentines, this continued to represent American short-sightedness and hypocrisy; U.S. officials pressured for open trade and finance policies in Argentina, but when the Argentine government acceded, the Americans seemed always to want more. No evidence exists to suggest that, had the U.S. government been more supportive of

Argentina financially and otherwise, Argentina's growing economic problems through the early 1960s might have been solved. Even so, American policy in Argentina contradicted Washington's strong support for democracies in the Americas as an antidote to a cold war "communist menace." According to the historian Stephen G. Rabe, in the lead-up to and in the aftermath of the military overthrow of the Arturo Frondizi presidency in 1962, "the Kennedy administration silently watched the destruction of the democratic process in Argentina."[2]

Nuclear Dangers

Argentine strategic planning reflected cold war influences. This was most evident in the launch and early development of a nuclear program that was a function of U.S. nuclear policy but also tested its limits. Between the discovery of nuclear fission in 1938 and the First International Conference on the Pacific Use of Nuclear Energy in 1955, nuclear power became central to American military strategy and foreign policy. With the bombings of Hiroshima and Nagasaki, a growing number of scientists and others pressed the U.S. government to develop a supervised international system of nuclear technology dissemination. A government-sponsored study group led by David Lilienthal and including the atomic scientist Robert Oppenheimer concluded that it would be impossible to keep nuclear technology an international secret. The group recommended the formation of a multinational body that would hold a monopoly over nuclear installations. Governments willing to abide by a set of international proscriptions on certain forms of research and all forms of nuclear weapons development would make their countries eligible for nuclear energy support from the United States and other nuclear powers. The new organization would also control the dissemination of fissionable material.[3]

In 1946, President Harry S. Truman sent his adviser, the financier Bernard Baruch, to pitch these and other ideas—including a unilateral American cessation of nuclear arms production—to the United Nations in what became known as the Baruch Plan. Escalating cold war conflict between the Soviet Union and the United States, the detonation of a Soviet nuclear device in 1948 and a British nuclear test four years later doomed the plan and the possibility of a cooperative international security plan. Both the Soviets and the Americans pressed ahead in their nuclear programs, developing nuclear fission technology and the hydrogen bomb. President Eisenhower's 1953 Atoms for Peace plan offered provisions for international cooperation in the supervision and control of nuclear proliferation. But this time, the Americans insisted on more direct control over who would have access to nuclear technology and offered no provision for their own weapon reductions. The 1955 Geneva Conference came out of Atoms for Peace and saw the sharing of a wide variety of previously guarded atomic secrets. It also led to the creation in 1957 of the International Atomic Energy Organization (IAEO) that had a dual mandate to facilitate and augment the contributions of atomic energy toward world peace and prosperity and to make certain that no assistance it offered led to military ends.[4]

Argentina launched its own nuclear program in 1944 in a context very different from the Manhattan Project, though as in the United States the Second World War and early cold war international tensions were a key backdrop. Like its Canadian equivalent, the Argentine nuclear program was tied to nationalist ambitions that linked industrial growth to strategic power, energy access, and the seemingly limitless potential of nuclear power more specifically. Writing in 1963, for example, Comodoro Fernando E. Barrera Oro argued that Argentine military strategy was directly linked to industrial development.[5] A long-standing association of naval officers with the Argentine government nuclear agency, the Comisión Nacional de Energía Atómica (CNEA), had parallels in other countries. Like naval officers in the United States and France, for example, Argentine naval officers believed in a strategic panacea based on the nuclear propulsion of warships and submarines. For military strategist Captain Fernando A. Milia, "as far as warships are concerned, atomic propulsion will mark their liberation from a long-standing [strategic and energy] servitude."[6]

There is no evidence that Argentine authorities ever developed or tried to develop nuclear weapons, though military governments in the

1970s did seek a level of readiness such that Argentina might always be within five years of producing a small nuclear arsenal.[7] But the U.S. government was always suspicious of Argentine nuclear intentions. At the same time, Argentines were wary of what they correctly suspected were close nuclear ties between Brazil and the United States. In 1945, the two countries signed a secret agreement that committed Brazil to supply the United States over a three-year period with three thousand to five thousand tons of monacite, a mineral containing uranium. A second monacite agreement was signed in 1952, and in late 1956 Brazilian scientists achieved the first nuclear chain reaction in Latin America with U.S. technical support.[8]

U.S. suspicions of Argentina came in large measure as a result of Perón's role in the early stages of the Argentine nuclear program. In 1951 Perón announced to the press that Argentina had successfully conducted controlled nuclear fusion reactions. The news spread like wildfire and was reported in both the *New York Times* and the *Times* of London. "What the Americans are now achieving in the detonation of a hydrogen bomb," Perón's chief nuclear physicist Ronald Richter told the press, "Argentina is achieving in controlled laboratory experiments."[9] "How is the explosion controlled?" a journalist asked Richter. "I control the explosion," he answered. "I've found a way to produce a slow and gradual explosion."[10]

As it turned out, Richter's nuclear fusion actions were a fantasy. The United States and Argentina signed their first nuclear cooperation agreement in 1953. This allowed Argentine access to information and assistance in the construction of a U.S.-designed Argonaut experimental reactor, completed in 1958.[11] In 1954, Perón offered the New York–based Atlas Corporation the opportunity to undertake aerial surveys of zones in Argentina where uranium thorium was thought to exist.[12] Argentina further integrated itself into the international atomic community in 1961 by negotiating a technical assistance agreement with Italian nuclear authorities. On the problem of Soviet-American nuclear tensions, the Argentine government took positions favoring the United States. In its instructions to the Argentine delegation to the 11 June 1963 meeting of the governing council of the IAEO, the Argentine Foreign

Relations Ministry noted that "Argentina is a western country, and . . . should support the western position."[13]

Though less openly in favor of the United States where U.S. policy might generate hostility in poor countries, after 1955 Argentina was generally unwilling to alter its "Western" policy position in favor of developing nations. Where conflicts might arise at the 1963 meeting between poor countries and the Western powers, Argentine delegates were to avoid disputes. Argentine leaders viewed their country as a "developing country with considerable need for technical and scientific assistance, but at the same time western with an independent foreign policy." Argentina participated in international conferences on outer space and launched a modest rocket program. The Argentine-designed Proson I rocket was tested in the province of La Rioja. Carrying fifty kilos of fuel, the rocket reached a height of fifty kilometers.[14]

Perón: The Third Position and the U.S. Embargo

Between 1948 and 1955, other areas of U.S.-Argentine relations followed the contours of Perón's presidency. As in the nuclear sector, Perón's policies more generally reflected unreasonable expectations that included prolonged rapid economic growth and international diplomatic leadership. Through 1949, Perón made anti-Americanism a hallmark of both his domestic and foreign policies. His "third position" policy charted a course for Argentina that would maintain the nation's independence both from the United States and the Soviet Union, while developing a leadership role for itself among poorer nations. Through his contacts in the armed forces, Perón buttressed relations with military rulers in Peru, Chile, and Venezuela. With ties to third-position diplomacy, the Asociación de Trabajadores Latinoamericanos (ATLAS), an arm of the Argentine Confederación General de Trabajo (CGT), tried to bring together unions from other countries against both capitalism and Communism. Railing against U.S. imperialism, the Argentine government promised $5 billion in development aid for the Americas as an answer to Washington's refusal to put in place a Marshall Plan for the hemisphere. Each of these endeavors came to naught. At the same time, with Spruille Braden's exit from the State Department in 1947, Argentina became far less important for U.S. policymakers. Preoccupied primarily with Europe, but concerned also with the creation of an anti-Communist, inter-American security system beginning with the Inter-American Treaty of Reciprocal Assistance drafted in 1947 in Río de Janeiro, the long-standing Argentina problem had become a nuisance. At the same time, the United States favored Brazil over Argentina in military and economic aid.[15]

Beginning in 1948, the Truman administration convinced European countries receiving Marshall Plan aid to import U.S. rather than Argentine grains. The result was disastrous for Argentina and helped precipitate a serious economic crisis there. Through the late 1940s, the State Department tended to understand Perón's anti-American rhetoric in a context of his domestic pressures more effectively than had Braden. But at the same time, the U.S. Economic Cooperation Administration (ECA) aggressively pressured Argentina. The British also used economic coercion against the Argentines, denying Argentina convertibility of sterling in 1947. This meant that Perón's economy minister Miguel Miranda could not get access to half the country's reserves, deposited in British accounts. The ECA set policy in early 1948—against the better judgment of the State Department—when the United States announced that European countries could not use funds from the Marshall Plan to buy Argentine exports.[16]

The Argentine government was alarmed at the danger of ECA policy to the country's growing economy. Perón lobbied U.S. ambassador James Bruce to help Argentina win Marshall Plan contracts and then sent a team of officials to Washington with the same objective. At one point, ECA administrator Howard Bruce suggested to Argentine foreign minister Juan Bramuglia that European Marshall Plan purchases in Argentina might reach $300 million. They never exceeded $21 million. James Bruce convinced his superiors to investigate the ECA; the State Department found thirty-three cases of discrimination against Argentina. Bruce argued that the U.S. government might regard these findings as an opportunity. A favorable trade and financial settlement for Argentina might strengthen the hand of those in Perón's government most interested in advancing good bilateral ties with Washington. But the ECA maintained its discriminatory tactics.[17]

In the face of U.S. economic hostility, Perón pursued better ties with the Soviets, sometimes to the consternation of Washington. But the Soviet Union exercised little influence in Argentina and never proved a source of much anxiety there for the United States. In 1946, a Soviet trade mission visited Argentina, and formal relations between the two countries were initiated. But despite bilateral commercial negotiations, they could not reach agreement on a treaty. The Soviet Union could not supply the machinery that Argentina urgently wanted. Perón negotiated a set of bilateral treaties with neighboring countries that promised an end to trade barriers. Conflict with Washington was renewed over a new Argentine constitutional guarantee protecting mineral wealth as an inalienable national domain. Argentina won a five-year trade agreement with Great Britain. Despite these developments and Perón's persistent harangues against the United States, commercial relations between the United States and Argentina improved steadily. By the end of the decade, Argentina sent more exports to the United States than to any other country, some 25 percent of total sales overseas. Moreover, U.S. exports to Argentina surged to almost ten times the value of prewar exports.[18]

Even so, the Argentine economy underwent a severe downturn at the end of the decade. Growing international trade deficits decimated the country's foreign currency reserves. Argentina entered a long period of persistent agricultural crisis that ground exports to a halt and ended Perón's ambitious plans for industrialization. Perón sought U.S. financial assistance at precisely the moment that the United States was stepping up its efforts to win firmer Latin American military commitments for hemispheric defense. In 1950, the Inter-American Defense Board brought in a new plan for Pan-American military cooperation, and a year later the U.S. Congress designated $38 million for direct military aid to Latin America. Also in 1950, the Export-Import Bank loaned a consortium of Argentine banks $125 million to be applied exclusively to the liquidation of debts due to American creditors. An agreement in principle followed from U.S. banks for a further credit of $75 million. But the United States expected, among other concessions in return, that Argentina would ratify the Río Treaty, which it did scarcely a month after news of the first loan. Perón also gave his backing to Washington in the Korean War, though that would later be withdrawn.[19]

The State Department supported the loan, not out of any confidence in Perón's stand toward the United States but out of concern for the steady decline of the Argentine economy. Initially, the State Department had pressed for additional concessions, including guaranteed Argentine purchases of U.S. agricultural machinery. Some in the State Department, including Assistant Secretary Edward G. Miller Jr., continued to feel that what the Americans viewed as Perón's "isolationism" was damaging to U.S. interests. Miller believed that Perón's request for a loan contradicted his refusal to join the International Monetary Fund (IMF), the Food and Agriculture Organization, and the International Wheat Agreement. But Washington hoped the loan might improve poor conditions for a number of large American companies in Argentina. U.S. packinghouses were in the midst of a dispute with the Argentine government over large sums the Argentines claimed the companies owed the government. In the late 1940s, foreign packers operated under strict government controls. The government fixed the values at which packers purchased livestock, the prices for finished products, and exchange rates on imports and exports. The packers argued that they had suffered significant losses because of government pricing at artificial values.

U.S. oil companies were in trouble as well because the state oil company, Yacimientos Petrolíferos Fiscales (YPF), had shut off their crude supplies. General Motors, General Electric, and other U.S. firms were routinely denied import permits for equipment necessary to keep their operations going.[20] At the same time, a government buying spree in the United States in 1948 drastically reduced Argentina's currency reserves, and as a result, Perón's government moved to effect greater control over the economy. There were new price controls, unprofitable barter deals, and new government regulation of financial transactions. The results further aggravated Argentina's economic woes. In May 1948, the government defaulted on payments of letters of credit, and by December 1949, it was behind in payments of $190 million, which included $50 million in unpaid profits, dividends, and royalties, as well as $20 million owed to International Telephone and Telegraph. A radical change in economic policy by the Perón government in early 1949 signaled the end to what the Americans saw as irresponsible economic policy and the beginning of improved bilateral ties.[21]

Hoping to sway Americans on the $125 million credit, new foreign exchange controls were set in place to avoid dollar indebtedness. Specific percentages of all government dollar receipts were set aside for repayment of dollar commercial arrears. The government reduced its control and profit margin on exports. For example, the government commission on canned beef exports dropped from 20 percent to 5 percent. Economic ties were further strengthened when a Joint Argentine–United States Committee on Commercial Studies began to meet in September 1949 in Washington. The committee quickly proposed a new taxation treaty between the two countries and a reciprocal bilateral income tax exemption on shipping lines. While Perón continued to express hostility toward Washington, there were indications of a thaw. At the founding meetings of the Organization of American States in Río de Janeiro in 1947 and in Bogotá in 1948 the State Department reported that the Argentine Foreign Relations Ministry had gone out of its way to give Americans detailed information on Argentine conference positions. In the United Nations, Argentine diplomats cooperated with the United States, and Perón made clear that in the event of a war between the United States and the Soviet Union, Argentina would join the U.S. side.[22] As the Argentine ambassador to the United States explained, Perón recognized that "Argentina's future lies with the United States."[23]

Cold War Cultures

In popular culture, there seemed little doubt that Argentina was increasingly following an American course. In keeping with the force of earlier American cultural influences, even at the height of the Perón-Washington antagonism in the late 1940s and the 1950s, Argentines followed a U.S. lead in the rapid cultural and ideological changes that accompanied cold war tensions in North America. In fashion, American styles predominated. In the early 1950s, women showed a newfound social independence by moving their skirt hemlines up to their knees or slightly higher. Male Argentine designers exalted women's curves, as did their U.S. counterparts. As in films, U.S. technology and culture found their way into Argentine radio. In the late 1940s, Argentines modeled radio programs on their American equivalents, with large studio audiences. Stories of Tarzan, Batman and Robin, and other American heroes were serialized in Buenos Aires. American companies sponsored programs and contests for listeners and audience members. In August 1949, for example, Perla M. Hyderman of Buenos Aires was the lucky winner of $25.00 from Colgate-Palmolive for having guessed the secret word in a local radio contest.[24]

In 1943, the government tried to control the diffusion of American cultural influences by limiting jazz on the radio. It didn't last. Jazz had been popular on radio and in nightclubs since the 1920s, and a broad range of U.S.-influenced jazz styles—from Louis Armstrong to Charlie Parker—caught the imagination of thousands of Argentines in the late 1940s and 1950s.[25] Television had powerful American influences. Before the first Argentine transmissions, the Buenos Aires press reported excitedly from the United States on the impact television was having. In 1951, the entrepreneur Jaime Yankelevich convinced Perón to allow the import of television sets and broadcast equipment from the United States. Yankelevich told the Buenos Aires daily *La Prensa,* "I'm going to the United States to bring back television. If the Argentine government agrees, fine, if not, I'm bringing it anyway." It's not that Yankelevich doubted Perón's authority. He simply recognized early what many other Argentines would see much later; American popular culture was powerful, influential, and likely unstoppable. In New York, he met representatives of RCA Victor, ITT, Dumont, and Federal Communications. David Sarnoff and Dan Panley introduced him to the mayor of New York. Yankelevich returned to Argentina with a transmitter, studio

equipment, an antenna, six Standard Electric cameras, and 450 Cape-
heart television sets. On 21 September 1951 his Channel 7 went on the
air. Advertising agencies had no more important or aggressive clients
than television manufacturers. According to Carlos Montero, an em-
ployee of the Pueyrredón Propaganda advertising agency, in the late
1940s and early 1950s "one of our clients was Standard Electric and our
principal preoccupation was selling television sets."[26]

The Argentine fascination with American television continued
through the 1950s and 1960s. In 1956, the first dubbed U.S. series reached
Argentina. They included *Cisco Kid; Boston Blackie,* starring Chester Morris; and *Patrulla de caminos* (Highway Patrol), with Broderick Crawford.
In the latter, Argentines watched enthralled by high-speed chase scenes
on U.S. highways, gunshots that almost never hurt anybody, and American story lines pitting good guys against bad guys. *Odol pregunta por
$1,000,000* (Odol's $1,000,000 Question), *La cabalgata Gillette de los cien mil
pesos* (The Gillette Cavalcade of One Hundred Thousand Pesos), *La cace-
ría de los quinientos mil pesos* (The Hunt for the Five Hundred Thousand
Pesos), and other game shows modeled on their American equivalents
went to air in 1956, as did the Argentine musical comedy *Field's College,*
in which actors appeared as how Argentines imagined U.S. teenagers
would dress, with leather jackets, poodle skirts, and bobby socks. Disney
Studios' *Zorro,* starring Guy Williams and Henry Calvin, reached Argentina in 1957. The show developed a cult following among Argentine
children, already primed by American adventure movies and comic
books. Inspired by the show's success, Argentine producers tried an adventure show of their own the same year. *El capitán Minverva* boasted
more than four hundred actors and horses for its elaborate action scenes
shot on a huge sound stage at Plaza Francia and on a pirate ship repro-
duction built in the port of Buenos Aires.[27]

In 1958, to boost sales of its cars, the U.S. firm Industrias Kaiser Argentina (IKA) sponsored a musical variety show whose star was the
American singer Andy Russell. *El Show de IKA* was the first to use cameras mounted high above the stage and was the most expensive television show produced in Argentina. A Kaiser Jeep was driven across the
stage during every show. Russell was accompanied by a fifty-piece

orchestra and a choir, and two dancers performed. In 1961, Argentine audiences first heard the dubbed song lines "caballo con voz/ no hay dos, no hay dos. / Solo Mister Ed tiene bella voz" that introduced *Mister Ed, el caballo que habla.*[28] By 1965, the four Buenos Aires channels used 230 hours weekly of foreign material, most from the United States. Almost all of what came to Argentina from the United States was dubbed in Mexico, Puerto Rico, and Miami. In 1966, responding to the concerns of some political leaders over that foreign presence, the Argentine Congress passed a bill requiring that 20 percent of foreign-language television programming that year be dubbed in Argentina. That figure was to rise by 20 percent each year through 1970, when all dubbing would be done in Argentina. But the Senate, pressured heavily by Argentine television executives, would not approve the bill. American television was in Argentina to stay.[29]

The Argentine literary world remained more reserved, and even hostile at times, toward the United States than did the television or film industries. A boom occurred in Argentine publications between 1944 and 1949. Many not only followed a government line openly hostile toward Washington but also made that line an ideological and thematic centerpiece of the work. The magazine *Dinámica Social,* for example, made Perón's third position a key theme in its articles. The left-leaning *De Frente* featured the anti-imperialist writings of radical Peronist John William Cooke.[30] But American ideological, political, and literary influences continued to mark the Argentine cultural landscape. Thousands of Argentines saw the world through *Life* magazine. Eva Perón grew up in the town of Los Toldos dreaming of movie stars and exchanging photographs of Hollywood actresses with her sisters. One of Argentina's most important twentieth-century writers, Manuel Puig, was one of many writing in the 1950s and 1960s who had similar experiences, drawing on cultural links to the United States throughout their careers. Ironically, like many Argentine authors, Puig wrote his best work outside Argentina. More striking still, he penned his most important work of fiction, *La traición de Rita Hayworth* (1968) in New York, coming to an understanding of his own society through the prism of Hollywood films and life in New York in the early 1960s.

Andy Warhol and Roy Lichtenstein were two of the many American influences on the vibrant world of Argentine modern art. In 1958, IKA organized a competition for Córdoba artists, and a year later the contest was expanded to the sixteen provinces of the center, north, Cuyo, and Littoral regions of Argentina. According to Kaiser, the decision to base a new and influential prize for the arts in Argentina's second most important city was an effort to find new artistic talent. It was also a political move on the part of the company to open a new cultural space outside of Buenos Aires that it might influence. In addition to building workers' housing, medical clinics, and schools—what Kaiser called public relations projects—the company was interested in advancing its reputation through fostering the plastic arts. IKA's interest in the arts was tied to a U.S. government and Organization of American States (OAS) vision that modern art—as a pure expression of free speech in a democratic society—might be used to counter Soviet cultural influences internationally.[31]

In 1961, José Gómez Sicre, head of the Visual Arts Division of the OAS, told Buenos Aires journalists that he was worried that "complots políticos internacionales" were at work in converting the Bienal de San Pablo art competition into a forum for the "wonders of Soviet bloc culture."[32] Gómez Sicre saw as his mandate to challenge that Communist presence in South America. In Argentina he served as a judge at both the first and second IKA-sponsored Córdoba exhibits, the Bienales Americanas de Arte.[33] The 1962 Bienal Americana reflected a cold war–influenced Pan Americanism.[34] Now expanded to include artists from Brazil, Chile, and Uruguay, prizes were handed out in a manner consciously meant to emphasize cooperation—a prize for an artist from each country participating. After Córdoba, the exhibit moved to several other locales, including Washington where critics acclaimed the entrants.[35]

Perón Redux: Friend of Washington

The growing popularity of American-style television programming by the mid-1950s dovetailed with Perón's political transformation. By mid-1950, Perón had overseen a rapid reversal of his strong stand against American capital. The Argentine government allowed Swift International to transfer its Argentine holding company from Argentina to the United States. It ended the ban on the importation of Hollywood movies. In 1951 it reached new agreements with U.S. oil companies. Perón also agreed to an auditing of American packinghouse books. This was meant to help clear up their long-standing disputes with the government. And he reopened air route negotiations with U.S. companies, stalled for four years. Perón also seemed newly keen on pressing for measures to fight Communism in Latin America. During a February 1950 visit to Buenos Aires, Assistant Secretary of State Edward G. Miller met with Perón, Foreign Minister Hipólito J. Paz, and several other Argentine officials who outlined a vision of international Communism as a menace to Latin America in keeping with Washington's point of view. Perón now insisted that third-position diplomacy had, in fact, been developed to "fight communism within Argentina." In August, when U.S. ambassador Stanton Griffis questioned Perón on persistent anti-Americanism in Argentina, the exasperated president responded, "Damn it, can't people realize that certain things are said for local consumption?" Citing Franklin D. Roosevelt's reforms, Perón insisted that his government meant only to reform capitalism in Argentina. Remarkably, in light of past conflicts, the State Department seemed to accept Perón's position at face value.[36]

But American uncertainty over Peronist ideology persisted. In the latter half of 1951, at the same time that Richter was boasting of his nuclear accomplishments, and through mid-1952, Perón's government escalated its anti-American rhetoric. Miller was among some that began to suspect that there might be Communist political influences close to Perón: "Argentine penetration in many levels of Latin American life under the guise of spreading Peronismo now appears to represent a more direct threat to hemispheric unity and democratic institutions than heretofore. This is particularly true because of the substantially increased program of Argentine propaganda in all of Latin America, a propaganda which often shows a striking parallel to that of communism."[37] Perón added to the uncertainty by pulling back from some of his earlier overtures toward U.S. business. On 8 July 1947 the Argentine Central Bank had closed the free exchange market. It was not until August 1950 that Perón took steps to allow American companies to begin to remit dividends again. At that time he permitted the transmittal of 5 percent on share capital. But that provision remained operative for only seven months. Miller now suggested a new set of tactics to help undermine Perón. These included fostering opposition to Perón in other Latin American countries, advocating improved living standards among the American Republics "through others' efforts as well as through our aid," and making use of the U.S. trade union movement's contacts in Latin America to neutralize Argentine anti-American activities in third countries.[38]

The election of Dwight D. Eisenhower to the U.S. presidency in 1952 held out the promise of greater American attention to Latin America. Eisenhower had criticized Truman's disinterest in Latin America during the campaign, and during Senate confirmation hearings, Secretary of State-designate John Foster Dulles promised to make the Americas more central to U.S. policymaking. More so than Truman, Eisenhower was increasingly preoccupied with the growth of strong nationalist politics in the Americas and the potential linkages between nationalism and Communism. At the same time, sentiment was growing in Latin America that in its focus on anti-Communism, the U.S. government was giving too little attention to Latin American development problems. The United Nations Economic Commission for Latin America (ECLA), under the direction of the Argentine economist Raúl Prebisch, spearheaded this critique. Prebisch's team countered the emphasis in U.S. policy on free markets and trade. Without wishing to limit trade, ECLA reasoned that individual countries needed to protect their interests with an aggressive program of state intervention in the national economy and import substitution industrialization, a program of action that had worked well for Argentina in the 1930s.[39]

For the Eisenhower administration, ECLA was anathema to good government and sound economic policy in Latin American countries. A strong state role in the economy was viewed with suspicion in Washington, as was the prospect of any control over private investment and free trade. In a move to shore up his prospects for successful policy initiatives in the region, the president sent his brother Milton Eisenhower on an information-gathering mission early in 1953. Milton Eisenhower's report gave credence to ECLA projects that backed fiscal conservatism for the region's governments and open trade, but the report also prompted the president to find a way to promote better economic relations between the United States and individual Latin American countries. Many of the recommendations remained unimplemented, but the president made better bilateral trade ties a priority of his administration. Even so, strong protectionist sentiment in the business community and in Congress slowed that initiative and made American policy on agriculture seem contradictory and duplicitous to Latin American leaders.[40]

Initially, Milton Eisenhower had decided not to include Argentina in his Latin American tour, but Dulles convinced him to go there as a goodwill gesture. There had been signals from Perón that the Argentine government now sought better relations with Eisenhower than it had had with Truman. A few days before Milton Eisenhower's arrival in Buenos Aires, Perón sent the Argentine Congress a bill liberalizing provisions for foreign company profit remittances, a long-standing sore point for U.S. business. Opposition among deputies was heated, and American companies complained that the legislation did not go far enough in redressing past wrongs. But the U.S. government took the legislation as a positive sign from Argentina. Perón's statements to the Americans during Milton Eisenhower's visit seemed cloying. He praised all aspects of U.S. policy in the Americas and pledged his support to American anti-Communist initiatives. A stream of American corporate executives from Westinghouse, John Deere, Kaiser, and International Harvester, among others, made their way to Argentina heartened by the new legislation and Milton Eisenhower's positive report. U.S. exporters lobbied the Export-Import Bank to expand its program of loans to Argentina.[41]

In conjunction with Perón's initiatives in the nuclear sector, the government launched a major expansion of energy production generally. In October 1953, Westinghouse won a contract from the Argentine government to supply equipment for a new power plant in Buenos Aires and then won a second important concession to sell equipment for a new steel mill. In each case, the company applied to the

Export-Import Bank to finance the project, and on each occasion, the bank was heavily pressured to deny the loans by the American and Foreign Power Company (AMFORP), which wanted to use negotiations to leverage the Argentine government into settling its outstanding conflicts with the U.S. firm. Despite pressure from Westinghouse and Argentine authorities, the Export-Import Bank dragged its heels until State Department officials began to worry that the delay might affect Argentina's position on the Guatemalan crisis.[42]

During the 1954 Caracas Conference at which Secretary of State John Foster Dulles won passage of his motion condemning Guatemalan Communism, Argentina abstained in the vote. In the lead-up to Caracas, the State Department fell back on a decades-old Pan-American tactic, rounding up the required majority in advance of the meeting. In June, U.S. ambassador Albert Nufer approached Perón to win Argentina's support for the U.S. plan to isolate Guatemala. Though Perón backed the conference on anti-Communism, he was uneasy about the political implications of backing Washington in so direct an attack on an OAS member. American officials believed that Perón was trying to antagonize them. In fact, he had suggested the alternative of using the same strong language in criticizing a "communist problem" on the continent, but without specifically targeting the Guatemalan case. Perón had no sympathy for Guatemalan Communism and only modest concerns over the U.S. intervention in that country. Again, though, and to the consternation of American observers who grasped the implications but could not accept them, Perón was not in a position to openly support U.S. policy in Latin America. *Peronista* senators and members of the Argentine Congress, as well as leaders of the Peronist-dominated Confederación General de Trabajo, took public positions that, if not openly favoring Guatemala, were nonetheless hostile toward Washington. Moreover, public sympathy was with Guatemala. In the city of Rosario, for example, police were unable to block protesters from smashing a United States Information Agency (USIA) exhibition.[43]

Tensions between U.S. companies and the Argentine government remained a sore point in bilateral relations through the 1950s. The American and Foreign Power Company could not resolve its disputes with Perón, and while Westinghouse eventually won the Export-Import Bank loan for its steel plant contract, the credit never became effective. With Argentina facing a power shortage, Perón liberalized investment and production rules for foreign oil companies. In September 1953, Perón spoke to Nufer about petroleum exploitation and the need to sidestep YPF in the granting of new concessions. But despite extensive negotiations with Esso, Standard Oil of California, and a handful of smaller companies, the Argentine government could not find a way of convincing American companies jaded by Argentine exchange controls that new investments could be lucrative.[44]

In 1954, the United States sought Argentina's support in challenging ECLA's growing policy influence among Latin American governments. In anticipation of a Pan-American economic conference to be held in Río de Janeiro in late 1954, Eisenhower, hoping to seize the initiative from ECLA, expanded the Export-Import Bank's lending capacity by $500 million. In response to senior administration members who opposed the change, Eisenhower framed his decision not only as part of how Americans had to do business successfully in Latin America, but also as a key component in the fight against Communism. Eisenhower did not go far enough in adopting ECLA proposals, according to Harold Stassen, the Foreign Operations Administration chief. But Treasury Department secretary George M. Humphrey opposed any concession to ECLA and was named by Eisenhower to lead the U.S. delegation to Río de Janeiro. Henry Holland made visits to several Latin American countries to try to build support for the United States. Reflecting the underlying strength of U.S.-Argentine trade ties—and in spite of persistent conflicts over a variety of trade and investment issues—Perón promised his support for the United States in Río de Janeiro.[45]

In the year before the military coup that overthrew him, Perón faced a declining economy for which his government could produce no viable remedy. Perón viewed his relations with the United States as better than ever, as did his nationalist critics. A January 1955 multimillion-dollar agreement with Henry Kaiser to build an automobile factory in Córdoba was important both symbolically and materially. Other foreign contracts existed with firms from Europe and the United States. These included one with Merck & Co. for the building of a cortisone factory and one with Monsanto to manufacture polystyrene. None of this satisfied American officials that Argentina had, in fact, "come around" to a pro-U.S. business stand. American investors and government officials were troubled when, in March 1955, Argentina signed a Trade and Payments Agreement with Great Britain that offered British companies profit remittance concessions that the American companies did not have. James H. Drumm, the national councilor for the Chamber of Commerce of the United States of America in the Argentine Republic, echoed the sentiment of many American entrepreneurs tired of Perón's supposedly capricious politics. While British companies had been offered new dividend remittance provisions tied to a British loan to Argentina, U.S. companies continued to be treated poorly despite a recent $60 million Export-Import Bank credit.[46]

U.S. officials largely failed to recognize that bilateral commercial and financial relations were sound and that Perón's rhetoric—when directed against Washington—had little if any impact on inter-American relations or American foreign policy in the region. Through mid-1955, as wages dropped, as labor unrest grew, the U.S. government continued to press Argentina on the slowdown of remittances by U.S. companies. A Peronist crackdown on political opponents in the Argentine Catholic Church prompted rebukes in the American press and some opposition in the U.S. Congress to Argentine-American cooperation. In June 1955, as Perón fought back an attempted military coup d'état, Henry Holland spoke with members of Congress at a secret meeting of the Latin American Sub-Committee of the House Foreign Affairs Committee. Despite his own reservations about Perón's slowness on remittances, Holland found himself defending what he described as Argentina's friendly politics toward Washington.[47]

Close Bilateral Ties during Military Rule

In August 1955, Argentina finally permitted the remittance by U.S. firms of $4.5 million in back profits. In September, disgruntled Argentine military officers seized power and sent Perón into exile. They acted from a litany of complaints, among them Perón's personalist political style and the Standard Oil of California contract, which was quickly abrogated after the coup. At best, Americans viewed Perón as a source of instability and were relieved to see him go. They saw the period after Perón's fall and before elected president Arturo Frondizi's term of office began in 1958 as a golden period in bilateral relations. Argentina's military rulers presented none of the complications of their equivalents a decade before; the specter of Nazism had passed, and Argentina's military seemed a strong potential ally in the fight against Communism in the Americas. Unlike his reserve in dealing with Hipólito Paz over remittances, Henry Holland's approach to the new Argentine ambassador in Washington, Adolfo Vicchi, was much more hospitable. Vicchi announced that he was pressing his government to join the IMF and the World Bank. He also indicated that it would be a priority of the new government to find new dollar earnings through increased sales to the United States. Holland was enthusiastic. Vicchi told him what he wanted to hear. U.S. companies would now be eligible to compete for contracts in the electricity sector, heretofore controlled by the government. A dispute between the government and IKA was settled happily for both sides. The company would make new investments in Argentina, and instead of producing passenger cars, it would build jeeps, trucks, and tractors.[48] Moreover, unlike Washington's relations with the previous administration, no serious misunderstandings existed over Argentine government public postures for domestic consumption and the real state of bilateral relations.[49]

Washington liked what it saw in Buenos Aires. Acting on the recommendations of Raúl Prebisch, the new military regime quickly ended a number of state strictures on the economy. Government spending was slashed, price subsidies on exports were cut, and export taxes were eliminated. Perhaps most significant, the new regime set in place an open foreign exchange market that allowed free capital movement in and out of the country. Both Holland and Nufer pressed hard in Washington for the U.S. government to back new Argentine loan requests, and Secretary of State John Foster Dulles made that case to the National Security Council. But others were more cautious. The State Department's Bureau of Economic Affairs wondered whether an American loan package that was too generous might unfairly disadvantage U.S. agricultural products in the face of Argentine competition on international markets. The State Department insisted that Holland make no quick commitments to Argentina. At the same time, de facto president General Pedro Aramburu made clear that the ambiguities of Perón's third-position foreign policy were at an end and that Washington would find staunch support in Argentina for its hemispheric anti-Communism.[50]

In 1956, Argentina ratified the OAS Charter, which the government had rejected as a pro-U.S. document in 1948. It signed on to the 1954 Caracas anti-Communist resolution. The military government became a member of the IMF and signed an Air Force Mission agreement with the United States. The Argentine Navy joined its U.S. counterpart in antisubmarine exercises. But old irritants continued to shape bilateral relations. Despite the dismantling of many Perón-era regulations, the military government was slow to negotiate an end to controls on profit making in the meatpacking sector. In January 1956, the government placed IKA on a list of interdicted companies—a Perón-era device—for supposedly improper business practices. Though nothing came of the accusations, Americans remained wary of what had happened. The Aramburu regime tried again, unsuccessfully, to convince Washington that Argentine beef exports were safe and that foot-and-mouth disease was no longer a threat in Argentina.[51]

Relations stalled also as Argentine authorities continued to pressure Washington for loans to help jump-start the Argentine economy. On 22 June 1956, Argentine Central Bank president Carlos Coll Benegas came to Washington to negotiate public and private financing. In more than six weeks of discussions with the International Bank for Reconstruction and Development (IBRD), the Export-Import Bank, and a handful of New York banks, Coll had nothing to show. In mid-August, the Export-Import Bank told Coll that although it would not fund a loan to help reform and modernize the Argentine transportation sector, it would help fund the power sector, but only as part of an agreement by which AMFORP's stake in electricity generation in Argentina would expand. In September, the bank reversed itself and extended a $100 million credit to Argentina, with $85 million dedicated for public transportation and $15 million in private capital. In return, the Americans expected "progress toward the solution of several problems before any further credit could be considered in the public sector."[52]

In April 1957, at a Buenos Aires luncheon for the Argentine heads of General Electric, Ford, National City Bank, and a handful of other U.S. firms, Finance Minister Adalberto Krieger Vasena reaffirmed that Argentina would return to a completely open free enterprise system with one exchange rate. Subsidies would be eliminated, foreign capital would be treated fairly, and everything possible would be undertaken to attract new investors. But Krieger Vasena wanted more help from Washington. He lectured guests about how disappointed he was at the hesitancy of Americans to invest in Argentina and how "parsimonious and tight-fisted" the Americans were behaving toward his government. Krieger Vasena found remarkable that, although the Aramburu regime was getting nowhere in Washington, even as Perón had continued to unleash his anti-American diatribes in 1951, he had been granted a $60 million Export-Import Bank loan for the San Nicolás Steel Plant.[53] What Krieger Vasena was missing was that, despite a generally positive U.S. perspective on the military regime in Argentina, Americans continued to be driven by unresolved business disputes and remained suspicious of Argentines and Argentine democracy. In 1957, anticipating the 1958 Argentine presidential elections, U.S. ambassador to Argentina Willard L. Beaulac described presidential candidate Arturo Frondizi as Argentina's "outstanding demagogue since Perón." Despite that Frondizi bore none of the authoritarian tendencies that had characterized Perón's government, the two were linked in Beaulac's mind because both were critical of foreign oil companies.[54]

Frondizi, Economic Crisis, and the Cuban Revolution

Between late February, when Frondizi won the presidential vote, and 1 May 1958, when he took office, the president-elect toned down his preelection nationalist rhetoric. He also made clear both to the outgoing government and to U.S. officials that he intended to work effectively with the United States to resolve outstanding problems and promote economic growth in Argentina. Frondizi hoped to use the period between his election and his inauguration to help settle the business conflicts that had strained bilateral relations for years. But by 1 May, nothing had been settled.[55]

Frondizi came to the government convinced that Perón's advocacy of import substitution was essentially a sound policy but should be directed at specific sectors of the Argentine economy. Labeled *desarrollismo* (developmentalism), the president's new economic plan gave priority to heavy industry.[56] Faced with annual expenditures of $250 million on oil imports and $150 million on foreign steel, Frondizi targeted these sectors as well as coal and iron mining. But the new government faced problems at least as serious as those encountered by its predecessors. Dollar earnings were scarce. The foreign debt had reached $930 million. Debt service payments for 1958 were $95 million, almost half of which were in dollars.

Moreover, Frondizi understood that he had an even narrower political window than did the Aramburu regime. His election had been founded in part on the split of his Radical Party. The party of Yrigoyen and Marcelo T. de Alvear was still essentially a centrist party dedicated to the interests of the urban middle class. The break in the party led to the formation of the Unión Cívica Radical del Pueblo (UCRP) under Ricardo Balbín and the Unión Cívica Radical Intransigente (UCRI) led by Frondizi. One key issue divided the two groups. Although Balbín favored a continued appeal to voters on the basis of the party's differences from the working-class-based Peronist movement, Frondizi moved toward a tacit alliance with Peronism, in part to take advantage of the proscription of Peronism from national politics in the aftermath of the 1955 coup d'état.

Frondizi had won the 1958 election with Peronist backing. But in the months that followed, and in the absence of substantive prolabor policies from the new government, many of his supporters bolted to Balbín. To make matters worse, the military, which had given Frondizi his opening by calling elections, continued to be wary of the president for his proximity to the Peronists during the election campaign. Frondizi would need to produce political results quickly in order to get a chance to implement his medium- and long-term economic projects.[57]

The president moved quickly to raise wages and to restore collective bargaining and other Confederación General de Trabajo (CGT) rights denied by the military. He also invited American oil companies to compete for new exploration and development contracts. During his goodwill tour of Latin America, U.S. vice president Richard Nixon had attended the May inauguration. Frondizi had told him that he intended to do all he could to attract foreign investment. Nixon stressed the possibility of U.S. companies investing in oil exploration, and Frondizi acted on that suggestion. Despite his having been a strong and vocal defender of YPF's role in oil exploration, Frondizi now believed that the state petroleum company simply did not have the resources to find and extract enough oil to reverse Argentina's persistent energy crisis. Frondizi personally took charge of secret negotiations. In late July, he announced new contracts with several foreign drilling and production companies including Carl Loeb, Rhodes & Company, Pan American International Oil Company (Standard Oil of Indiana), and Williams Brothers. Contract terms varied, but in each case, companies would deliver oil found to YPF and would receive compensation in a combination of dollars and pesos. By December, the Argentine government had reached agreements as well with Esso and Shell. In light of past antipathies to foreign oil companies in Argentine politics, the agreements were particularly lucrative and generated loud protests against Frondizi having sold out his principles. YPF's agreement with Esso promised the company thirty years of exploitation rights to a petroleum-rich 4,800 square kilometers. Although YPF would pay for Esso's oil in pesos, a crucial provision of the agreement made clear that the Central Bank would convert those profits to dollars on request.[58]

Remarkably, and despite opposition criticism, the new government moved faster and more effectively than any government since the 1920s in reversing the country's economic nationalist policies. Frondizi wanted to clear the books of all outstanding disputes with foreign companies. In May, the government gave back to German investors property that had been expropriated more than a decade earlier. In September, Frondizi quietly reached an agreement with AMFORP by which outstanding claims would be settled, and the U.S. firm would build a new plant in Buenos Aires.[59] In December, the Argentine congress passed Frondizi's Law 14.780, which ended controls on profit remittances and assured capital repatriation. The Industrial Promotion Law that followed offered lower taxes and other incentives for foreign investors. Frondizi's speed and lack of hesitation in settling issues that had irritated U.S.-Argentine relations for more than a decade had a strong impact in Washington. In July, Export-Import Bank representative Vance Brand had gone to Buenos Aires to study Frondizi's economic policies and actions in reference to a new Export-Import Bank loan. Frondizi wanted money for a new steel plant. Brand was uninterested and unconvinced that the project would be viable. But just a few months later, Brand had changed his mind on the basis of the oil contracts and the AMFORP settlement and other issues. He favored an Export-Import Bank loan for $250 million.[60]

In late 1958, U.S. government agencies cobbled together the most aggressive American assistance package in the postwar period. The Treasury Department provided $50 million in credit to back exchange support. The Export-Import Bank offered a balance-of-payments loan of $24.75 million and provided a further $100 million for specific project financing. The Development Loan fund added $24.75 million in credits for imports from Argentina. Private banks made loans of $54 million and $75 million more by the end of 1959. By mid-1961 Export-Import loans to Argentina had reached $486 million, $230 million of which had been disbursed. But the Argentine government expected still more. Between May 1958 and April 1961, the Argentine government approved $323 million in foreign capital investment proposals.

But all of this came too late for Frondizi, and even if it had come earlier, it may not have saved him politically. In November 1958, Peronist unions mounted a general strike to back oil sector workers in Mendoza protesting worsening living conditions and what they viewed as Frondizi's oil patch giveaways to the Americans. Frondizi responded to the crisis by invoking a state of siege. His Peronist backers were right in finding the measures excessive and authoritarian; Frondizi's actions broke the support of his Peronist backers. Many suspected him of an ulterior motive in calling for a state of siege. Shortly before issuing his decree, Frondizi had decided to accept tough IMF guidelines demanded by public agencies and private banks in the United States as a condition for their bailout package. These measures would have been anathema to previous cold war–era Argentine governments. They included an end to restrictions on imports, a wage freeze, a single exchange rate system for foreign currencies, and projections for a balanced budget based in part on substantial firings in the public sector. Frondizi announced that decision shortly after the initial thirty-day state of siege was called, and then extended it indefinitely. It continued through the end of Frondizi's period in government.[61]

Early in 1959, the embattled Frondizi found momentary solace in a visit to the United States—a first for an Argentine president. The trip was a diplomatic and public relations success. Congress and the Eisenhower administration lavished praise on Frondizi as a model Latin American leader. Meanwhile, in the president's absence, acting president José María Guido exacerbated labor unrest by sending in the armed forces to suppress striking workers. On his return to Buenos Aires, Frondizi faced months of political and social turmoil. The military high command began to contemplate a coup d'état, and some officers spoke openly about the possibility of a coup, further destabilizing the government. IMF-sanctioned adjustments brought severe recession and inflation characterized by a 133 percent cost of living rise in 1959. In spite of the crisis, Frondizi hoped to press ahead with plans to accelerate industrial development and production in oil and other sectors. A split in his administration pitted those backing Frondizi's aggressive position against others, including Economy Ministry Under Secretary Roberto Alemann, who opposed moving ahead on capital-intensive projects, requiring further massive borrowing from the United States, until current economic problems were solved. Though concerned about stronger Argentine-Soviet trade ties and a 1957 Russian credit to the Argentine oil sector for $100 million, U.S. officials held back from backing further loans to the Argentine government, partly on the advice of the IMF.[62]

With the military threatening a takeover in June 1959, Frondizi accepted an armed forces demand that the fiscally conservative Alvaro Alsogaray be named economy minister. That appointment gave the military firm control of economic policy and made explicit the threat that if labor peace and economic stability could not be maintained, the armed forces would assume command of the government. Since his January visit to Washington, Frondizi had backed the military's efforts to secure massive U.S. assistance to counter what Argentine officers increasingly saw as a dangerous internal Communist menace. Late in 1959, the Americans approved an $11 million loan to finance the Argentine purchase of military equipment. Funds were designated in part for the purchase of F-86 fighter jets, as well as tanks and armed personnel carriers.[63]

Argentina's balance-of-payments problems remained tied to what Argentine leaders continued to believe was American intransigence on foot-and-mouth disease and beef imports. In 1959, U.S. restrictions became even more stringent when research conducted at the USDA showed that a wet salt-cure method employed on beef in Argentina could not destroy the foot-and-mouth virus. Not only did Argentine officials protest the new ban on cured beef, but they continued to press a long-standing case that the United States should amend its prohibition on fresh and frozen meats from Argentina to exclude Tierra del Fuego and Patagonia, where they maintained there was no foot-and-mouth. Americans remained justifiably skeptical. But in 1961, Argentines held that a resumption of cured beef shipments might mean as much as $40 million in sales annually, this in the context of Argentina's 1960 exports to the United States having only reached $90.5 million.[64]

Frondizi's diplomatic rapprochement with Washington in 1959 proved brief. In the aftermath of the Cuban Revolution, the United States hoped to gain Argentina's backing for its Cuba policy. The reaction to the revolution in Argentina was mixed. Middle- and working-class Argentines knew the Batista regime for the repressive, U.S.-backed regime that it was. As in much of Latin America, the ouster of the dictator was welcomed. At the same time, though, the mostly anti-Communist Peronist workers movement was unsympathetic to more left-leaning Cuban workers. More suspicious than ever of popular politics, middle-class Argentines were wary of the Cuban Revolution, as were their political leaders.

Frondizi was no supporter of Fidel Castro. Even so, American policymakers disliked the Argentine president's independent approach, like that of many other Latin American leaders, to what Washington regarded as a major inter-American crisis. Beginning in early 1960, the United States tried to shore up support in Latin America for its stand on Cuba, beginning with a trip to South American by President Eisenhower in February. But as American officials became more and more preoccupied with Castro and the purported dangers he posed to political stability in the Americas, the Frondizi government pushed harder still for loans to alleviate the ongoing economic crisis in Argentina. In mid-1960, Frondizi tied the Cuban situation to the Argentine government's need for more credits from Washington. He told U.S. chargé d'affaires Maurice Bernbaum that Argentina and the United States were "in the same boat." If Argentina's austerity program failed, in the absence of stronger American support, this would embolden those who believed in the Cuban way. U.S. officials were sympathetic, but there was no more money for Argentina.[65]

In mid-1960, when, through the OAS, the United States proposed the creation of a $500 million Social Progress Trust Fund for Latin America, Frondizi and President Juscelino Kubitschek of Brazil were critical. Frondizi argued that the program, intended as a solution to the purported threat of more Cuban revolutions in the Americas, was inadequate. As in the case of Argentina, what was needed was a sustained program of U.S. public and private investment in industrial infrastructure. In 1961, as the United States worked within the Organization of American States to isolate the Cuban revolutionary government, American leaders saw Frondizi as a key obstacle to their diplomacy. While the State Department acknowledged that Argentina had openly criticized Castro as well as the intervention of the Soviet Union in the Americas, it focused on Frondizi's position that the U.S. relationship with Castro was clearly distinct from that of other Latin American governments with the new regime. Frondizi viewed the problem as more "Latin American" than based on the cold war. For the United States, the Cuban Revolution was essentially a dilemma in the long-standing Soviet-American confrontation. Frondizi, on the other hand, more clearly than most other Latin American leaders concerned with U.S. pressures, understood the Cuban Revolution as a social movement whose external component was complicated by strong support among many Cubans. For the United States, this stand marked a worrisome deviation from the inter-American security line that Americans were advancing within the OAS and that entertained no room for a gray area on cold war conflict.[66]

To Washington's annoyance, in March the Argentine Foreign Relations Ministry had tried to mediate U.S.-Cuban tensions without having consulted the Americans in advance. In August 1959, at the meeting of the Inter-American Economic and Social Council in Punta del Este, Uruguay, U.S. treasury secretary Douglas Dillon had presented what would become President John F. Kennedy's most important foreign policy initiative for the Americas. The Alliance for Progress, a plan for massive financial assistance, was to help lift Latin America out of poverty. At the meeting, the pro-American Argentine journalist Jacobo Timerman had brokered a secret meeting between Che Guevara and Kennedy envoy Richard Goodwin. Despite this, the Americans reacted badly when Guevara went on to Buenos Aires after the meeting and met with Frondizi. To make matters worse, in Punta del Este the Argentine president had told U.S. ambassador to the United Nations Adlai Stevenson that he blamed the Bay of Pigs fiasco in part for unfavorable conditions within the OAS and for collective action on the Cuba question. Frondizi also told Stevenson that without real economic and social progress in Latin America tied to the Alliance for Progress, the OAS would be unlikely to take any sort of action.[67] The State Department thought Frondizi did not understand the gravity of the Cuban threat. Americans disliked the implications of what he was saying for the prospects of collective hemispheric action against Castro.

In 1961, the U.S. State Department Bureau of Inter-American Affairs described Argentina as having worked harmoniously and productively with the United States after the fall of Perón. Frondizi was hard at work on a "courageous" stabilization and recovery program. Argentina had "proved" its alignment with the "West." Moreover, for the bureau, it was a "tribute to Argentina that it is endeavoring to rise above nationalism, neutrality, sensitivity, egocentricity, and fancied rivalry with the United States for hemispheric leadership." For American leaders, the key issues that defined good bilateral relations had always been clear. Once specific business and commercial problems had been settled satisfactorily for the United States, relations were considered good. For the bureau, Argentina's "current improved and productive state may be ascribed in large part to the fact that Argentina needed United States sympathy, cooperation, and financial support to rebuild the country following Peron's overthrow, and that the United States was willing to forgive the past and extend help."[68]

The Argentine high command was appalled at the government's position on Cuba. Officers demanded that Frondizi break diplomatic relations with Cuba, which he did. This and a failed electoral strategy in early 1962 helped create an opening for the military's removal of Frondizi from power. In the hope that his party could defeat them, Frondizi permitted Peronists to participate in congressional and gubernatorial elections. The results were disastrous for the president. Peronist candidates won ten of fourteen provinces contested. This helped convince the military that Frondizi would not be able to keep Peronism out of politics, a precondition for their remaining on the political sidelines. The military ousted Frondizi and imposed a regime headed by Senate president José María Guido.[69] Democratic government and the prospect for economic stability had come to an end and would not reappear for more than two decades.

5   The Sixties: Military Ties, Economic Uncertainties

One day in 1961, at the training grounds of the Colegio Militar, Argentina's equivalent to West Point, two key figures in Argentina's cold war fight against Communism confronted one another over old and new strategies. Both men were already dedicated cold war warriors and followers of the U.S.-led fight against Communism in the Americas. Their disagreement came as a reflection of the growing influence of American military strategy and ideologies in Argentina. At the time, Jorge Rafael Videla, future de facto president and leader of the first junta that followed the coup d'état of 1976, was a lieutenant colonel and commander of the Cadet Corps at the Colegio Militar. The young officer and military instructor, Mohamed Alí Seineldín, served beneath him. During the 1976–83 dictatorship, or Proceso de Reorganización Nacional (Proceso), Seineldín was one of the military regime's most fervent ideological defenders. A Falklands/Malvinas War hero, Seineldín won a more ominous notoriety in 1990 by helping to lead a failed coup d'état attempt against the Argentine government. In 1991, from his prison cell on the Campo de Mayo base outside Buenos Aires, he told the story of his 1961 run-in with Videla.[1]

On the day in question, Videla's order of the day called for Seineldín to lead his troops in a frontal attack maneuver. Seineldín, convinced by National Security Doctrine analysis that Argentina's next war would be fought against an internal subversive threat, altered the plan.[2] He instructed cadets to remove their insignia; training began in counterinsurgency warfare to capture guerrilla warriors. But Videla appeared in a surprise inspection and did not like what he saw:

"What is called for in [today's] plan?" he demanded.

122

"A conventional maneuver, a frontal attack, colonel," Seineldín replied.

"Why aren't you doing that?" Videla continued.

"What's coming is a revolutionary war, lieutenant colonel."

In the early 1960s, Seineldín was among many of Argentina's fastest rising young officers committed to cold war models of National Security Doctrine and counterinsurgency warfare. Just as in Brazil and other South American countries, junior officers pressed their superiors to reconsider what they viewed as dated strategic and tactical models. Seineldín was among many that saw traditional troop movement training as outdated and irrelevant to Argentina's current threats. In keeping with how the U.S. military defined the most prescient threat to Latin American nations in the aftermath of the Cuban Revolution, Argentine officers looked increasingly for the enemy within the country's borders. In retrospect, Argentine officers identified the late 1950s and early 1960s as the point of departure for an internal subversive war against Argentine authorities, led by the Frente Revolucionario Indoamericano Popular (FRIP) and the Montoneros, among others.[3]

Facing what they believed was a global revolutionary Communist threat, Argentine and American officers had never worked more closely together or with a more clearly common set of military objectives. While Argentine popular opinion reflected a strong opposition to U.S. involvement in Vietnam not unlike equivalent hostility in Western Europe and Latin American countries, the Argentine military strongly backed American objectives and actions in Vietnam. Argentine officers shared the frustration of their American counterparts over what both groups saw as a civilian leadership in the United States unwilling to deploy the force necessary to win in Vietnam. Speaking with a journalist over a cup of coffee in August 2001, retired general Mariano Jaime de Nevares reminisced about the Argentine military observer mission he led to Vietnam in May 1968 and about the war more generally. "If one goes to war, all means available must be employed with maximum energy and speed to defeat the will of the adversary. Over there, in Vietnam, the Americans fought piecemeal."[4]

U.S. Military Initiatives

By the time of the Juan Carlos Onganía dictatorship, beginning in 1966, Argentine military leaders considered their cold war international position as one of staunch support for what the secretary of the Argentine National Security Council, General Osiris Guillermo Villegas called at the time the "Western and Christian line."[5] As an indication of the growing importance in Argentina of U.S. military strategy and influence, Argentine military and naval strategic planning for external war came to be strongly based on American models, far more so than at any time previously.[6] But the American military impact was far more profoundly felt in Argentina's growing preparation for internal war.

Under Eisenhower, American policymakers had begun to speak of counterinsurgency and internal security. Kennedy "aggressively pushed to make such concepts essential parts of his Latin American policy."[7] In September 1961, he instructed the secretary of defense to find ways to establish better ties between U.S. and Latin American armed forces. More specifically, Kennedy saw the imperative for Latin American soldiers to be taught to "control mobs and fight guerrillas." By radically increasing military aid to Latin America, Kennedy reversed his stand on restricting arms spending in the region. A November 1961 report from the Joint Chiefs of Staff argued to the president that an increased U.S. supply of training and equipment to Latin American militaries could improve those militaries' ability "to conduct counter-insurgency, anti-subversion, and psychological warfare operations."[8]

Kennedy supported U.S. military initiatives to bring more Latin American officers to American military schools. At the same time, though, he was unable to resolve a crucial policy contradiction in how the U.S. military approached Latin America. While preoccupied with a surge in leftist insurgencies in the Americas, U.S. officers planned for their Latin American counterparts to be stalwart supporters of American-style democracies. At the same time, however, American military policies in the Americas encouraged Latin American officers to fight a style of warfare that turned their countries into war zones, tore down the barriers between dictatorship and constitutional rule, and contributed to horrific and unprecedented repression in most Latin American countries. During the 1960s, some thirty-five hundred Latin American soldiers attended American military schools each year. Several of the fiercest ideologues and repressors of the Argentine military regime that came to power in March 1976 were graduates of the School of the Americas who acknowledged the influence of National Security Doctrine on their thinking, including Mohamed Alí Seineldín, Colonel Carlos Alberto Martínez, second in command of military intelligence at the time of the coup, and General Roberto Viola. Viola and General Jorge Rafael Videla were the chief military coconspirators in the months preceding the March coup.[9]

There was a more immediate impact of National Security Doctrine anti-Communism on the generation of Argentine military that controlled national politics after 1963. In 1962–63, conflict within the Argentine military boiled into open warfare between two factions, the *colorados* (reds) and the *azules* (blues). Despite the fact that this struggle was not explicitly about counterinsurgency warfare, internecine tensions within the officer corps were partly the product of fears that emanated from the Cuban Revolution and a putative leftist insurgent menace in Argentina. As much as any other single factor, the *colorado-azul* divide can be attributed to a growing divergence of opinion within the officer corps on the roles of the armed forces in promoting modernization, anti-Communism, professionalism, and democracy—all themes tied to National Security Doctrine.[10]

The rise of General Juan Carlos Onganía to the top of the Argentine armed forces in 1963 and his coup d'état in 1966 confirmed the ascendancy of U.S.-inspired National Security Doctrine analysis and strategy within the Argentine military. According to Videla, under Onganía's leadership "political infighting in the armed forces came to an end" (if only through the mid-1960s). Onganía's consolidation of power politically and militarily in Argentina after 1962 was undertaken with what the authors María Seoane and Vicente Muleiro describe as the "anti-Communist catechism that had its origins in the School of the Americas and the Pentagon."[11]

Onganía was the first Argentine commander to see his mandate for national defense as an essentially internal struggle. Speaking at West Point in 1964 in a thinly veiled threat to the constitutional authority of governments in Latin America, Onganía maintained that armies pledged to defend their national constitutions could never ignore the threat of "exotic ideologies." In other words, the fight against Communism might take constitutional democracy as a casualty. In 1966, after the coup d'état that brought him to power, Onganía put theory to practice. While the violence of his regime would pale in comparison to that of the dictatorship that would come ten years later, Onganía's repression was unparalleled and imagined an internal enemy of the sort that National Security Doctrine had identified. The military's attack on perceived opponents in Argentine universities ("The Night of the Long Sticks"), the crackdown on labor unrest in 1969, and dozens of other violent attacks on civilians all stressed the threat of subversion, as well as the destruction of a democratic opposition to military rule.[12]

American military assistance and Argentine purchases of U.S.-made matériel rose dramatically. Beginning in 1963, the two countries began negotiating toward a program of military sales under the American Military Assistance Program (MAP). Robert McClintock, U.S. Ambassador to Argentina, came up with the figure of $7.5 million in aid for 1964 and $10 million for the following year. Negotiations led to a memorandum of understanding signed by McClintock and Argentine foreign minister Miguel Angel Zavala Ortiz on 10 May 1964. The document specifically referenced the Communist threat in the Americas as an internal threat to Latin American countries: American military assistance would be apportioned in a manner that reflected the "incompatibility of communism to the inter-American system." The U.S. government seemed to regard the agreement in part as compensation for Argentina's support for the American blockade of Cuba at the time of the missile crisis. Secretary of State Dean Rusk envisioned the Argentine assistance package as commensurate with that for Brazil.[13]

The Argentine services had a long list of requests tied to Washington's MAP in Latin America. In early 1965, the Argentine Navy asked for $7,566,000 worth of equipment that included twelve T-28-C training aircraft, a catapult for the aircraft carrier *Independencia,* and twelve AD6 Skyraider aircraft. The air force wanted a broad range of spare parts, electronic equipment, and other materials worth $5 million. In addition, the Argentine armed forces wanted the United States to provide $90.5 million in credits to fund a battalion of tanks, a squadron of heavy transport aircraft, antiaircraft missiles, a squadron of medium helicopters, and a "squadron of light helicopters . . . for counterinsurgency operations."[14]

U.S. Cold War Diplomacy and Argentine Political Structures

Anti-Communism and cold war conflicts informed more than the military aspects of Argentine-U.S. relations. Beginning in the early 1960s, and in conjunction with the Alliance for Progress, American planners understood aid to Argentina as they did elsewhere in Latin America as part of an anti-Communist crusade. Although Americans did not identify Argentina as a potential cold war flash point equivalent to Central America or northeastern Brazil, they did believe in a persistent Communist danger in Argentina. In 1961 and 1962, members of the American Jewish Committee asked for the State Department's help in pressuring the Argentine government to crack down on the Argentine anti-Semitic, neo-Nazi group Tacuara. Despite there being no supporting evidence, the U.S. embassy in Buenos Aires supported the position of the Buenos Aires police that Communists could well be using recent anti-Semitic outbursts to help discredit the government.[15]

After the introduction of the Alliance for Progress, the United States identified dozens of projects for funding in a drive to block Communist penetration in Argentina. U.S. Agency for International Development (USAID) funding was used to modernize agricultural schools and create new courses in agricultural economics and marketing through the Ministry of Agriculture. The U.S. Information Agency (USIA) funded the Lincoln Library in Buenos Aires, which operated a branch in the working-class neighborhood of Avellaneda. American officials also began to initiate contacts with Peronist labor leaders in an effort to derail possible

Communist influences among Argentine workers. In late 1962, relations between U.S. and Argentine labor groups were poor. Americans were suspicious of what they believed wrongly was the pro-Nazi heritage of Peronist labor. At the same time, Argentine union bosses found their U.S. counterparts aloof. Hugo Belloni, a leader of the Light and Power Workers Union (Luz y Fuerza) whom Robert McClintock described as a "Peronist hack," called Serafino Romualdi an "Italo-Yankee gangster" and the American Federation of Labor–Congress of Industrial Organizations (AFL-CIO) an "agent of Wall Street Imperialism."[16]

Generally in Latin America, U.S. efforts after 1959 to curb Communism in labor movements were heavy handed and cumbersome, and they likely did little to reduce Communist influences. Beginning in the mid-1950s the AFL-CIO, with support from the Central Intelligence Agency and other U.S. government bodies, began to fund national and international anti-Communist labor groupings in the Americas. The most prominent of these were the Hemispheric Free Labor Organization (ORIT) and the American Institute for Free Labor Development (AIFLD). But in Argentina, Belloni's comments hint at the American inability to distinguish between Communism and militant labor Peronism. In May 1964, Esteban Torres, an international representative of the United Auto Workers, told U.S. embassy officials in Buenos Aires that within the powerful Unión Obrera Metalurgica (UOM), "there was no respect for ORIT." Torres saw ORIT secretary general Arturo Jaúregui approach UOM head Augusto Vandor to suggest a meeting. Vandor simply said no. The UOM regarded AIFLD as an "imperialistic arm of the capitalist class in the United States and considered the unions that associated with it to be traitors."[17]

Although Peronists saw themselves as anti-Communist, Americans tended to view Confederación General del Trabajo (CGT) militancy and hostility to the Argentine government as a threat equivalent to Communism in other countries. A 1964 State Department report attributed continued "chilly" relations between the American labor movement and the CGT to a "recrudescence of Peronista militancy and the CGT challenge to the [Arturo] Illia government." Whether the failed American opportunity to "moderate" Argentine labor might have changed much is unclear; unlike Bolivia, for example, the Trotskyist and Communist movements in Argentina never counted on the support of many workers.[18]

Argentine Arms Policies and the Weakening of Pan-Americanism

Ironically, while Argentine arms-control policy was heavily influenced by U.S.-led anti-Communism, American leaders never backed some of Argentina's most important arms stands. Though American and Argentine leaders shared anti-Communism as a policy priority, they were divided in how they conceived of Argentina's role in the cold war. While the Americans viewed that role as relatively insignificant, Argentines felt differently. In the late 1960s and early 1970s, Argentina's military chiefs fought arms controls, worked effectively to nullify the OAS role in arms regulation, and expanded Argentina's access to armaments from overseas. For Argentina, arms control was linked to authoritarian rule and related problems faced by military governments after 1966. Such problems included the maintenance of a militarized national security state, labor violence, the appearance of a terrorist menace, and the ideological and policy urgencies of convincing other governments that Argentina was a democratic nation.

The United States backed an OAS arms control regime, emphasizing the control of nuclear weapons. But Americans made no strong effort to limit the sale and dissemination of conventional weapons to right-wing authoritarian regimes intent on maintaining social order through the use of force. On the contrary, the United States had become an enthusiastic arms vendor in Latin America. U.S. ambivalence on arms control bolstered already strong bilateral relations during the period of military rule in Argentina—perhaps the strongest of the cold war era. In addition, the inability of the OAS to establish an arms limitation regime marked one of many cases of failure for cold war Pan-Americanism.[19]

Argentina had been a key promoter of Article V of the previously negotiated Antarctic Treaty that prohibited explosions of any sort in

Antarctica. In August 1963, when the Treaty of Moscow for the Partial Prohibition of Nuclear Testing was opened for country signatures, Argentina was among the first to sign. The treaty blocked nuclear arms testing under a wide range of conditions.[20] Just three years later, Argentina's enthusiasm for nuclear arms control had disappeared. While Mexico joined the United States in pressing hard for the Tlatelolco Treaty, preventing nuclear dissemination in Latin America, the two most advanced nuclear powers in the region, Brazil and Argentina, opposed the accord as a serious impediment to their active nuclear programs. Treaty negotiations lasted three years and could not reconcile Brazilian and Argentine ambitions with the Mexican-led consensus in Latin America against nuclear explosions of any sort.[21]

In Geneva, during the simultaneous negotiations of the Nuclear Nonproliferation Agreement, Argentine officials were even more explicit in their rejection of what they perceived as international efforts to limit the free functioning of Argentina's peaceful national nuclear program. According to the chief Argentine negotiator, José María Ruda, "my delegation considers that this treaty proposal unreasonably limits the functioning of non-nuclear powers in a complete line of research in regard to nuclear explosions with peaceful ends."[22] On 12 June 1968, the UN General Assembly approved the Nuclear Non-proliferation Agreement. Argentina abstained from the vote. Later that year, Ruda summarized his country's disaffection with UN nuclear nonproliferation politics by terming it "el desarme de los desarmados."[23]

Negotiations for arms safeguards in Latin America during the 1960s conformed with the inter-American security system and, for some political leaders, the recuperation of Latin American power lost to the United States in the 1947 Río Pact and the OAS constitution of 1948. All OAS members ratified the pact in 1948, but a number of Latin American leaders had since expressed their reservations at different times over U.S. power within the inter-American system. In 1957, several countries rejected Washington's proposal to link the OAS and the North Atlantic Treaty Organization (NATO). In 1954, after the *golpe* against the Guatemalan president, Jacobo Arbenz, many Latin Americans began to see U.S.-led nonproliferation projects in the Americas as a means for

Washington to maintain a monopoly on nuclear and nonnuclear arms classes.

Once established in 1967, the Latin American nuclear-free zone did win Argentine backing. This was an Argentine policy anomaly. During the cold war, Argentina tended to be a strong supporter of arms control initiatives beyond the Americas, but not within the hemisphere. In 1957, for example, Argentina supported a UN initiative for an immediate end to various forms of nuclear testing. In addition, during the 1950s and 1960s, Argentine disarmament politics beyond the Americas tended to coincide very closely with Washington's policies toward the Soviet Union and China. On the one hand, then, Argentina was opposed to what its leaders saw as American efforts to limit Argentine nuclear independence. Like others in Latin America, and despite their anti-Communist affinities for Washington, Argentine leaders suspected U.S. designs on power in the Americas. They also believed that American nonproliferation positions would limit Argentina's prospects for development and modernization. On the other hand, Argentine leaders backed U.S. stands on arms reduction outside the Americas, as part of a larger anti-Communist initiative.

After the coup d'état of 1966 and the beginning of military rule, the Argentine military developed a Pan-American policy that advanced its authoritarian ideology. The Onganía regime instructed its OAS negotiators to act in a manner that supported the prestige of the Argentine armed forces. Diplomats were also told to keep aware of potential popular reactions in Argentina to foreign influences over domestic policies. Argentine negotiators were to counter the impression overseas that dictators ruled Argentina. In February 1967, with the backing of Brazil at the Third Extraordinary Inter-American Meeting of Foreign Ministers, Argentine foreign minister Nicanor Costa Méndez supported making the OAS Consultative Defense Committee permanent. The proposed change implied a greater role for Latin American militaries in determining Pan-American security questions. It also represented a middle position between a U.S.-Brazilian proposal for a joint, supranational OAS military force and Chile's rejection of any sort of OAS coordination of the military affairs of individual nations in their war against internal subversion. The Argentine proposal failed. A majority of Latin American representatives were concerned that Argentina and Brazil would dominate the proposed inter-American force.[24]

In April 1967, at a meeting of OAS foreign ministers in Punta del Este, delegates approved an Argentine-sponsored motion to limit arms proliferation on the basis of the argument that more resources should be directed toward development. But the new convention had little impact because the Argentine proposal was a vague, watered-down version of the approach diplomats had advanced under Illia. Also in 1967, the Colombian government tried to push the OAS toward a more concrete plan for conventional arms limitation. Among other elements in the Colombian proposal was a regime of responsibilities and obligations among states that de-emphasized the size and military differences between nations. Argentina opposed the Colombian plan as discriminating against regional powers. At a meeting of the OAS disarmament committee in 1968, the Argentine delegate confronted the Colombians with the argument that a regional arms accord would be impractical. The Argentines conceded that regional arms accords might well have value in other contexts—in the Middle East, for example—but not in the Western Hemisphere.

In the Americas, Argentine military rulers not only worked for an OAS that would not interfere in Argentina managing its security state independently, but advanced Pan-American projects that would enhance the strength of repressive judicial, military, and political structures in Argentina. Three key events shook Argentina and heightened the sensitivity of the Argentine military to security concerns within the OAS. In May 1969, a strike in Córdoba quickly escalated into a riot involving thousands, the largest urban revolt in twentieth-century Argentina. The Cordobazo not only undermined the military mythology of a nation under social peace but also raised doubts about the government's ability to suppress turmoil. In March 1970, guerrillas of the Frente Argentino de Liberación kidnapped the Paraguayan consul in Posadas, Argentina. In June, the Montoneros burst onto the Argentine polity by kidnapping and executing former de facto president General Pedro E. Aramburu. In response, the Argentine government complemented an internal crackdown on civil society with diplomatic initiatives within the OAS intended to prompt other Latin American nations to take similar actions. More specifically, in an ominous precedent to Operación Condor—by which South American dictatorships cooperated after 1976 in the assassination of supposed subversives across international borders—Argentines targeted Montonero-like movements in neighboring countries.

In 1970, Argentine government analysts suggested that the OAS Assembly set standards for the obligation of members to take preventive action against the kidnapping of diplomatic and consular officials accredited to member states. That same year, Argentine diplomats attending the First Extraordinary General Assembly of the OAS used the opportunity to propose a human-rights-based condemnation of terrorism. The Argentine government wanted terrorism included on the General Assembly agenda, particularly with reference to kidnapping with an intent to extort, as a violation of the American Declaration on the Rights of Man. As in its diplomacy to derail an inter-American disarmament regime, Argentina had the firm backing of Brazil. But in addition, other dictatorships, including those in Nicaragua, Haiti, and Guatemala, lined up behind the Argentines while left-leaning administrations in Chile and Bolivia strongly opposed the Argentine initiatives.[25]

A weak democracy returned to Argentina in 1973, lasting less than three years. The government made an about-face on several foreign policy positions, joining the nonaligned movement, taking up the cause of decolonization, and reviving Frondizi-era developmentalism. But on arms control the damage was done. The OAS never recovered the initiative on arms limitation to an extent sufficient to implement or supervise any kind of weapons control regime. While the United States continued to back arms control in the Americas, its policy message remained unclear. Argentines saw in the Nixon Doctrine—which left primary responsibility for local development and security planning to the discretion of each country—a justification for their antidisarmament stand. During the 1970s, Argentina continued to make the distinction between its opposition to regional disarmament and its support for global nuclear arms reduction projects. What eventually held back to some extent

Argentine weapons purchases and its nuclear program after 1976 was not the OAS, but policy shifts in the United States during the Carter administration and equivalent changes in Canada and Western European states.[26]

The Alliance for Progress and Cuba

While military power politics were a cornerstone of U.S.-Argentine relations in the 1960s, as in the past, economic problems shaped bilateral ties. Mario Amadeo's work as UN ambassador stressed Argentina's key cold war foreign policy equation: Without development in Latin America, Communism would likely gain a foothold. In May 1961, Amadeo warned the World Affairs Council of Northern California that "communist propaganda had achieved important successes in its effort to identify Marxist revolution with the social revolution of underdeveloped peoples." The day that the Soviets succeeded in convincing those peoples that Communists were their friends, "world conquest will have become a reality." While religion and national traditions represented important anti-Communist defenses, the only sure defense was an immediate, massive U.S.-led mobilization against poverty in the Americas.[27]

In theory, the Kennedy administration was in agreement. But the discrepancies between Argentine and U.S. positions on how U.S. aid, investment, and finance might help end poverty and prime growth echoed long-standing differences in how leaders in the two countries imagined an American assistance role in Argentina. Before the Cuban Revolution and the alarmed U.S. interest in a forceful development program for the Americas, the Argentine government had worked with Brazilian authorities on Operación Panamericana, a major aid package for the region and a precursor for the Alliance for Progress. But Brazilian president Juscelino Kubitschek's proposal for massive U.S. investment and aid in the Americas to spark development and help eliminate poverty was more radical than what Argentine leaders imagined. Ironically, by the late 1950s, Brazil's decades-old amity with Washington had begun to show severe cracks, while Argentine suspicions toward

American policy in Argentina and the Americas were more muted than they had been in the past.[28] In 1958, the Argentine and Brazilian governments began working for an inter-American meeting of national leaders that the Argentine foreign minister hoped, in confidence, would avoid "a lyrical affirmation of love for western democracy and the repudiation of communism."[29] Conference themes would include the promotion of national development in each Latin American country, new trade treaties, a common market in the Americas, and foreign aid. But through contacts with Willard Beaulac and Roy Rubottom, Argentina was working toward a plan more closely aligned with U.S. objectives in the Americas than was Brazil, a plan that would not go as far as Kubitschek wished in bringing real economic reform.

Kubitschek imagined new and revolutionary levels of U.S. aid for the region. But for Argentina, the "principal objective of the projected meeting . . . is not to reformulate the problem of relations between Latin American countries and the United States, but to reformulate the problem of relations among and between the nations of the Americas." Argentine leaders recognized that despite their ongoing bilateral tensions with the United States over economic and business issues, the tone of their dialogue with Washington would likely be less hostile than those of Chile and Brazil, for example, over copper and coffee, respectively. In fact, compared to other countries in Latin America, the Argentine Foreign Relations Ministry saw Argentina's relations with the United States as more "comfortable"; its trade was not as extensively tied to the United States as that of most Latin American countries. Argentine leaders did not see themselves as anxious as their equivalents in neighboring countries for a radical reworking of U.S.–Latin American economic ties.[30]

Frondizi's initial response to the Alliance for Progress was enthusiastic. During its first year the Alliance targeted $150 million for Argentina to be spent for the most part on debt refinancing with the Export-Import Bank ($50 million), road construction ($56.7 million), balance of payments financing ($20 million), and housing (12.5 million).[31] Relations between Argentina and the new Kennedy administration at first seemed very strong. In public, the presidents seemed to get along well.

Each saw in the policy objectives of the other the opportunity for improved bilateral relations. But the Cuban Revolution slowly chipped away at U.S.-Argentine relations. Before Kennedy's election, Frondizi had reacted to the revolution by offering Argentina's help in mediating the U.S.-Cuban conflict. He renewed that offer in March 1961 to the consternation of the Argentine military, which saw any position not explicitly supportive of Washington as dangerous. According to U.S. secretary of the navy Gastón Clement, Argentina's position was one of "absurd neutrality in the face of communist penetration in the Americas."[32]

Late in April, after the Bay of Pigs invasion and despite the doubts of American policymakers and the Argentine military, now firmly committed to the National Security Doctrine and U.S. thinking on Cuba, Frondizi reaffirmed his foreign policy position at a meeting with Brazilian president Joao Quadros. In a dilemma reminiscent of Argentine positions during the First and Second World Wars, Argentine policy, though strongly supportive of the United States, was viewed as suspect in Washington because it did not coincide exactly with U.S. policy on the crisis of the moment, this time Cuba.

In May, an Argentine-U.S. working group was set up to address economic issues of interest to both nations. The industrialist Adalberto Krieger Vasena led an Argentine mission to Washington. The working group held talks for three weeks on a broad range of topics. Topping the list was an Argentine request for $200 million in aid for road construction, airports, and other projects. At the August meeting of the Inter-American Economic and Social Council in Punta del Este, the United States went further than it had before in committing itself to a massive aid and investment effort for Latin America. The United States promised more than $1 billion in assistance for Latin America by April 1962. Argentina received $1.4 million in aid and $76.9 million in loans from the Export-Import Bank, USAID, and the International Development Bank. This was a remarkable sum, bearing in mind that between 1946 and 1962, Argentina had received only $596.5 million in economic aid (more than $591 million in loans) and $44 million in military aid. In economic assistance, Argentina now ranked fourth in Latin America behind Brazil, Chile, and Mexico.[33]

In Punta del Este for the 1961 meeting, Che Guevarra wanted to speak with the Argentine president. Frondizi agreed. On 18 August the two had a seventy-minute conversation at the presidential residence in Olivos. Though the meeting had no great impact on the Cuba-U.S. conflict, Argentine military officers were livid that their president had spoken with Che. Two days later, Frondizi went on national television to try to limit the political damage the meeting had caused and make clear his opposition to totalitarianism. It was too late. Many officers now believed the country would be better off with Frondizi out of office.[34]

When Frondizi visited the United States again in September 1961, Kennedy told the Argentine president in a private meeting that although he wanted to provide Argentina with a generous aid package, his hands were tied. "The situation in Congress," he argued, "is not favorable." Kennedy explained to Frondizi that Congress had slashed the international aid budget from $5 billion to $3.9 billion and that half the latter figure would go to military assistance to Korea, Taiwan, Turkey, and a handful of other countries. "Now we don't have money for the Alliance for Progress."[35] When Kennedy tried to press Argentina for a stronger position against the new government in Cuba, Frondizi moved the conversation back to aid: "I believe that the solution to the Cuban question lies in setting in motion urgently and effectively plans for the Alliance for Progress." Kennedy hedged: "I'm sure that the social and economic development generated by the Alliance might have a favorable effect against the political agitation that has followed the Cuban Revolution." Frondizi held firm in his focus on the present. "It's not a question of waiting for final results," he told Kennedy. "On the contrary, it's a question of showing the immediate start of programs that will have a positive impact on the standard of living of Latin American peoples."[36]

Kennedy was not swayed. Frondizi and his team left Washington concerned about Kennedy's assessment of the congressional priority for arms over aid and the absence of adequate funds for the Alliance for Progress. Despite the fact that Kennedy was the "boldest man of the moment" as far as aid and development in Latin America were concerned, he seemed to the Argentines to be flying by the seat of his pants.[37] Frondizi had, in fact, identified an essential contradiction in U.S. cold war policy toward Latin America. Kennedy encouraged his advisers to think amply about the possibilities for Latin America and models for growth and prosperity. He asked scholars and academics to join the administration in planning for a more prosperous future in Latin America. But the models and policies for change were flawed in a manner that Kennedy could not appreciate. The White House distinguished clearly between an administration like Frondizi's, military rulers, and personalist political leaders. However, the Americans were unable to appreciate the complexities of Frondizi's political situation— a democrat dependent on the "personalist" Perón's politics and boxed in by an Argentine military anxious over internal discord and the purported emergence of a subversive enemy inside Argentina. Moreover, as flaws in the alliance quickly showed, the Kennedy administration was never able to find the practical means to connect the components of their development plans for Latin America—democracy, economic growth, and modernization.

Guido and Illia

Early in 1962, the United States moved to have Cuba excluded from the OAS. The Argentine government abstained from the OAS vote. Frondizi's ouster by the military came shortly after, and in March 1962, Senate president José María Guido took over for a term that lasted 562 days. His economic policies were less visionary that Frondizi's; Guido and his economy ministers were fiscal conservatives and shied away from confrontation with the United States.[38] European and Latin American governments were slow to recognize Guido. McClintock favored quick recognition by the United States, but some in the Kennedy administration, including Arthur M. Schlesinger Jr., urged caution. Guido sent newspaper editor Francisco Guillermo Manrique on a secret mission to the United States to gain Kennedy's support for the new government. Arguing that Argentina might well fall into the hands of a military regime or a Communist-Peronist popular alliance, the Argentine embassy in Washington convinced Kennedy to receive the envoy. Manrique managed to convince the administration that Guido—even though he owed his presidency to a military intervention and was clearly under the supervision of the armed forces—represented a moderate, pro-U.S. position between the army and political chaos.[39] On 18 April 1962, the United States recognized Guido despite the fact that the military clearly directed policy from behind the scenes and that Guido had broken and continued to break constitutional provisions for democratic rule.[40]

Unlike the issue of Cuba's expulsion from the OAS, the Cuban missile crisis held no controversy for the United States as far as Argentina was concerned. The Guido government quietly affirmed its support for the U.S. position. At this point the Americans no longer considered Cuba relevant in any significant way to the OAS but rather looked on Cuba as a battleground for its confrontation with the Soviet Union. Now, the OAS was much more supportive of Washington. On 23 October 1962 the OAS council passed a resolution backing the U.S. blockade of Cuba. Five days later, the Argentine diplomat Rodolfo Weidmann informed the OAS that Argentina would contribute the deployment of the destroyers *Rosales* and *Espora*, already en route for the Caribbean, to the U.S. cause. Without the approval of the Argentine Defense and Foreign Ministries, the Argentine Air Force offered to join the United States in potential military actions over the missiles in Cuba.[41]

Much more important than Cuba to Argentine-U.S. bilateral relations, Argentine foreign relations more generally, and the Argentine economy was the rapidly worsening problem of economic instability and Argentina's foreign debt. Facing short-term payment deadlines on several loans, Economy Minister Álvaro Alsogaray tried to buy time. He sought a major restructuring of Argentina's foreign debt, more than twenty-six million dollars of which was held in the United States. But by 1962, U.S. Treasury and State Department officials no longer believed in Argentina's short- and long-term ability to put foreign financial support to good use. There was a sense of alarm among leading Argentine entrepreneurs in contact with American diplomats. In June, a handful of Argentina's principal manufacturers, including Siam di Tella and

Fabril Financiera, each owed about twenty million dollars on short-term loans overseas. Normally, such loans were automatically renewed. But for the first time, renewal was no longer a certainty.[42]

In July, IMF officials told Dean Rusk that Argentine economic stabilization efforts appeared to be collapsing as a result of Argentina's failure to make a "serious" effort to set in place IMF austerity programs. Rusk blamed Argentina's debt problems on the "near-complete failure" of the government to cut spending as promised. Moreover, the Americans believed that Alsogaray seemed not to understand the enormity of the Argentine crisis. When confronted with these and other questions from Rusk, Alsogaray made no defense of his policies other than "the familiar one that he had inherited [the] situation" and that he was the only Argentine leader who had the ability to prevent economic crisis and political chaos. Rusk was further troubled that Alsogaray was underestimating the threat of inflation and the risk of labor unrest while overestimating Argentina's ability to secure new loans from overseas.[43]

Early in 1963, Foreign Minister Carlos Muñiz led a mission to Washington to try to win American support for a new restructuring plan. Muñiz saw himself as a supporter of U.S. policy in Latin America. In January 1963 he announced that, in support of the Alliance for Progress, Argentina would send teachers to poor countries in the hemisphere and would make available new spaces in its normal schools to train Latin American teachers.[44] In Washington, Edwin M. Martin (assistant secretary of state for Inter-American Affairs), Teodoro Moscoso (coordinator of the Alliance for Progress), and Robert McClintock (U.S. ambassador to Argentina) met with the Argentines. Muñiz argued that growing popular dissatisfaction in Argentina over tough economic conditions was an ongoing threat to Guido. Initiating a virtual constant in U.S. policy toward Argentina for the next four decades, American policymakers conditioned their support for Argentine loan restructuring on the premise that Argentina was mismanaging its economy and had to make crucial changes. In keeping with IMF demands, Moscoso countered that before the U.S. government would back Argentina, the Guido government would have to make major policy changes including a reduction of subsidies to YPF and to the transportation sector, as well as a more determined effort to collect unpaid taxes. Moreover, USAID loans were now subject to IMF agreement.[45]

Elected president in July 1963 by barely 26 percent of the electorate, Radical candidate Arturo Illia inherited an economy in recession and moved economic policy to the left. Economy Minister Eugenio Blanco stressed raising consumption while controlling the country's balance of payments abroad. Sharp salary increases for state workers initially helped push up the national deficit, while the government implemented a plan for rapid industrial expansion. The gross domestic product grew 10.3 percent in 1964 and 9.2 percent in 1965. Industrial growth registered 18.9 percent in 1964 and 13.8 percent in 1965. Illia inherited from Guido a high foreign debt level and a severe recession. Illia's minister of the economy proposed to solve the country's economic difficulties by expansive monetary and spending programs and by reintroducing exchange controls. According to then president of the Argentine Central Bank, Félix G. Elizalde, the IMF reacted with alarm. Elizalde and Blanco tried to reschedule IMF loan repayments. But while a 1965 IMF report criticized Argentine economic policy, Illia's policies hardly represented a radical departure from those of the preceding government.[46]

Despite the IMF's struggles with Illia's economic policies and Argentina's relative independence internationally, Illia's election changed little in the fundamentally strong relations between the United States and Argentina. Economic issues remained at the core of bilateral ties, and for both countries, the key problems remained unchanged. Argentine leaders wanted a stronger commitment from private U.S. investors and more aid from the U.S. government. The Americans pressed for austere monetary and economic policies. Illia was as much a developmentalist as Frondizi and was seen as just as much a threat by the Argentine military for that reason. But although the rhetoric of developmentalism remained strong, policymakers in the Illia administration were less willing even than the relatively conservative Frondizi government to adopt programs and policies at odds with Washington's concerns. In part, this was because of the growing importance of the IMF and the World Bank in establishing the terms for Argentine economic policy.[47]

New sources of bilateral friction developed. Illia refused to ratify the previously negotiated Guaranteed Investment Accord with the United States that would have protected American investors from the sorts of losses they had faced in Cuba from expropriation or insurrection. Illia saw the accord as a sellout to American companies. Though never substantiated, a May 1964 report by the U.S. Chamber of Commerce in Argentina attributed a year-long drop in foreign investment in Argentina to Illia's decision. Far more important was Illia's plan to abrogate Frondizi's pathbreaking YPF contracts with American companies. Despite the fact that Argentine oil production had doubled between 1958 and 1962 thanks, according to many Argentines, to the Frondizi contracts, Illia opposed them for two reasons. First, he felt obliged to carry through on a campaign promise to end the agreements. Second, his weak government felt beholden to economic nationalists inside and outside his Radical Party. Illia and the head of YPF, Facundo Suarez, staked out what they believed was a moderate position on ending the contracts. They proposed to indemnify Shell and Esso fairly. When the president's decision was announced in November 1963, he faced opposition both from nationalists, who opposed what they believed were the generous terms of the contract abrogation, and from liberal developmentalists who saw no reason to alter the current arrangement.[48]

Contracts were broken with a handful of American and other companies that included Esso Argentina (Standard Oil of New Jersey), Tennessee Argentina (Tennessee Gas Transmission Company), Pan American Argentina International (Standard Oil of Indiana), Marathon Oil Company, the Continental Oil Company, and Cities Service. In November 1963, immediately following Illia's decision, Senator Bourke Hickenlooper introduced an amendment to the Foreign Aid Bill before the Senate that would suspend assistance to countries that nationalized or otherwise seized American property or capital without indemnity. On 14 November, the Senate drastically cut Alliance for Progress funds.[49]

One day after Illia's announcement, McClintock told the president that the United States would suspend aid to Argentina effective immediately because of the contract cancellation. This, coupled with the blow to the funding for the Alliance for Progress in the U.S. Senate, marked an end to the illusion of cooperative friendship between Frondizi and Kennedy. While the U.S. Congress applied the Hickenlooper Amendment without delay, the State Department was more cautious, wanting to see the results of Illia's promise to indemnify before pursuing any policy shifts toward Argentina. But Alsogaray had been right. Illia's decision cost Argentina the confidence of Washington policymakers as well as foreign financing and investment. As a result of the contract cancellation, Argentina received no credits from the World Bank or the International Development Agency for more than two and a half years.[50]

The Dominican Invasion

While the oil contract cancellation and Argentina's ongoing inability to secure adequate foreign credits were in keeping with long-standing tensions in U.S.-Argentine economic ties, Argentina kept backing U.S. foreign policy stands in other countries. Early in 1964 when violent anti-American protests in Panama City led to the suspension of U.S.-Panamanian diplomatic ties, Panama charged the United States with aggression before the OAS and the United Nations. Argentine foreign minister Miguel Angel Zavala Ortiz expressed Argentina's "solidarity" with the Panamanian people and backed an OAS investigation of the conflict. But Argentina sought a solution that avoided identifying one or another party as responsible for the conflict. The Argentine foreign minister was deliberately ambiguous, so as not to offend either party in the dispute. The Argentines refused a seat on the OAS-mandated investigating commission. In December 1964, with the announcement of a new canal treaty, Zavala Ortiz told Panamanian president Marco Aurelio Robles that he hoped a just solution could be found to control of the canal. Argentina's position was equally ambiguous when the Venezuelan government accused Cuba of backing terrorists in Venezuela. Although Zavala Ortiz was a fervent anti-Communist, alarmed at what he viewed as a terrorist threat in Argentina's northwest, his position reflected both Argentina's support for Washington and its unwillingness to aggravate inter-American tensions. In July 1964, Venezuela took its complaint against Fidel Castro to the Ninth Meeting of OAS Foreign Ministers. Argentina abstained on votes for the OAS to apply sanctions to and rupture ties with Cuba but voted with the majority on declaring Cuba's actions against Venezuela as aggression.[51]

The U.S. invasion of the Dominican Republic was more complicated for Argentine leaders. In 1965, American forces went into the Dominican Republic to support what Washington viewed as the anti-Communist side in a Dominican political and military conflict. Zavala Ortiz committed Argentina to an OAS decision to send in a multilateral military force in support of U.S. objectives to restore stability on the island. Though in public Zavala Ortiz was less dire in his assessment, privately the Foreign Relations Ministry viewed the Dominican Crisis in part as a stark anti-Communist struggle; President Juan Bosch was a subversive engaged in psychological warfare backed by pro-Castro guerrillas hoping to establish a Cuban style regime in their country. But Argentine policymakers had no illusions about U.S. intervention. Foreign Relations Ministry officials saw American policy in the Caribbean basin as confused. They also believed that the American military had landed on the island in haste and had not been able to count on a hoped-for anti-Bosch popular sentiment.[52]

Argentina's delegates to the OAS, Hugo Gobbi and Ricardo Colombo, Defense Minister Leopoldo Suárez, and Commander of the Armed Forces General Juan Carlos Onganía were among a number of highly placed Argentine officials who backed the foreign minister's position on sending Argentine troops. Illia was included among a number of Radical Party politicians (mainly members of Congress and the Senate) who opposed it.[53] As the public conflict within Radicalism deepened over the Dominican Crisis, Zavala Ortiz appealed directly to Argentines in the Buenos Aires daily La Nación. His statement is a revealing insight into Argentine cold war policy. The foreign minister defended his position with reference to earlier Argentine peacekeeping missions in Lebanon and Congo. He also criticized those who damned the United States for unilateral action in this and other cases but who refused now to support Argentine participation in the multilateral force. "Let us mobilize that national dignity," Zavala Ortiz wrote, "so that it does not always appear that the United States is the only country that undertakes something for others or blocks the expansion of the world-wide revolutionary war."[54]

Illia refused to back his foreign minister by sending a bill to the Argentine Congress favoring the country's participation in a multilateral force. Zavala Ortiz—with the support of a military hierarchy already positioning itself for a possible coup d'état—went directly to the legislature. He tried unsuccessfully to organize a meeting of Southern Cone foreign ministers to win backing. A raucous debate in congress over U.S. intervention in the Dominican Republic led to a congressional declaration on 14 May that condemned U.S. intervention, demanded the withdrawal of American troops from the island nation, expressed the solidarity of Argentines with Dominicans, and affirmed the principle of nonintervention in the Americas. The motion reaffirmed the need for legislative approval before the executive could send troops overseas.

Illia's victory was Pyrrhic. At the Tenth Meeting of Consultation of Foreign Ministers that month, Zavala Ortiz was unable to play a leading role in planning for and effecting the inter-American force. But at the same time, the Argentine military viewed Illia as a dangerous ideologue. Moreover, Onganía, Defense Minister General Ignacio Avalos, and Naval Chief Admiral Benigno Varela saw Argentina's nonparticipation in the force as a failed opportunity to work closely with the United States on a military mission that might potentially lead to military assistance.[55] Ironically, though, it was the emergence of Brazil as the nation that would lead the Inter-American Peace Force in the Dominican Republic that led quickly to a "dwindling enthusiasm" in the project on the part of Argentine officers.[56]

Military Rule

Illia's overthrow in June 1966 ushered in a period of military rule in Argentina under three presidents, Juan Carlos Onganía (1966–70), Roberto Marcelo Levingston (1970–71), and Alejandro Agustín Lanusse (1971–73). The justification for the coup came in part from the National

Security Doctrine. The nation, according to Onganía, was in danger of falling to collectivist totalitarianism. With far more popular support than the military regime of the late 1950s, Onganía took on the problems of economic stagnation, the so-called Communist menace, internal security, and the need for a new model of stable participatory democracy. Some in the new administration expressed a nationalist hostility toward the United States through alarm over U.S. designs on Argentine primary materials. Even so, the de facto government sent a cooperative message to the Americans by naming Alvaro Alsogaray ambassador to Washington (1966–68). Onganía's economic policy centered on economic liberalization and free trade. It was meant to push Argentina much closer to the United States.

Washington was initially cautious. Led by Senators Robert Kennedy and Jacob Javits, Congress blocked American recognition of the de facto regime for eighteen days. Ironically, from exile in Madrid, Juan Perón told Argentines that this latest example of U.S. intervention in Argentine politics was unacceptable.[57] Although the United States banned the sale of some weapons to Argentina as a result of the coup, and even though the Argentines detained an American academic, Warren Ambrose, in July, U.S.-Argentine ties stayed strong. A visit to the United States that same month by Alsogaray alleviated the concerns of some Americans over new reports of anti-Semitism, the end of democratic rule, and economic policy.[58]

Onganía's coup coincided with a new free-market policy push in Washington. A State Department memorandum to the U.S. president in October 1966 characterized Latin America as being at a crossroads. Although there had been some modest economic progress since the start of the Alliance for Progress, those developments would not avert severe social crises over the next two years. The State Department urged the United States to press still faster for regional economic integration and higher Alliance standards on education, agriculture, investment, and trade.[59] The coup brought immediate positive signs for American business in Argentina. Prior to the 28 June coup, the Illia government finally reached settlement agreements with six of the foreign oil companies whose contracts had been annulled in November 1963. The agreements called for a cash settlement in return for the companies giving up their contract areas to YPF. Disputes with Pan American International Oil Company and Cities Service remained unresolved. Onganía reached much more favorable accords with these firms. Each would be allowed to continue local oil exploration and extraction at least through 1978.[60]

American business in Argentina supported the Onganía regime, feared the small political left, blamed labor agitators for problems on the shop floor, and shared Onganía's impatience with Argentina's social and political uncertainties. Before the coup, U.S. business leaders in Argentina, like the Argentine military, saw the radical left as dangerous. In September and October 1964, Chrysler Argentina fired almost 10 percent of its fourteen-hundred-person hourly wage workforce for supposed affiliation with the Communist Party and agitation at the plant. On 12 October, after the dismissals, a police cordon turned back protesting workers who marched on the plant with water cannons. On 2 March 1966, the John Deere Company locked workers out of its Rosario factory. The dispute centered on what management called a new "incentive plan" that union representatives told the AFL-CIO was no more than a speedup. John Deere's Argentine president told the U.S. embassy that "radicals" were at the root of the strike and that when production began again, the company would lay off a large number of "undesirables."[61]

The positive response of the American business community to the Onganía regime dovetailed with the friendly relations between the two nations' militaries. Between 1964 and 1970, more than two thousand Argentine officers received military training in the United States and the Panama Canal Zone. The response of the Argentines in these programs was generally positive, and the result was an ongoing strengthening of bilateral military ties. In May 1967, with the Bolivian government seemingly unable to control an internal guerrilla threat, Argentine ambassador to the United States Alsogaray approached U.S. assistant secretary of state Lincoln Gordon with a possible solution. Julio Alsogaray, the ambassador's brother and the commander in chief of the Argentine Army, believed that the Bolivian military was incompetent and that "the point might be reached where foreign assistance would be necessary." He offered that Argentina might "take the lead in providing such assistance in place of the United States so that the United States could avoid political complications."[62]

Foreign Minister Nicanor Costa Méndez was never as enthusiastic as Alsogaray about the United States. Moreover, when Economy Minister Adalberto Krieger Vasena implemented his strongly pro–U.S. austere stabilization program in March 1967, there was considerable opposition from within the Onganía administration, as well as from two architects of the Revolución Libertadora, Admiral Isaac Rojas and Pedro Eugenio Aramburu. Krieger Vasena's orthodoxy survived, but in late 1968 and 1969, popular unrest developed in Argentina over Onganía's austerity and economic stagnation. Terrorist attacks gripped Buenos Aires and La Plata. Massive strikes shut down the industrial cities of Córdoba and Rosario. Student protests erupted throughout the country. To some extent, this unrest came as part of a global wave of upheaval. But Onganía wrongly attributed the opposition to his regime to leftist insurrection. His response was to repress the dissent. Brigadier General Alejandro Lanusse, on the other hand, led a movement both inside and outside the military to oust Onganía and move Argentina back toward constitutional rule.[63]

Although Lanusse can scarcely be described as anti-American, his role in the ouster of Onganía depended on a nationalist appeal both inside and outside the armed forces that stressed what many believed was an exaggerated strength of the United States in Argentina and in the Americas. In August 1966, the U.S. Embassy in Buenos Aires had reported on the distinct positions held by Onganía and the more moderate future president, Lanusse. Addressing representatives of Latin American armed forces and echoing the long-deposed Frondizi, Lanusse argued that socioeconomic bankruptcy in Latin America had produced Castroism, "a pragmatic home-grown communism more dangerous than [the] purely ideological kind." Without naming the United States, Lanusse criticized Washington by noting that Latin American countries should not depend on one country with military supremacy in the region. Such dependence had fostered Communism. This position varied from the one advocated by the United States,

Brazil, and Onganía, which had favored a NATO-like inter-American defense structure (under U.S., Brazilian, and Argentine leadership) over a broader-based "inter-American peace force."[64]

Through the late 1960s and early 1970s, the United States continued to try to influence the Argentine labor movement, meeting with no more success than it had in the past. In June 1968, the AIFLD finally implemented a five-year-old loan project for low-cost worker housing in Argentina. The $13 million loan, guaranteed by USAID, went to four unions for the building of sixteen hundred dwellings. Between 1964 and 1968, AIFLD also trained more than sixteen hundred workers in courses and seminars in collective bargaining and labor law.[65] Despite the replacement of both Costa Méndez and Krieger Vasena in June 1969, U.S.-Argentine relations experienced no significant change. A year later, Lanusse succeeded in having Onganía removed from office, and the developmentalist economist Aldo Ferrer was appointed economy minister. Ferrer implemented a plan that included an "Argentinization" of the economy that would highlight importation restrictions to stimulate industry and an expansion of the credit market that would send a shudder through Washington. But in the context of Argentina's pro-U.S. cold war positions and the persistence of strong economic ties, the 1960s had produced little controversy in bilateral relations.

6   Descent to Dictatorship, 1970–1983

During the 1970s, Argentine-U.S. relations experienced their most strained period since the first Perón presidency. During Jimmy Carter's presidency, the United States established human rights as a foreign policy priority. Americans turned their attention to the abuses of the Argentine dictatorship (1976–83) and punished the military by prohibiting the sale of military equipment and working to isolate the regime diplomatically. Carter's human rights emphasis, though, was anomalous. The 1970s represented a high point in bilateral ties in other areas. Cultural relations were never better. Moreover, the Argentine military took its inspiration from National Security Doctrine and U.S. military training in its war on a growing domestic terrorist menace. In addition, and despite a period of economic nationalism in Argentina that reflected a forceful anti-Americanism, commercial and financial ties remained strong throughout the decade and into the early 1980s.

Cultural Ties

During the 1970s, U.S.-Argentine cultural ties continued to expand and deepen. Boxing reached an apogee in Argentina both for fan support and the number of exceptional champions who fought. Ties with the boxing world were never stronger. On 30 June 1975, in a remarkable night at New York's Madison Square Garden, the Argentine Carlos Monzón—possibly the best middleweight fighter in history—successfully defended his world title against Tony Licata. On the same card, the Argentine middle heavyweight Víctor Galíndez also retained his world title. A product of the Luna Park gym in Buenos Aires, super bantamweight Sergio Victor Palma won the Argentine championship in 1977. But to win the world title he had to consciously retrain himself as an American-style fighter. This meant doing away with his cautious and defensive style of jab-and-run in favor of a more aggressive "American" technique that he modeled after Joe Louis. Palma began to attack in close, relying much more than he had in the past (or than did other Argentine fighters) on quick combinations of upper cuts.[1] In 1980, Palma put what he described as his American tactics to work in winning his world title over the American Leo Randolph in Spokane, the first Argentine to win a world championship in the United States.

American musical influences in Argentina were vital. During the 1970s, Argentine rockers, the most influential of whom was Charly García, took their lead from American musical forms. But the sway of Argentine "Rock Nacional" remained limited by military government censorship. With the return of democracy in 1983, there was a deluge of foreign popular music, most notably American rock and pop. One consequence of the rapid entry of music from the 1960s, 1970s, and early 1980s that had never been heard before was that Argentines had little sense of the chronology of American rock. As a result, many musical groups in the 1980s and 1990s that were influenced by American music, including Los Fabulosos Cadillacs and Bersuit, frequently mixed a broad range of compositional, performance, and interpretive styles that drew on different periods in the era of rock. Bersuit, for instance, played in a range of U.S.-influenced styles that included tejana, heavy metal, and rock ballads.[2]

While less popular than rock, jazz was even more subject to American influences. Unlike rock, jazz remained below the radar of nervous military leaders during the 1970s. Its exponents were freer than rock artists to follow foreign trends. Many Argentine jazz musicians continued to play the music of the American greats to modest followings in Buenos Aires nightclubs. Having played jazz professionally since the 1930s, Enrique "El Mono" Villegas now emerged as Argentina's most dynamic interpreter of Cole Porter, Duke Ellington, Fats Waller, and a range of other American jazz icons. After a year in the United States, Villegas made his return to Buenos Aires in 1971, where he played

George Gershwin's "Rhapsody in Blue" at the Teatro Colón opera house to overwhelming acclaim.[3]

If "El Mono" represented an older generation of American-style jazz in Argentina, Gato Barbieri became the cutting edge. A tenor saxophonist, Barbieri was South America's most innovative jazz composer and artist in the 1970s. Profoundly influenced by Miles Davis, Charlie Parker, and Astor Piazzola, among others, Barbieri consciously wove together Argentine folk music styles with 1950s- and 1960s-era American jazz to produce a new sound that was in many respects a precursor to world music. In 1973, at the height of his innovative talents, Barbieri was approached by the American Broadcasting Corporation's Impulse! label to record an album. In part, Impulse! producer Ed Michel viewed Barbieri as a hot commodity for having recently finished composing music for Bernardo Bertolucci's *Last Tango in Paris*—music that was never used in the film. Barbieri, in turn, was excited at the prospect of working for the label that jazz legend John Coltrane had helped make famous.

Michel flew to Buenos Aires. Barbieri assembled a tango band. According to Michel, "we began with an ensemble in support of a tenor saxophonist with one foot in John Coltrane, one foot in the broader history of jazz, one foot in Tango, one foot in Pan-Andean folklore, and one foot reaching Samba-wards."[4] What Gato recorded, with Michel producing, was astonishing. He not only used jazz to bridge different forms of Argentine folklore, but long before other Latin American artists had begun to explore the fusion of music from more than one nation, Barbieri used jazz to meld Argentine with Brazilian music. Gato made two albums during these sessions. The first, recorded in Buenos Aires, focused on Argentine rhythms, traditional instruments, and instrumentations. At the end of the album, Gato recorded a brief track called "To be Continued." Over music made by a new set of instruments associated with samba, bossa nova, and other Brazilian music styles, Barbieri spoke about moving on to Rio de Janeiro to record a second part to his Buenos Aires work. In another 1973 album, *Bolivia*, this time produced by RCA Victor, Barbieri combined jazz, Argentine folk music, and Bolivian musical forms. Writing at the time, the American jazz critic Nat Hentoff called it "the highest point yet of his passionately expressive achievement."[5] Not coincidentally, Barbieri made his most important music during a very short period of cultural openness in Argentina sandwiched between military rule in the early and mid-1970s. His innovations came on the eve of the most restrictive censorship on international cultural contacts in Argentine history.

Diplomatic Cooperation

As had been the case in earlier decades, U.S.-Argentine diplomatic, military, commercial, and political relations followed the contours of burgeoning cultural contacts. Bilateral ties had never been better during the Onganía presidency. Nicanor Costa Méndez served as foreign minister from July 1966 through June 1969. He aligned Argentine foreign policy more closely with American interests than at any other time in the twentieth century. Argentina stepped up its activity within the Organization of American States, participating in key efforts to bring stability to the hemisphere. Argentina played an important role in both mediating the Honduras–El Salvador Soccer War and in providing military support for OAS peacekeeping in Central America. Sympathetic to U.S. interests in both cases, Costa Méndez also took the initiative to help mediate U.S. conflicts with Peru and Bolivia over American oil company contracts. Under Foreign Minister Juan Martín's direction (June 1969–June 1970), the Argentine government became still more involved in the OAS and United Nations. Argentine diplomacy turned toward commerce; Argentine missions were directed to sell Argentine products. Diplomats took university-level commerce courses for the first time as part of their professional training.[6] Both Martín and his successor, Luis María de Pablo Pardo, promoted a tougher Argentine stand on terrorism, which was also supported by the United States. With the Americans, Argentine diplomats at the OAS special conference of February 1971 pressed for a new international agreement on combating terrorism. When delegates moved toward drafting what de Pablo Pardo deemed an ineffectual compromise accord, the foreign minister walked out of the meeting to protest OAS weakness.[7]

In 1970, an informant gave the U.S. Embassy in Mexico information on Buenos Aires as a major transit destination for heroin coming into South America with the United States as a final destination. Shortly after, the two governments launched a long-term cooperative project to stop the international drug trade through Argentina that included U.S. Drug Enforcement Agency training programs in Argentina for Argentine police and the supply of military equipment to break the traffic in cocaine.[8] As Argentina experienced a rapid rise in left-wing political violence, American officials turned increasingly to strong Argentine anti-Communists for political advice and information. Despite Argentina's spiral into severe political turmoil between 1970 and 1976, U.S. government and business officials were uncharacteristically calm and lucid about the Argentine polity. Information gathered was extensive.[9] In January 1971, in a remarkable reflection of strong U.S.-Argentine diplomatic ties, Mario Cámpora, the political counselor at the Argentine embassy in Washington, went to the State Department to predict the overthrow of de facto president Roberto Levingston by the military. The State Department instructed the U.S. Embassy in Buenos Aires to keep confidential that Cámpora was the source for this information.[10]

Economic Nationalism, Anti-Semitism, and American Calm

Americans kept their heads in the face of developments that would certainly have been viewed as crises a generation earlier. After Héctor Cámpora was elected president in 1973, the Argentine government immediately improved relations with Communist countries and legalized the Argentine Communist Party. When Juan Perón took presidential office a few months later, he made no quick moves to alter Argentine foreign policy. Even so, American observers remained grounded. In November 1973, embassy chargé d'affaires Maxwell V. Krebs wrote that "Argentina under Perón is in no danger of moving into the Communist orbit. . . . Perón is above all a pragmatist . . . [and] appears to be under no illusions as to the fact that Argentina's substantive interests lie with the West."[11] In their dealings with Perón during the brief period of his last presidency, the State Department never doubted these credentials.

Ten years before, at the height of a wave of anti-Semitic violence in Buenos Aires, and in the aftermath of the Israeli government kidnapping of war criminal Adolf Eichmann from Argentina, the U.S. government had become concerned about the safety of Argentine Jews in the face of right-wing attacks.[12] Now that concern had dissipated. In May 1971, the U.S. ambassador in Argentina, John Davis Lodge, wrote to the State Department criticizing Rabbi Morton Rosenthal, Latin America section head of the Anti-Defamation League of B'nai B'rith (ADL). According to Lodge, Rosenthal was spearheading a "concerted campaign in the United States to create the belief that a serious anti-Semitic problem exists in Argentina."[13] The Argentine government, according to Rosenthal, was indifferent at best to the anti-Jewish attacks. In response to that sort of publicly expressed opinion, Argentine authorities approached Lodge to find a way to call off Rosenthal. Both Lodge and the Argentines feared that what they viewed as Rosenthal's exaggerated reports of anti-Semitism could limit Argentina's access to international loans and investment. The State Department responded cautiously but sympathetically to Lodge's concerns; Washington urged the ambassador to speak with U.S. Congressman Joshua Eilberg about Rosenthal's statements. Eilberg was a leading defender of Jews oppressed in the Soviet Union and in other countries. He had visited Argentina and maintained close ties to the ADL.[14]

During the 1976–83 dictatorship, Rosenthal would emerge as the single most important voice anywhere decrying state-sponsored anti-Semitism in Argentina. His criticisms of the Argentine junta helped equate the Argentine military in the international community with anti-Semitism. Moreover, after the March 1976 coup d'état, Argentine military rulers identified Rosenthal as a significant threat to their relations with other governments and expressed similar concerns to those Lodge raised—accusations of anti-Semitism risked undermining Argentina's prospects for foreign loans and investment. In October 1972, in conjunction with a visit to Argentina by fifty members of the ADL that included Rosenthal, the U.S. Embassy in Buenos Aires produced a report on anti-Semitism in Argentina. The embassy found that terrorist attacks against the Jewish community had diminished significantly over the preceding three years with the seeming dissolution of Tacuara and Guardia Restauradora Nacionalista, two right-wing ultranationalist groups that had previously targeted Jews. There were ongoing attacks on Argentine Jews. But unlike Morton Rosenthal, the embassy believed that those attacks could be attributed to a range of causes. "It is increasingly apparent that those Jews who are among the current targets of terrorist bombing attacks do not seem to be singled out because they are Jews, but are businessmen, targeted, in extremist rhetoric, as 'exploiters of the workers,' regardless of their religion or nationality."[15]

As they did other aspects of Argentine politics and society, Americans now saw the question of anti-Semitism through a national security prism that underlined a Communist threat in Argentina. The embassy went on to report that members of the Argentine Jewish community had identified some Jews as participants in "extremist activities, not in the name of Jewry, but in order to bring down the present government and effect revolutionary changes in Argentine society." Argentine Jews, according to the embassy, were less "Jewish" political actors and increasingly political players in the context of a left-wing revolutionary threat to Argentine stability.

Economic instability in Argentina contributed to new problems for U.S. business, such as hyperinflation and new threats of economic nationalism. But in contrast to their reactions a decade earlier, Americans no longer viewed economic nationalism as a dangerous menace. They distinguished, for example, between what they believed was the overwhelming menace of Salvador Allende's Chile and the generalized trend in South America to growing state intervention in the national economy. The U.S. share of Argentine imports was 25 percent in 1970, $419 million. The United States was Argentina's largest single supplier and its third largest customer. In the eighteen months ending in December 1971, the U.S. Embassy in Buenos Aires estimated that a stagnating economy had cost $350 million in potential investment. Increasingly restrictive Argentine import controls appeared to be impacting upon U.S. exports to Argentina. But the data were not yet conclusive, and American officials seemed unconcerned in comparison to how they had responded to Argentine oil sector problems a decade before. By 1972, imports from the United States had dropped to 19.2 percent of total imports.[16]

In June 1972, the chairman of the Board of Governors of the U.S. Federal Reserve System, Arthur F. Burns, visited Buenos Aires for four days. Highlighting the generally strong economic ties between the two countries, Burns's stay was unremarkable and presaged a decade of the heaviest lending ever by U.S. banks to Argentina. The Americans perceived problems in Argentine finance markets. There was an ongoing threat of government nationalization of foreign banks, and American firms faced what they believed were severe and unfair limitations on their access to credit. Even so, U.S. banks had recently approved a new $145 million loan, tied to $210 million more from Japanese and European financial institutions. Burns viewed the loan as having been made under "exceptional circumstances in order to support the [Argentine] government": Argentine government financial projections extended not even a year, to the first quarter of 1973. "We have no idea what the overall foreign debt position of the country is, nor do we have good information on scheduled debt repayments." And the loan was made despite the fact that "the future political outcome of the country is far from clear."[17]

Military Aid, Organized Labor, and the Rise of Terrorism

Early in the 1970s, U.S. military sales to Argentina soared, as they did to other South American countries. On 9 April 1971, President Richard Nixon approved a waiver on the congressionally imposed $75 million ceiling on military assistance to Latin America for fiscal 1971.[18] Secretary of State William Rogers made the case for the waiver, arguing that military equipment sales would foster U.S. security interests by bolstering the "counterinsurgency capabilities" of South American countries, which, in turn, would enable socioeconomic development to take place "within a more stable environment."[19] Two years later, Acting Secretary of State Kenneth Rush made an identical request of the president, this time specifically citing Argentina, Chile, Brazil, Colombia, and Venezuela as potential buyers of the Northrop F-5E fighter jet. Northrop had developed the F-5 "Freedom Fighter" a decade earlier specifically for the U.S. government Military Assistance Program in Latin America. But in 1967, reacting against the sale of sophisticated weapons to poor nations, Congress had passed a series of amendments blocking such sales. As a result, there were no exports of U.S. aircraft to Latin America until 1970. Recognizing that Argentina and four other South American countries had bought Mirage fighters from France, partly because of the U.S. export ban, Washington reconsidered its policy. In May 1973 the president approved another waiver, and extended credit to Argentina, Brazil, Chile, Colombia, and Venezuela for the F-5E aircraft purchases.[20]

Bilateral labor ties were never better. Relations between the AFL-CIO and the CGT were uncharacteristically close. The U.S. Embassy in Buenos Aires identified the Peronist labor movement as profoundly anti-Communist. Despite some persistent anti-American sentiment among Argentine workers, many Peronist-controlled unions began participating for the first time in U.S. government–sponsored programs and affiliating with pro-U.S. inter-American labor organizations. In November 1971, for the first time since Perón took charge of the CGT in the 1940s, the labor central sent delegates to the AFL-CIO annual convention under the auspices of the U.S. Leader Grant Program.[21] As American officials became more accepting of mainstream Peronist politics, inside and outside of the labor movement, they also became more active in tracking the rapid emergence of violent left-wing revolutionaries. In January 1972, the U.S. Embassy in Buenos Aires reacted to public accusations by eighteen political prisoners who had alleged that police and the military had tortured them. The American position heralded both coming political violence in Argentina and U.S. indifference to state-sponsored torture and other human rights violations. Ambassador Lodge made three important points. First, although police torture was not unknown in Argentina, this was the first accusation that the military was abusing civilians. Second, it was a "safe estimate" that the accusations were valid. And finally, "police/military tortures and parapolice/military kidnap squads" represented means of combating terrorism.[22] Lodge's remarks underscored what would be a key policy difference between the American approach to Chile and Argentina during the 1970s. Although the U.S. government had sponsored and supported the 1973 coup d'état in Chile, in Argentina there was no such overt backing.[23]

Through the early 1970s, U.S. businessmen in Argentina faced a growing threat of terrorism. In April 1973 the Fuerzas Armadas de Liberación kidnapped Anthony Da Cruz, a Kodak Argentina manager. He was released five days later for a ransom of $1.5 million. In October, David B. Wilkie, president and general manager of the Amoco Argentine Oil Company was kidnapped. He was freed ten days later for $1 million. There were daily bombings in Buenos Aires and other cities. The Argentines did not request U.S. assistance in fighting what it called "subversion," but Washington continued to provide military assistance that was directed at the growing internal war. Moreover, American officials quickly accepted Argentine government definitions of "subversives" even as Argentine authorities became less interested in human and civil rights guarantees, and less able or willing to distinguish between those responsible for violent acts and a host of other "enemies."[24]

In 1972, the Argentine military government acceded to Argentina's first open presidential election since Perón's ouster in 1955. Peronist candidate Héctor Cámpora won the presidency in March 1973. At first Washington worried about the possibility of a radical shift to the left in economic policy and international diplomacy. Cámpora surrounded himself with economists who favored a severe reduction in the influence of foreign capital. The government-elect announced plans to establish diplomatic relations with the Democratic Republic of Vietnam, North Korea, and Cuba. Cámpora also made clear that he would back Panamanian claims to sovereignty over the Panama Canal at a particularly sensitive period in U.S.-Panamanian negotiations. Despite these and other irritants, American diplomats and policymakers showed none of the alarm that had marked earlier dealings with Perón. Lodge wrote that he had no intention of doing other than watching from the sidelines, and he was particularly concerned that there be no hint of a Spruille Braden–like intervention in Argentine politics.[25]

Soon after coming into office, Cámpora had announced that Perón would return to Buenos Aires from Madrid and that there would be new presidential elections. Perón reached Argentina in June 1973, and again Lodge urged that despite past antagonisms, the U.S. government should give Perón the benefit of the doubt.[26] In October, with Perón now in office as president, Secretary of State Henry Kissinger met with Argentine foreign minister Alberto Vignes in New York. The meeting was friendly. On the question of Argentina's ties with Cuba, Vignes asserted that his government was strongly anti-Communist. Links with Cuba were a matter of commercial importance and nothing more. Americans expressed no doubts in response, impressed by Perón's strong anti-Communism and his determination to stamp out left-wing political violence.[27]

Like most Argentine political and military leaders, Americans remained alarmed at the ongoing increase in terrorist acts in Argentine cities through the mid-1970s. In January 1974, the CIA reported on what it believed were credible plans by the Montoneros or another revolutionary group to assassinate the first secretary of the Chilean Embassy in Buenos Aires and the Argentine head of Lan Chile, the national airline of Chile. A month later, the CIA argued that the Chilean left was being strengthened by the appearance of Argentine subversives at Chilean summer beach resorts and by the return of exiled Chilean activists from Argentina. While these accusations seem preposterous in light of the ferocity of the Augusto Pinochet regime in 1974, that same year the offices of Eli Lilly, Firestone, Goodyear, Xerox, and Pepsi-Cola in Buenos Aires were all bombed. In addition, Argentine police were providing the U.S. Embassy with twenty-four-hour-a-day protection from potential leftist attacks.[28]

In the aftermath of Juan Perón's death, the political situation became increasingly unstable. One source of problems was José López Rega.[29] A shadowy figure with strong ties to extreme right-wing groups in Italy and other countries, López Rega had been Perón's chief adviser. In the government of Isabel Perón that followed, he assumed still greater powers as "Isabelita" lost control of the military, the police, and other important government bureaucracies. At the end of November 1974, a U.S. State Department mission told Argentine counterparts that they believed that the USSR was no longer aggressively interested in promoting revolutionary conflict in the Americas and that Soviet ideology was not a "danger for the American continent." But in light of what became the open competition between the Argentine military and López Rega to run the country through the entirely ineffectual president, Americans believed that the Argentine polity was spiraling out of control. Political violence escalated. In April 1974, leftist terrorists tried to kill Alfred Laun, a United States Information Service operative in the city of Córdoba. U.S. Embassy officials were worried. U.S. Counselor William Sowash informed the Argentine Foreign Relations Ministry that the Americans had information on the existence of a "massive action plan to eliminate all American functionaries" in Argentina. On 16 April, Sowash sent the Foreign Relations Ministry's Department of North American Affairs a photocopy of two threatening cards from the revolutionary Ejército Revolucionario del Pueblo addressed to General John G. Wagener, chief of the U.S. military mission in Argentina. By September 1975, according to Robert A. Fearey, chairman of the Working Group/Cabinet Committee to Combat Terrorism, "the most virulent terrorism in Latin America is in Argentina."[30]

The Coup

American officials were more circumspect in the lead-up to and execution of the 1976 overthrow of civilian rule in Argentina than they had been in their overt backing for the Pinochet coup three years earlier. Unlike the Chilean case, there is no evidence of CIA participation in the Argentine coup. But Secretary of State Kissinger and other U.S. officials supported the military takeover. At least as early as June 1976, the CIA tracked the formation and functioning of Operación Condor, a secret assassination and intelligence squad managed jointly by military officers in Chile, Argentina, Bolivia, Peru, and Paraguay.[31] American officials not only knew the coup was coming long before March 1976, but they also had extensive and accurate information on the machinations of the generals through the latter half of 1975 as the military plotted. At the same time, it is not clear they knew more than dozens of politicians, reporters, and others in Argentina, including the editor of *Opinión*, Jacobo Timerman, from whom the Americans gleaned a good deal of information.[32]

The State Department sympathized with the military's objective of restoring order to the Argentine polity; but so did many middle-class Argentines worn down by years of political chaos and violence. Ambassador Robert Hill maintained frequent contact with General Jorge Rafael Videla, head of the Argentine Armed Forces, throughout the six months leading up to the coup, as he did with General Roberto Viola, the key political strategist for the *golpista* faction within the Armed Forces. Both Videla and Viola, future de facto presidents during the military period of government, had received extensive National Security Doctrine training in the United States. Videla had made the first of several professional visits to the United States in 1957 when he served at the Inter-American Defense Board. Viola had trained in counterinsurgency tactics at Fort Gulick in the Panama Canal Zone.[33]

Ambassador Hill wrongly assessed the March 1976 coup d'état as representing a victory of moderates within the military over what he termed "hawks." He underlined the common interests of the U.S. government and the new Argentine regime. Hill also pointed out that Videla had immediately promised the U.S. Embassy that he would quickly create a climate for investment more favorable to U.S. interests. This was true, but that policy shift came with an enormous cost to Argentines brutalized by the dictatorship. Through the period of dictatorship many American policymakers continued to rely on the dictatorship for an accurate estimate of the leftist security risk to Argentina and to its neighbors. In August 1976, for example, the State Department was circumspect in responding to intelligence information that Operación Condor was responsible for the assassinations of political opponents in

South America. If "rumor" were true, "this would create a serious moral and political problem." Though the State Department did not wish for any U.S. government agency to be responsible for "finger[ing] individuals who might be candidates for assassination attempts," it did advocate intelligence exchanges with Condor operatives. A month later, the U.S. Department of Defense credited "streamlined intelligence organization" in the Southern Cone for "much of the success enjoyed recently in the battle against subversion." In October, the CIA reported on the "rumor" in no uncertain terms. "Special teams" from various countries had been deployed to assassinate opponents. These teams were "structured like a U.S. Special Forces Team."[34]

In an October 1976 meeting between the U.S. secretary of state and the Argentine foreign minister, César Augusto Guzzetti, Kissinger gave his unequivocal support for both the goals and methods of the Argentine military's Dirty War. He urged a quick finish to the military's internal war, largely because of growing popular sentiment in the United States against the dictatorship. On the same visit U.S. president Gerald Ford met with Guzzetti. There was no American criticism of government killings and torture. On the contrary, the White House staff briefed Ford on Argentina being the "most violent state" in Latin America but blamed leftist terrorism for the violence and having "already claimed 1,000 lives this year"—an absurd overestimate. Ford's briefing paper blamed "right-wing vigilante organizations," not the military government, for the killings of hundreds (a dramatic underestimate) of leftists and others. The closest the White House came to addressing the military's rampant human rights abuses was an oblique reference to "a number of unexplained disappearances and murders, with apparent knowledge or complicity of some government officials."[35]

Ford's talking points made no reference to state-sponsored violence but did praise the work of Economy Minister José Martínez de Hoz, who had undertaken a dramatic restructuring of Argentine economic and monetary policies. The changes included a free exchange rate, an end to price controls, a new investment code that favored foreign capital, and a refinancing of the Argentine debt with $500 million from U.S. banks. Over the next two years, with the ending of protections on domestic production, Argentina experienced its most rapid and pronounced deindustrialization of the twentieth century, as the country's foreign debt soared. At the same time, bilateral trade soared. In 1977, Argentina exported $382.6 million worth of goods to the United States. In 1978 that figure reached $536.6 million, and in 1980, $696 million. Imports from the United States also rose sharply from $771.7 million in 1977 to $1.89 billion two years later. Primed by the demand for industrial goods, imports surged to reach $2.37 billion in 1980.[36]

Carter, Human Rights, and Cold War Politics

Beginning in 1977, U.S. policy toward Argentina changed to reflect the emphasis of the incoming Jimmy Carter administration on human rights and a transformation in many Americans' perception of such rights.[37] Along with Chile, Nicaragua, and Uruguay, Argentina emerged as a central diplomatic target for the United States on human rights. Aid and military programs were delayed and cut back because of human rights violations. At the same time, Assistant Secretary of State for Human Rights and Humanitarian Affairs Patricia Derian was among several administration officials who made a point of repeatedly and specifically attacking the Argentine junta. Carter's policy had an impact. After Export-Import Bank credits to Argentina had been eliminated in 1978, a promise from de facto Argentine president Jorge Rafael Videla to allow a visit of the Inter-American Commission on Human Rights to Argentina restored the funding. But at the end of the 1978 fiscal year, the Pentagon informed Argentine officials that they had been denied nearly $100 million worth of U.S. equipment because of human rights abuses.

Argentines responded with alarm to American pressures. Moreover, Argentina suffered economically and militarily from the U.S. stand, and there may well have been specific cases of prisoners freed or moved from illicit detention to the formal penal system as a result of the Carter-era human rights shift. But the thrust of the Argentine response was to deny, to obfuscate, and to claim a high ground on human rights. This

Argentine campaign in defense of its human rights record failed. But so too did American pressures to end human rights abuses in Argentina. Richard Holbrooke, Zbigniew Brzezinski, and others both inside and outside the Carter administration had questioned the efficacy of the U.S. policy on human rights at the time. In the case of Argentina, their suspicions of inefficacy were justified—though in the end, Carter administration hawks contributed to that ineffectiveness. But in addition, it is hard to say whether U.S. pressures substantially reduced human rights violations after 1976. Such violations declined, to be sure. But there is no clear way of establishing how American pressures measured up to other factors in the minds of the Argentine military, including the pressures of other governments and international human rights agencies as well as a range of domestic factors.[38]

Through late 1976, the U.S. government registered dozens of protests over human rights abuses in Argentina.[39] But in the months after Carter's election, American policymakers and politicians pressed the Argentine military still harder on torture, disappearances, and the breakdown of judicial fairness. Conditioned by long-standing military ties with the Pentagon, U.S. support for the Pinochet coup in Chile, and American cold war anti-Communism, the generals believed that Carter marked a temporary aberration in U.S. policymaking. They anticipated correctly that if they could handle Carter for the short term, human rights would return to a much less significant place in American foreign policy. In response to Carter, and to even stronger and earlier pressures from European governments, the junta moved to fabricate an international image of Argentina as a defender of human rights. As in the case of Pinochet's Chile, part of this strategy involved thinking through human rights problems in a context of pre-1973 UN politics, and in a manner that ignored current accusations.[40]

Even though human rights represented the most public area of contention between the United States and Argentina, there were other emerging bilateral problems. After the coup d'état in 1973, Chile had remained a member of the nonaligned movement in name only; its delegates simply stopped attending meetings. By contrast, and to the surprise of many, a faction within the Argentine military government that included Foreign Minister Nicanor Costa Méndez prevailed in keeping Argentina inside the movement. Although Argentina stayed a strong supporter of Carter administration policy toward the Soviet Union on disarmament and on other important U.S. cold war policies, the Americans were puzzled by the extent of Argentina's contacts with Cuba, Yugoslavia, and other nonaligned states. In 1978, for reasons that had little to do with human rights, and in the wake of Argentina's long-standing refusal to sign the Nuclear Non-proliferation Treaty, the United States aggravated bilateral relations by restricting nuclear ties with Argentina. And despite heavy diplomatic pressure on Argentina to join an embargo on the Soviet Union in the wake of the Afghanistan invasion, the Argentines refused to curtail their trade ties—particularly in grain— with the Russians. None of these sore points in bilateral relations indicated the sort of conflict that had marked the strongest bilateral antagonisms of the Perón period.[41]

Ironically, in light of U.S. cold war politics and Argentine fears that the Soviets and their allies were behind the Argentine revolutionary left, the junta felt almost no pressure on human rights from Communist states. Shortly after the coup, the Cuban government assured the Argentine military that although Cuba had intervened in the domestic politics of some countries in the Americas, Argentine military intelligence would find no links between Argentine insurgents and Cuba. Cuba insisted privately to the generals that it had had and would have nothing to do with the Argentine revolutionary left. Cuba understood that such links would jeopardize valued, friendly Argentine-Cuban relations. Remarkably, the Cuban government conceded secretly to the Argentines that although it opposed coups d'état, it considered the Argentine coup a "necessary change" in that some "bandits" (meaning the previous government of Isabel Perón) had taken over beforehand and had eliminated security for the general public. The Cuban acceptance of the supposed need for military intervention in Argentina was the same as the American stand in March 1976.[42]

U.S. pressure on Argentina over human rights abuses mounted through 1978, but at the same time, U.S. diplomats in Argentina continued to advise the State Department that the Argentine dictatorship was "moderate" and that military cooperation between the two countries should continue.[43] Argentine military leaders and diplomats tried to exploit what they believed were divisions and uncertainties in the Carter administration. In early 1978, for example, the Argentine ambassador in Washington, Jorge Aja Espil became particularly worried about Deputy Assistant Secretary of State for Human Rights and Humanitarian Affairs Mark Schneider. Schneider was among those in the administration most favorable to human rights as a core foreign policy guideline; those less interested in human rights viewed him as blocking the emergence of a supposed democratic opening of the Argentine political system. Schneider was right. There was no opening in 1978, simply a modest relaxation in repression. But based on their contacts with more conservative policymakers in the Carter administration, the Argentines hoped to dupe Washington into believing democracy was coming.

The Argentines misunderstood how the Carter administration formulated human rights policy, ascribing too much to factors that likely had little impact on thinking in Washington. In 1978, for example, Argentine military leaders distinguished themselves from their Chilean counterparts in several spheres as far as Washington was concerned. In part because Pinochet had been a prototype in the popular imagination of many peoples for brutality in South American dictatorship, the Argentines believed wrongly that human rights problems counted less for Argentina than for Chile in the minds of U.S. policymakers. They also attributed the difference to Videla having been in Washington during the signing of the new Panama Canal Treaties, to what they believed was a more measured and dignified international Argentine diplomatic conduct, and to there having been no Argentine equivalent to the assassination of Chilean Orlando Letelier.[44]

U.S.-Argentine tensions over human rights came to a head over the 1979 visit of the Inter-American Commission on Human Rights (CIDH) to Argentina. The visit came as a direct consequence of Carter administration arm-twisting of Videla on human rights—representing an important, if limited, policy success of such U.S. pressures. Although the Argentine military approved the mission, it immediately set about creating a false image of human rights in Argentina and cracking down on groups that might leak the truth to commission members. The Argentines worried about the specifics of the CIDH itinerary requests—including meetings with high-profile prisoners such as the journalist Jacobo Timerman and ex-president Isabel Perón—as well as the potential ambiguities and surprises that the visit might hold. Argentine officers gathered information from their contacts elsewhere in Latin America in anticipation of the kinds of problems they might face. Argentine Naval Intelligence reported in September 1979, for example, that the executive secretary of the commission, Edmundo Vargas Carreño, had visited ex-president Eduardo Frei in Chile at which time the two men had discussed human rights in a manner critical of the Argentine regime.[45]

Argentina had received a generally positive assessment in 1976 from the CIDH, whose annual report had cited Argentine responses to a commission questionnaire as evidence of the country's support of the American Human Rights Declaration.[46] But as criticism mounted in the United States and other countries, Argentine authorities refused to participate in the next annual CIDH survey. The country's relations with the OAS regarding human rights deteriorated as they did with the United States. Argentine officials linked Carter to the CIDH, particularly through the commission's strongest and most prominent defender of human rights, the American jurist Tom Farer. Various steps were taken to ensure that the CIDH would see only what the government wished them to see. In loco visits would proceed only with commission members respecting Argentine sovereignty—meaning that they would not be permitted to question what Argentine authorities offered as evidence of the state of human rights. The visitors would be permitted to interview whomever they wished in federal or provincial police custody.[47]

The CIDH visit, which came in part as a consequence of U.S. government pressures on Argentina, reflects both the limited successes and more dramatic failures of Carter administration human rights policies in Argentina. The CIDH met with a broad range of human rights activists in Argentine cities, and although members were carefully kept from the worst Argentine atrocities, the commission issued a scathing condemnation of the regime in early 1980.[48] The Argentine government reacted as it had in the lead-up to the visit. Officials from a number of ministries denied what they could. The Foreign Relations Ministry claimed the CIDH conclusions were wrong, that they reflected a dangerous foreign interference in Argentine domestic affairs, and that they jeopardized the effective functioning of the OAS and its associated agencies. Military officials organized a campaign to discredit the CIDH visit that included winning (or giving the appearance of having won) the public backing of Argentine professional associations, unions, the families of victims of so-called subversion, and immigrant groups. As evidence of supposed Argentine sympathies for human rights, for example, the Immigration Department was charged with featuring in the media the hundreds of Vietnamese "boat people" that Argentina had accepted as residents.[49]

The mounting importance of human rights to U.S.-Argentine relations during the late 1970s and early 1980s came with two accompanying developments in the United States. First, because of the Carter administration policies, the extent of human rights abuses in Argentina, and the widespread reporting of those abuses in newspapers and other media across the United States, thousands of Americans had a better (if still limited) understanding of Argentina than at any time before or since. From Iowa to Texas, from California to New York, in their churches, in their schools, and in a host of other venues, Americans who had never thought much or at all about Chile or Argentina took an interest in how to stop the killings and tortures in those countries. Second, how Americans understood the violence in Argentina became increasingly associated with the persecution of Jews. Morton Rosenthal became the harshest and perhaps most effective critic of the junta outside Argentina. His characterizations of the Argentine generals as "Nazis" were repeated frequently in the U.S. Congress and in the media. Rosenthal understood that in the context of American concerns at the time for the mistreatment of Soviet Jews, and the cultural impact in the United States of the Holocaust (and the American role in the defeat of Nazism), the Argentine dictatorship was most vulnerable on accusations of Nazism. In those accusations, Rosenthal became unrelenting.[50]

A sentiment among American leaders that the Argentine government was run by Nazi thugs was reinforced in April 1977 when the prominent

Argentine Jewish journalist Jacobo Timerman was arrested and detained. It was a public relations nightmare for the Argentine government. Protests from the United States played a major role in Timerman's release from prison, the military's denial of his citizenship, and his expulsion from the country the following year. Once liberated, he became the first Argentine to appear on the cover of the *New York Times* Sunday Magazine. His book *Prisoner without a Name, Cell without a Number* appeared in 1980. Its descriptions of the anti-Semitic vitriol Timerman faced while in captivity energized opponents of the Argentine regime in the United States.[51]

Ironically, while Timerman accused Argentine Jewish community leaders of complacency in the face of dictatorship anti-Semitism, an American rabbi became the strongest voice of Jewish protest in Argentina. The American conservative rabbi Marshall Meyer had reached Argentina in 1959 and remained until 1985. Loud and uncompromising, Meyer made many in the Argentine Jewish establishment nervous. His sermons at Bet El Synagogue in Buenos Aires featured regular attacks on military violence and drew Jews and non-Jews. In the United States a number of prominent American Jews pursued accusations of anti-Semitism against Argentine authorities primed by the ADL. In September 1976, Burton Levinson, president of the Latin American Affairs Department of the ADL came before a special session of Congress to report that anti-Semitism represented an important factor in illicit detentions. The ADL excelled not only at exposing how the dictatorship targeted Jews, but also in associating the dictatorship with human rights violations in the minds of Americans and defining those violations first and foremost in the context of anti-Semitism.[52]

Argentine government efforts to counter the American charges of anti-Semitism were ineffectual. This contributed to Argentine government paranoia that Jews were controlling policy in the Carter presidency. In 1977, as a result of human rights abuses in Argentina, section 620B of the America Foreign Assistance Act (Humphrey-Kennedy Amendment) ended U.S. military training programs in Argentina and the sale of some military equipment. The Argentine government linked

Jewish organizations to the Carter administration and even blamed them for Carter's pro–human rights stand in Argentina.

In response to a stated objective of the visit—to learn more about the state of the Argentine Jewish community—Argentine officials believed that it would be impossible for the delegation to "learn" anything. ADL held a firm position and was unlikely, according to Argentine officials, to change its accusatory tone. Moreover, the government worried that the proposed visit would likely generate conflicts within the Argentine Jewish community because, following Jacobo Timerman's lead, ADL had repeatedly criticized Argentine Jewish leaders for downplaying anti-Semitism and had accused the Argentine Jewish community of collaborating with the dictatorship. The Interior Ministry reasoned that although the visit might be approved, the Argentine government should establish contact in advance with both the local Jewish community and the Israeli Embassy to avoid a new round of negative publicity on anti-Semitism. As late as May 1981, Foreign Minister Oscar Camilión wrote to Interior Minister General Horacio Tomás Liendo that the power of Jewish influence in the U.S. Congress was such that the Argentine government should release Jewish prisoners from detention, including Deborah Benshoam and Natalio Mehlul.[53]

In January 1979, the head of the state security and internal intelligence agency Secretaría de Inteligencia del Estado (Secretary of State for Intelligence, SIDE) determined that the Timerman case was the most pressing issue in U.S.-Argentine relations in the area of human rights. Although SIDE blamed the "Jewish community around the world" for the campaign to free Timerman, it found that international pressure went far beyond the Jewish community, organized simultaneously in the United States and Western Europe. As in other human rights episodes involving Jews and non-Jews, Argentines saw a conspiracy against their country. They also worried about international perceptions of Argentina—as though, somehow, without these annoying episodes of human rights critiques, Americans would view the generals in a positive light. In the Timerman case, SIDE singled out the work of *New York Times* writer Juan de Onís as particularly damaging, noting that he had abandoned his journalistic objectivity toward Argentina in his reporting of the Timerman case.[54]

After Timerman's release, the Argentine government tracked his activities and assessed his effectiveness through his contacts with Jewish organizations. Argentine intelligence observed in 1981 that the volume of pro-Timerman material in the international press was declining. In mid-1982, SIDE charted Timerman's waning influence and effectiveness. It pointed out as well that in Israel, he was being attacked for his connections to the "Graiver terrorist group" and for his "false pro-Zionism." "Timerman," SIDE reasoned, "has the support of only one Jewish group in the United States, that uses him to attack the Reagan government from the perspective of his old terrorist ties." It noted also that while working to promote his book *Prisoner without a Name, Cell without a Number,* he regularly tried to show that Jews were being persecuted in Argentina. "In this latter area," SIDE observed, "he has not achieved the desired result. In general each of the Jewish organizations in the countries that he has visited have rejected his accusations. Because of this, Timerman and his campaign will continue to wane quickly."[55]

The Argentine military watched for signs that its international propaganda suggesting a pro–human rights regime in Argentina was having a positive impact abroad, particularly in the United States. SIDE reported enthusiastically, for example, on a breakfast meeting of the National Committee of American Foreign Policy on 3 November 1981 at which Rabbi Robert Scheiner spoke on the topic "Argentina 81." Scheiner had interviewed de facto president Roberto Viola and reported at the meeting that within twenty-four hours of his interview with Viola, the Argentine government had released a satisfactory declaration condemning all forms of religious intolerance. SIDE also reported that Scheiner had praised the freedom with which the Argentine media published the statements of the Mothers of the Plaza de Mayo and had pointed out that priests, pastors, and rabbis were regularly able to visit political prisoners in Argentina. Scheiner discredited Timerman, pointing out that there was no connection whatsoever between Argentina and Nazi Germany.

While Argentine leaders struggled to counter anti-Semitism charges, they also pressured the Carter administration in other areas. Despite ongoing provisions of the Humphrey-Kennedy Amendment, Argentine leaders believed that by standing up to the Carter administration call for an embargo on grain sales to the Soviet Union in 1979, Argentines had contributed to a thaw in bilateral relations at the end of the Carter presidency. That year, Argentine foreign minister Carlos W. Pastor had a series of long conversations with Secretary of State Cyrus Vance. According to Pastor, these changed Vance's thinking on Argentina, led to the visit of General Andrew Jackson Goodpaster to Buenos Aires as a special presidential representative, and revived cooperation between the Argentine military's Escuela Superior de Guerra and Escuela Superior Técnica with the U.S. armed forces. At a 1980 meeting, Pastor convinced Secretary of State Edmund S. Muskie that the Argentine intervention in the 1980 coup d'état in Bolivia had been necessary to maintain order.[56]

Transition to Reagan and Argentina's Central American Intervention

Argentine authorities approved of what they saw as the links between American Jews, the Reagan administration, and a thaw in U.S.-Argentine relations at the end of the Carter administration. Before Jeanne Kirkpatrick was named U.S. ambassador to the United Nations, for example, Argentine leaders expressed hope privately that, as a key foreign policy adviser to Ronald Reagan, Kirkpatrick would work to end human rights pressures from Washington. The Argentines were familiar both with Kirkpatrick's positions on dictatorships and her interest in Argentina.[57] Relations did improve quickly. The Reagan administration pressed for and won the repeal of Kennedy-Humphrey in December 1981.[58] It based a decision to improve ties with Argentina on the CIDH, having found no official policy of anti-Semitism in Argentina. Though the administration conceded that a disproportionately high number of Jews had disappeared during the dictatorship, according to the Reagan White House, this was due to what Robert Hill had signaled before the dictatorship—their high representation in terrorist groups.

Moreover, in 1981 Reagan took Viola's comments at face value when, before the Senate and House Foreign Relations Committees, Viola stated that he was aware of anti-Semitism in Argentina and was taking action against it. In reference to a major human rights prize Timerman received from Columbia University, SIDE established that the U.S. ambassador to Argentina, Harry W. Shlaudeman, had specifically announced that this private initiative would have no impact on U.S.-Argentine ties, which were "excellent in all regards."[59]

Between the inauguration of Ronald Reagan in early 1981 and the collapse of the Argentine military regime two years later, there were two key developments in bilateral relations. When the Argentine military invaded the Falkland/Malvinas Islands in April 1982, they fully expected U.S. support in their war with Great Britain. Not only did Washington's support for the British expose a critical strategic miscalculation by Foreign Minister Nicanor Costa Méndez, a key Argentine advocate for the war, but the dramatic British military victory over the Argentines helped speed the military's exit from government the following year. Through the end of the dictatorship and the early period of democratic rule that followed, the war served as the basis for Argentina's main Pan-American goals. Argentine diplomats made a priority of convincing OAS delegates to build on a resolution passed at the Twentieth Consultative Meeting of Foreign Ministers on 29 May 1982. That resolution had condemned as "unjustified" the armed attack of Great Britain on the islands once the Argentines had occupied them. The resolution had also characterized as "coercive" measures adopted by the United States and members of the European Economic Community to try to force Argentina off the islands.

According to the Argentine government, the resolution had "reinforced Latin American solidarity with regard to Argentina." That solidarity represented a diplomatic wedge. It created conditions that Argentine leaders believed would allow Argentina to "exercise a growing continental pressure in favor of a fast and just definitive solution to this sovereignty dispute."[60] In late 1983, the Foreign Relations Ministry's main Pan-American objective was to increase pressure over the next year on other OAS member states toward obtaining "an even more categorical OAS pronouncement [on Falklands/Malvinas] with greater political content." One reason the Argentine military moderated its support for the United States in Central America in 1982 was the perception that U.S. intervention in the region could be tied to the British "invasion" of the Falklands/Malvinas with regard to Pan-American principals of nonintervention. After the Falklands/Malvinas War, Argentina joined Guatemala and Venezuela in reasserting its opposition to admitting new members to the OAS with ongoing Commonwealth ties to Great Britain. The basis for the position centered on nonintervention. No country with formal links to Britain should be allowed to join the OAS because that would give the British a voice in Pan-American affairs.

The war remained a lingering trauma for many Argentines after 1983, though memories of U.S. support for the British faded quickly with the return of democracy. At the same time, because of the U.S. stand, the war helped bring to an end four years of U.S.-Argentine cooperation in counterinsurgency warfare in Central America. In early 1982, there were twenty-five hundred Nicaraguan Contras under the command of Argentine military officers. After June, Argentina reduced its Central America activities.[61]

Before the Falklands/Malvinas War, the Argentine military had become active in Central America as an extension of its internal war on so-called Marxist subversion and, after November 1980, as an expression of support for Ronald Reagan's rightward foreign policy shift in the Americas. The political scientist Ariel C. Armony has argued that Argentina's involvement in Central America focused initially on "targets perceived as sources of anti-Argentine propaganda." He also points out that in the minds of Argentine military leaders, the Central American initiative was tied to a fierce anti-Marxist conviction that the regime was fighting the first battles of a third World War against international Communism. This was inspired in part by National Security Doctrine connections to American cold war–era anti-Communism. But the link between the action in Central America and anti-Communist ideologies also derived from growing ties between General Carlos G. Suárez Mason, General Luciano Benjamin Menéndez, and other regime hard-liners and Stéfano Delle Chiaie, Pierluigi Pagliai, and a host of violent neofascists from Italy and elsewhere. After the 1976 coup, Delle Chiaie visited Buenos Aires and Santiago several times to help coordinate the work of Italian neofascists with that of the regimes in Chile and Argentina. All shared a sense of immediacy around combating international Communism.[62]

A 1981 Argentine intelligence report characterized the Reagan administration's struggle in Central America as a national security priority for Argentina. For the Argentine military, the key distinction between Carter and Reagan was that the latter had redefined U.S. foreign policy in a manner that had ceased to "contemplate the advances of subversives with disinterest and had begun, with no uncertain measure, to support friendly governments threatened . . . by Nicaragua." This Argentine approval of the U.S. escalation of military aid to El Salvador, Guatemala, and Honduras was less telling than what the Argentine military now believed was a set of global connections to Central America that Washington both faced and, according to Argentine intelligence, understood. U.S. support for right-wing repression in Central America was directly tied to Cuban and Soviet expansionism. Related issues included the kidnapping of U.S. general James Dozier by Red Brigades operatives in Verona, the threat to NATO from the Warsaw Pact countries, the possible revival of the Weather Underground in the United States, and a variety of other international leftist threats, mostly imagined. These were precisely the kinds of chilling and far-fetched connections that had shaped Argentina's internal war since 1976, and that the Argentines now believed Ronald Reagan, a kindred spirit, was making.[63]

According to the Argentine intelligence officer and repressor Leandro Sánchez Riesse, with the help of the CIA, the Argentine government set up a business front in South Florida to move money and arms to Central America between 1978 and 1981. Beginning in 1977, the Argentine government tried to prop up the ailing Anastasio Somoza dictatorship in Nicaragua with arms shipments and military advising, this in the face of Montonero financial backing for the Sandinista rebels.[64] In 1978, the Argentine military sent a team to Nicaragua to hunt down

Argentines working with the Sandinistas, three of whom were apprehended by the rebels when they captured Managua in July 1979. Beginning in 1979, in cooperation with American operatives and military officers in El Salvador and Guatemala (and in seeming contradiction with the Carter administration human rights policies), Argentines participated in the fight against leftist insurgents in those nations. In August of that year the Argentine Foreign Relations Ministry sent instructions to its Central American embassies to provide intelligence on "the participation of the Montoneros in the recent Nicaraguan revolutionary process."[65]

In December 1980, Argentine-trained exiled Nicaraguan guardsmen attacked a short wave radio station in San José, Costa Rica. Ostensibly, the station was run by Montoneros, who were denouncing human rights violations in Argentina. According to a former Argentine intelligence officer, "the CIA provided the Argentines with intelligence and logistical assistance for the attack on the radio."[66] This attack coincided with the start of Argentine military training of former Nicaraguan guardsmen in Guatemala and Buenos Aires. Contra chief Enrique Bermudez recognized in 1988 that the Argentines had offered crucial assistance to their anti-Sandinista crusade at its earliest stages. In August 1981, Honduran military officers met with Argentine intelligence officials and CIA representatives to hammer out a covert accord in support of the Contras. By the terms of this agreement, the Argentines would provide "organization, administration, and military training."[67]

The Central American incursions mark the last important anti-Communist offensive by an Argentine military regime already faltering under growing international pressure to step aside. There is little evidence, though, that Argentina's role in Central America had a decisive impact on developments on the isthmus. Moreover, Argentine authorities were both intent on and seemingly successful at maintaining the secrecy of their operations. In 1979, on the eve of the Sandinista victory, Panamanian president General Omar Torrijos complained to both the Brazilian and Argentine ambassadors in Panama: South American militaries were letting Nicaragua fall into the Communist orbit by not helping Somoza. The head of the Panamanian National Guard, Colonel

Florencio Flores, invited the Argentine military attaché in Panama to join him in visiting Nicaragua immediately to see "the real situation that [Nicaragua] is living."[68]

Though Torrijos regarded himself as a staunch anti-Communist, his relations with the regimes in Chile, Argentina, Brazil, and Paraguay were tentative in light of these latter regimes tending to have supported the U.S. positions on the Panama Canal. At the same time, it bears noting that he seemed to have no idea that Argentina was involved militarily in propping up Somoza. Secret correspondence between Argentina's diplomats and the Argentine Foreign Relations Ministry between 1978 and 1983 gives no indication that they were aware of the extent of the Argentine military roles in Central America. In July 1979, Horacio S. Ballestrin, the Argentine ambassador to Panama, wrote an incensed letter to the newspaper *Crítica* in response to an article accusing the Argentine Air Force operatives of actively supporting the Somoza dictatorship in its last desperate struggle against the Sandinistas. The Hercules c-130 aircraft referred to in the article, according to Ballestrin, was sent laden with food and medicine as a humanitarian gesture toward the Nicaraguan people.[69] Stranger still, in December 1980, the U.S. ambassador in El Salvador, Robert E. White, told his Argentine equivalent that he had information that Argentine military officers were in El Salvador participating in the anti-Communist struggle. Victor Bianculli, the Argentine ambassador to El Salvador, responded that he had no information on any of this. "I have to add," he told the Argentine Foreign Relations Ministry in a secret telegram, "that this is the second time White has brought to my attention the question of Argentine military advisors."[70]

While the Central America initiative was significant for several reasons, it clearly ran counter to other important elements of Argentine foreign policy. Despite Argentine military cooperation with repressive Honduran officers, in December 1982 the Argentine Foreign Relations Ministry advocated that Argentina take a neutral stance in the event of a military conflict between Nicaragua and Honduras.[71] In November 1982 the Foreign Relations Ministry's director of the Central America and Caribbean Department visited Managua as a "starting point toward maintaining an open door to dialogue with the Sandinista authorities, and anticipating a high level rapprochement between the two governments." In addition, as early as February 1983, the Argentine Foreign Relations Ministry anticipated the policies of the Radical Party government that followed the military into office at the end of the year. Within the Argentine government, it promoted the Contadora regional peace plan for Central America. The Central America and Caribbean Department of the Argentine Foreign Relations Ministry supported an international diplomatic effort that would "go beyond the animosities between the ideologies of leftist guerrillas and rightist terrorism, and . . . avoid . . . the probable military intervention of the United States."[72] That Yugoslavia and Cuba were among the first nations to come out in favor of Argentina during the Malvinas/Falklands War reflected Argentina's growing economic cooperation with "Communist" nations within the nonaligned movement. The U.S. embargo on the Soviet Union in the aftermath of the Afghanistan invasion led directly to a rapid increase in Argentine grain sales to the Soviets.[73]

With the fall of military rule in 1983, the elected government of President Raúl Alfonsín set about reversing Argentina's sinister reputation on human rights. But both Alfonsín's administration and that of his successor, Carlos Menem, had problems closing the book on the country's authoritarian past. Alfonsín presided over both the prosecution and imprisonment of top dictatorship generals but also agreed to the controversial Final Point and Due Obedience laws that allowed many more military repressors to walk free.[74] In international forums, Argentine diplomats followed a cautious line that stressed a strong public opposition to racial or ethnic discrimination of any kind but that reflected a pragmatic tendency to avoid any confrontation with the United States. Menem's inability or unwillingness to solve the mystery of the Asociación Mutua Israelita Argentina (Israeli Argentine Mutual Association, or AMIA) bombing of 1994 reminded many of Proceso-era anti-Semitism. In one particularly poignant political inheritance from the last dictatorship, the Argentine government quietly fought a Jewish family in the 1990s over a violent episode from the dictatorship period. Under military rule, the Tucumán businessman José Siderman had lost his property to the military government under a brutal and unlawful seizure. More than ten years later, the Siderman family filed a civil suit in the U.S. District Court for the Central District of California against the Argentine government for damages. The Argentine government quietly settled for six million dollars in 1996, but not before fighting the Sidermans and trying to discredit their claim. In one particularly unsavory strategy, the Menem administration tried to show that Siderman had, in fact, sold his Gran Hotel Corona to someone else before the military seized it. The Siderman family victory in a California court came in spite of the efforts of Argentina's elected government, not because of those efforts.[75]

7 The Forging of a New Relationship, 1984–1999

At 1:30 p.m. on 15 October 1988, a concert began at the Malvinas Argentinas Stadium in Mendoza, Argentina, that featured Peter Gabriel, Sting, Youssou N'Dour, and the Americans Tracy Chapman and Bruce Springsteen. There were twenty-seven thousand people in the stadium, and that night, at the El Monumental Stadium in Buenos Aires, sixty-two thousand more heard the five rock superstars. It was the end of a thirteen-nation pro–human rights concert tour organized by Amnesty International and underwritten by a $5 million infusion of cash from Reebok. "I consider myself a citizen of the world community," Tracy Chapman told the Argentine press, "and as such I feel I have a responsibility." "Rock makes you feel free," Bruce Springsteen told Argentine journalists, "and that's what Amnesty International does as well. Also, I think music can change the way people think."[1]

Argentine singers joined their foreign counterparts on stage. Springsteen grinned at the Argentine folksinger León Gieco as they played a traditional *cueca* together. In reference to victims of state-sponsored killings during the dictatorship, Tracy Chapman dedicated her performance to "those who aren't here today." The concert was the first occasion on which two American musicians with mass followings, at the height of their popularity, joined Argentine counterparts on stage. It also highlighted the singular importance of the Argentine dictatorship in how people around the world had come to imagine and understand the politics of human rights during the 1980s.

Democracy and the Flood
of American Popular Culture

After 1983, the attraction of American musicians for Argentina was sporadic. But with the end of the dictatorship and Argentina's cultural opening of the 1980s and 1990s, the American cultural impact in Argentina was never greater. The Amnesty International concert in Mendoza and Buenos Aires was the country's largest-drawing musical event in 1988. Also that year, the top-grossing movie in theaters was *Fatal Attraction*, while *Miami Vice* was the second most popular television program.[2] In 1984, the La Urraca publishing house in Buenos Aires launched the magazine *Fierro*. The publication not only featured cutting-edge cartoon art from around the world but also provided a monthly forum for Max Cachimba, Carlos Nine, Kike Sanzol, and other Argentine cartoonists. Cartoons and story lines were deeply influenced by a range of American art forms including Art Spiegelman's *Maus: A Survivor's Tale* (first serialized four years earlier in the American magazine *Raw*) and the science fiction of the film *Blade Runner* (1982).[3]

American television programming influenced the creation of dozens of new programs in Argentina, from the first aerobic exercise program starring María Amuchástegui in 1986 to Jerry Springer–like sexually explicit exposé programs to a series of reality shows produced after 1999 modeled after *Survivor* and other American creations. American television shows were all over the airwaves. They included current productions like the prime-time soap opera *Dallas* and the action drama *The A-Team*, which ranked second among the most watched television programs in Argentina in 1984 and 1985. But also shown were a variety of old reruns such as *El Superagente '86 (Get Smart)*. Although this and other shows were period pieces in the United States—an early 1960s cold war spoof in the case of *Get Smart*—American programming entered Argentina as a wave. Much of it was entirely new to Argentine viewers. The Cable News Network (CNN) began broadcasting in October 1987. With the opening of Argentina to unfettered foreign investment in 1991, U.S. investors took control of major Argentine media corporations. This helped accelerate the increase of American content on

Argentine television. In 1994, Citicorp Equity Investment made its first major play in the Argentine communications sector, spending ninety-six million dollars for a 30 percent share of Multicanal, one of Argentina's largest television networks. That same year the TCI corporation bought 80 percent of Canalvision, Argentina's most important cable television provider.[4]

Raúl Alfonsín, Dante Caputo, and the Sur-Sur Foreign Policy

In the two decades after the dictatorship, as American cultural influences poured in, Argentine-U.S. relations changed substantially. After 1983, the new Argentine democratic government spoke critically of U.S. policies on nuclear arms production, counterinsurgency warfare in Central America, and the international debt. The Argentine government backed the Contadora Peace Process in Central America, putting it at odds with the Reagan administration. But bilateral relations improved substantially with an end to military-era human rights violations and the end to American perceptions that Argentina was anti-Semitic. On 12 March 1984, little over a year after the government of Raúl Alfonsín had taken office, Foreign Minister Dante Caputo met with the U.S. ambassador to Argentina Frank Ortiz on priorities in Argentine foreign policy. As far as the United States was concerned, the message was mixed. Caputo, a socialist member of Alfonsín's government, seemed critical of Washington at times. This came in a context of Caputo's having been the architect of Argentina's "Sur-Sur" foreign policy, where Argentina sought stronger commercial and strategic relations with the poor nations of the Southern Hemisphere, particularly through the nonaligned movement. But the foreign minister also took pains to point out areas where the two nations' foreign policies intersected. "Argentina should not be a theatre for conflict between the United States and the Soviet Union," he argued in the context of turmoil in Central America. In regard to Argentina's strong support for democratic governments in the Americas, Caputo suggested to Ortiz that "democratic regimes were the only ones in which rational thought prevailed." Democracy was crucial to preventing "the infiltration of the Cuban and Soviet regimes." At the same time, Caputo urged the United States to recognize that in some cases Latin American interests would simply not dovetail with those of Washington. In such instances, Latin American countries would have to be left alone. In his criticism of U.S. involvement in Central America, Caputo suggested that Argentine objectives were not dissimilar to those of the United States. He explained to Ortiz that U.S. aggression in Central America was destabilizing the region, which was benefiting the Soviets. In his meeting with Ortiz, Caputo cast himself as a pro-U.S. cold warrior.[5]

There was an immediate and rapid acceleration of bilateral contacts with the swearing in of the Alfonsín administration. Lines of communication between the two countries became stronger at all levels, and bilateral dialogue did not come to an impasse over areas of conflict, including differences on nuclear policy and repeated U.S. threats to impose commercial sanctions on Argentina for its financial support of agricultural exporters. Despite disagreement over Argentina's immense foreign debt, Argentina never adopted a radical nonpayment policy. And for the most part, the U.S. government helped Argentina win new credits from the IMF and private banks. Argentina and the United States coincided in their stand in favor of democracy and against dictatorship. Early in the new government, Argentine authorities sent a strong message on human rights and relations with the United States by taking a strong stand on anti-Semitism.[6]

In the United States, Alfonsín was celebrated as a human rights hero. On 21 May 1983 the Pan American Development Foundation named the president Man of the Year. On 1 June, he won the Americas Society's Gold Insignia. At a meeting in November 1984, U.S. deputy secretary of state Kenneth Dam reached agreement with Argentine secretary of state Jorge Sábato on a shared policy commitment to democracy in the Americas and jointly fighting the international drug war.[7] Liberals in the U.S. Congress who had forcefully criticized the generals now lined up to make contact with the new Argentine government. In January 1984, for example, Representative Stephen Solarz visited Argentina. Solarz had opposed the junta vociferously over the regime's anti-Semitism, the Falklands/Malvinas War, and human rights abuses. The Argentine Foreign Relations Ministry perceived that Solarz's visit presented an opportunity to establish a common public critique with the Democratic Party of the Reagan administration's Central America policy. Despite Caputo's private assertions on the Soviet threat in Central America, liberal Democrats in the United States and the Argentine government favored the Contadora negotiation process, while the Reagan administration took a harder stand against leftist insurgencies in El Salvador and elsewhere.[8]

Despite opposing the U.S. position on Contadora, in private the Argentines were more supportive of Washington. The Argentine government recognized in 1985 that the presence of "modern weapons or missiles" in Nicaragua constituted a serious security problem for the United States. Although the Argentines were in favor of regional disarmament in Central America and the withdrawal of foreign advisers and soldiers from the region, Argentina refused to criticize the U.S. military presence openly. Argentina supported the Sandinista government as legitimate but viewed democratic elections as necessary. Argentina rejected U.S. support for the Nicaraguan Contras as untenable for Latin America.[9] Bilateral ties were strained by the Argentine government's launching of the Cóndor missile program in January 1984. Cóndor I and Cóndor II missile production was sanctioned in April 1985 by a secret presidential decree, and in August 1987, the government secretly authorized the export of Cóndor missile technology through a new corporation controlled by the Argentine Air Force, Integradora Aeroespacial S.A. (INTESA).[10] Throughout the Alfonsín administration, Washington pressured Argentina to eliminate the program. Argentina refused, but as with economic questions, the Argentine missiles were neither a crisis nor a priority for the United States. Bilateral military ties improved during the 1980s, though it was not until 1988 that the two countries participated in joint naval exercises in the South Atlantic.

Despite the U.S. backing for the Nicaraguan Contras and Argentine ties with the Sandinistas, it mattered little to Washington that Argentina supported the Sandinistas. Shortly after Alfonsín came into office,

Argentina granted a $45 million credit to Nicaragua as well as a $5 million donation of grains. When Alfonsín reviewed the "Kissinger Report" on Nicaragua, he pointed to what he called positive aspects of the document. It recognized the severe economic and social problems that impacted upon Central America, the need to support political democracies in the region, and the urgency of international support for human rights. But the Argentine president also feared that because Kissinger had placed so great an emphasis on military assistance and security, these issues might overwhelm any possible international consideration of social and economic problems in Central America. Alfonsín also worried that the U.S. emphasis on the East-West conflict in understanding unrest in Central America would subsume other key issues, notably the crisis in local democracies and political processes. Because the Kissinger Report did not discard the possibility of U.S. intervention in Central America, Alfonsín believed that it would be "important for the United States to make absolutely clear that a socialist government is not necessarily a security threat."[11] Alfonsín and Caputo announced that they would not join the Contadora group but would support its aims for peace in Central America. The Argentine government also defended the Pan-American principle of nonintervention in the region and expressed the hope that the United States would not try to invade Nicaragua as they had Cuba twenty years before.[12]

Nuclear Ties

The only area of strong contention between the United States and Argentina was in the nuclear sector. Even here, although the United States took exception to Argentina's independent nuclear program, it was scarcely a policy priority for Washington. At the end of 1983, Alfonsín announced that Argentina had developed the technology to enrich natural uranium. There were quick condemnations from the United States. On 22 November 1983, Senator Edward Kennedy sharply criticized the news at a meeting with Argentine ambassadors Esteban Takacs and Lucio Garcia del Solar. In January 1984, both the State Department and

Senator Charles H. Percy wrote to the Argentine government insisting that it adhere to comprehensive international nuclear safeguards and to the Nuclear Non-proliferation Treaty. During a U.S. Senate debate on 28 February, Argentina was one of the countries most cited as a potential nuclear proliferation threat. Former president Jimmy Carter made two visits to Buenos Aires during the 1980s to try to persuade the Argentines to drop their nuclear program. The Reagan administration hoped that Carter, as a naval officer, a nuclear engineer, and an American leader whose pro–human rights stand had made him immensely popular in Argentina, might be able to convince a broad range of Argentine policymakers to dismantle their nuclear program. Like other Americans, Carter was ineffectual. Despite nuclear tensions, on the basis of the return to democracy, President Ronald Reagan certified Argentina as eligible to purchase a broad range of military equipment withheld from the previous government. In early 1984, a new State Department annual report on human rights appeared giving Argentina high marks. Congress shifted from criticizing the violence of the military regime to praising the new government and expressing hope for Argentine growth and development. In part as a result of what he learned on a trip to Buenos Aires, Representative Claude Pepper urged Congress to press the Reagan administration to negotiate more generously on debt reduction for poor nations.[13]

Argentine nuclear policy overlapped with Caputo's Sur-Sur policy. The Americans disapproved of Argentine efforts to improve ties with its nonaligned movement partners. In 1985, Argentine authorities announced plans to build a research reactor in Algeria. The U.S. government expressed its concern through the late 1980s when the reactor was built, even as Algeria descended into civil war.[14] The Algeria case typified new directions in Argentine foreign policy under Alfonsín, what Argentines considered U.S. misunderstandings of Argentine foreign policy goals, and perceptions in Washington that Dante Caputo and other policymakers in Buenos Aires were loose canons in the nonaligned movement. First and foremost, despite U.S.-Argentine differences on Algeria and other poor countries whose governments Washington mistrusted, the U.S.-Argentine difference of opinion was never more than that—a disagreement that did not impact significantly on bilateral ties. For Washington, Argentina was selling nuclear equipment and technology to a nation whose government could not be trusted not to develop a nuclear weapons program or supply other states with nuclear ambitions. For Argentina, Algeria represented a series of opportunities.

In pursuing nuclear ties with Algeria and other states with which the United States, Canada, and France were reluctant to maintain such ties, the Alfonsín administration was carrying through on a policy priority of the previous Argentine government with some of the same objectives. Argentines believed with good reason that their long-standing differences with the United States and other nuclear powers over adherence to international nuclear safeguards agreements such as the Tlatelolco Treaty drew on American mistrust of Argentines. U.S. policymakers did not believe that Argentines were capable of managing their nuclear sector safely and making certain that nuclear secrets did not fall into the "wrong" hands. Argentines resented the slight. But more important, in the context of U.S. policy, they recognized a niche in the international nuclear products market. Just as the Americans and other wealthy nuclear powers were wary of nuclear technology in Argentine hands, they were even more suspicious of Iran, Cuba, Indonesia, and a host of other countries with nuclear aspirations. Beginning in the 1970s, Argentine civil servants and scientists adapted their nuclear program to sell effectively in poor countries where competition with Westinghouse, General Electric, and other nuclear providers would be minimal in light of U.S. government proscriptions on dealings with those nations.[15]

Nuclear ties with Algeria, then, would not only strengthen the Argentine nuclear sector through millions of dollars in revenue but would also help shore up Argentina's international position on nonproliferation and the rights of poor nations to develop their nuclear sectors in the face of U.S. suspicions late in the cold war. In early 1984, Dante Caputo was among several high-ranking Alfonsín administration officials who viewed the Argentine nuclear sector with suspicion. He believed it was a sinister creation of the dictatorship that he suspected had wanted to build nuclear weapons. But only months later, Caputo came around to the military's vision of the nuclear sector as a means of generating millions of dollars in trade and advancing Argentina's strategic position within the nonaligned movement. Beyond these questions, Argentine policymakers viewed nuclear politics as a wedge.[16]

Still more worrisome for Washington was Argentina's improved nuclear cooperation with Cuba. In 1985, Argentine intelligence reported secretly that Cuba planned to build an atomic bomb of the sort dropped on Hiroshima in 1945. Despite this information, Argentina and Cuba signed a nuclear cooperation accord in November 1986 that called on Argentina to assist Cuba in quality assurance, regulatory research, nuclear facility operations, and emergency preparedness. Some Americans viewed Argentina's plans as undermining U.S. efforts to isolate Cuba in the Americas. Others complained that as a major debtor nation, Argentina was not in a position to offer Cuba roughly $600 million in credits for bilateral trade. But on the whole, Argentine-Cuban nuclear ties remained inconsequential to U.S.-Argentine relations.[17]

The Alfonsín administration blamed the military government for a "lack of foresight and reasonable conduct" in policy toward the United States. According to Argentine secretary of state Jorge Sábato, the absence of democracy in Argentina's recent past had led to the explosion of terrorists "with connections to Cuba and the United States." Taking a pro-U.S. cold war line, the new Argentine government pitched democratic rule in Argentina as the only way to avoid the future infiltration of Cuban and Soviet influences. Argentine authorities wanted American policymakers to understand that U.S. and Argentine interests would not always coincide. The Argentines wished for Americans not to read bilateral disagreements as an indication of Argentine antagonism. As Alfonsín took a personal interest in aligning Argentina more closely with India, Yugoslavia, and other leaders in the nonaligned movement, Argentina became a vociferous critic of the U.S.–Soviet nuclear rivalry. But it did so cautiously, never taking any action specifically critical of U.S. strategic or foreign policies. Despite U.S. pressures for Argentina to adhere to U.S. Middle East policies, Argentina refused to take as strong a position in favor of Israel as the United States.[18]

At the same time, in pushing for nuclear disarmament, the Argentine government made no concession to the Soviets that might prejudice relations with the United States. In mid-1984 the Soviets asked Argentina to support an initiative to have neutron and binary weapons condemned by the international community. The Argentines refused to take action against these "American" weapons, arguing to the Soviets that in its fight for international disarmament, Argentina would not single out any particular weapons system. The Argentine Foreign Relations Ministry also rejected the Soviet emphasis on international declarations against a "first strike." Although Argentine policymakers supported that stand, they found it of no particular use in preventing nuclear war.[19]

Economic Relations

Through the 1980s, Argentines were perennially disappointed at what they saw as U.S. disinterest in Argentina's increasing debt crisis, but in keeping with Argentine-U.S. relations over the preceding thirty years, bilateral economic and financial relations remained strong. In 1983, Alfonsín had campaigned for the presidency on a promise to politicize the debt problem. He promised voters that Argentina would only pay capital and interest on what his government determined had been debts legitimately incurred by the outgoing military rulers. Once in office, Alfonsín promised to suspend payments through mid-1984. Relations with Washington and with American banks were tense through the first months of 1984 as the latter waited to see how far the new Argentine government would go in confronting foreign bankers. During the period of the payment freeze the U.S. Treasury Department and private American creditors came up with $100 million to help Argentina cover loan payments that were overdue. At the same time, William Draper, the president of the Export-Import Bank, joined Treasury Secretary Donald Regan in insisting that there should be no new credits for Argentina until an agreement was reached with the IMF.[20]

Immediately, the debt crisis overwhelmed the Alfonsín administration. It became the government's most pressing foreign and domestic policy concern. But Donald Regan's 1984 enjoinder on banks to hold back new credits was the strongest criticism the U.S. government made of Argentine financial policies in the 1980s. In May 1984, Alfonsín expressed outrage over new rises in interest rates that made it impossible for Argentina to do anything other than slip further into debt. Economy Minister Bernardo Grinspun singled out the United States as responsible for helping to push Argentina into severe indebtedness. Moreover, he made clear that Argentina would no longer dip into its reserves to make overdue interest payments.[21] Financial relations between Argentina and the U.S. Treasury Department and American banks remained tense. Citibank advised 320 creditors in the United States that Argentina was unable to pay its financial obligations. On 18 June, private American creditors erased any doubts in the minds of many Argentines that the IMF, American banks, and the U.S. Treasury Department marched in lockstep by choosing to delay any decision on desperately needed new loans to Argentina until Argentina and the IMF had resolved differences on a medium-term plan for debt repayment.[22]

At the same time, the Argentine government told the Americans that the magnitude of the Argentine debt crisis was contributing to the social and political instability of the country. Argentina was a signatory to the Cartagena Consensus, an alliance of Latin American debtor nations that sought a solution to the debt crisis as a regional, multinational, political problem to be resolved at the highest levels of government. The United States rejected Cartagena Consensus premises including Argentina's policies that the foreign debt was due in large measure to extremely high interest rates between 1968 and 1980. But Argentines argued that 7 to 8 percent of their country's gross national product went to debt interest payments, and as long as the debt were treated by the United States as a "technical" rather than a "political" problem, it would remain unresolved. Alfonsín met Ronald Reagan in New York on 23 September 1984. At that meeting Alfonsín pushed Reagan on the problem of debt reduction. But the American president refused to be pinned down. "Only 37% of our production goes to the people," Alfonsín told his American counterpart. "In developed countries that figure is 50%. . . . We can't foster policies that lead to hunger and misery."[23]

A New Pan-Americanism and the Problem of Debt

The debt crisis and the Argentine policy position that the United States held considerable blame for the country's financial problems revived Argentina's interest in a Pan-American policy. The Alfonsín administration transformed Argentina's role within the OAS, rethinking it primarily as a forum for debt reduction advocacy during the 1980s. Under Alfonsín, Argentina continued to work for nonintervention and support for its position on the Falklands/Malvinas. But those goals were placed on the back burner. In preparation for the Sixteenth General Assembly of the OAS, Argentine policymakers identified two related priorities—the foreign debt of Latin American countries and Latin American cooperation toward development. Argentina staked out a harsh Pan-American position toward Washington on the debt. At the General Assembly, Argentine delegates took the position that even though wealthy countries had experienced recent moderate economic growth, they had not withdrawn recent threats to strengthen protectionist policies against imports from poor nations. The Argentine government argued in addition that Pan-American policies should be based on the premise that "the external debt had led to the persistence of a colossal net transfer of resources from Latin America to wealthy nations."[24]

The Argentines reasoned further that a new Pan-American policy should be based on the premise that "in our countries there is a legitimate pressure to recuperate standards of living that were common a decade ago and to expand the goods and services needed to most effectively serve large and growing populations" in Latin America. Argentine officials juxtaposed Latin America and the United States within the OAS. The Argentines wanted the OAS General Assembly to function as a forum in which to explore formulas that the United States might adopt to resolve the debt crisis and associated economic problems. Argentina saw this strategy as a means of avoiding future conflict between Latin America and the United States. The Argentines also advocated the strengthening of the OAS Special Commission for Consultation and Negotiation (CECON). This body's objective was to facilitate and foster trade between the United States and Latin America. But Argentina wanted the organization's mandate skewed toward supporting the interests of Latin American importers and exporters.

Through mid-1984, Reagan was sympathetic but offered nothing more than his vague support. Alfonsín promised Reagan that his government would reduce spending. Reagan asked the Argentine president to make public a statement of support for elections in Nicaragua, but Alfonsín wanted Reagan's backing for significant debt reduction first. Reagan ignored the overture.[25] Yet by and large, the Americans simply ignored what they viewed as Alfonsín's politicization of the debt crisis. The Reagan administration took a position similar to that of the U.S. government during the early 1970s. American policymakers resisted turning Argentine debt policy into a crisis or impasse in bilateral relations. They avoided harsh statements in response to the anti-U.S. rhetoric of Grinspun and other Argentine leaders. U.S. finance policy toward Argentina dovetailed with that of the IMF; as long as Argentina struggled to meet IMF guidelines for domestic economic and finance policies, short-term credits were offered to help get Argentina past the next payments. Beginning in 1984, on his first visit to the United States, Raúl Alfonsín took what the political scientist Roberto Russell called a realist position toward the Americans. He abandoned his election campaign promise to refuse payment on foreign debt amassed irresponsibly by Argentina's military leaders and now offered adherence to IMF guidelines.[26]

The softer line of Alfonsín and his foreign minister, Dante Caputo, bore fruit. With the friendly intervention of the Reagan administration, Argentina won a crucial standby loan from the IMF in December 1984. The new funds had no discernable effect on skyrocketing inflation and rapid economic decline in Argentina. On his second trip to the United States, Alfonsín announced a dramatic shift to the right on economic policy and policy toward the United States. The criticisms of the international banking community were unchanged, but the Argentine president now expressed a willingness to privatize important public sector enterprises as part of IMF-imposed guidelines for economic growth. In Texas he announced the "Houston Plan" as a first step toward major privatizations. Argentina would solicit new private investment in the oil sector.[27] In June 1985, under the stewardship of a new, more moderate

economy minister, Juan Sourrouille, the Argentine government implemented the Plan Austral, an economic austerity plan in keeping with
IMF cost-cutting recommendations. The U.S. government cheered the
new initiative, as did the IMF. Over the next three years, Washington
remained a strong supporter of Argentina in the latter's negotiations
with the IMF. But throughout this period, Argentina's debt increased
steadily, as did the country's economic woes more generally. In 1984,
Argentina's foreign debt stood at forty-three billion dollars. By 1988, it
had reached fifty-five billion dollars.[28]

Through his term as president Alfonsín worried about the destabilizing effect of the foreign debt on the economy. In turn, he feared that instability might lead to a coup d'état.[29] In 1987, renegade officers held the
nation hostage over the Easter weekend in an attempted takeover of the
government. Though the rising failed, Alfonsín was forced to concede
an end to prosecutions of military officers responsible for human rights
abuses during the dictatorship.[30] In light of the ongoing threat of military intervention in Argentina, Alfonsín made it a priority in his relations with the United States to convince the Americans of the importance of bolstering democracy in Argentina. Like Frondizi in his
dealings with Kennedy, Alfonsín tried in vain to have the Reagan administration understand that democracy in Argentina and in other
South American nations, supposedly a priority in U.S. foreign policy,
would not survive without social, economic, and commercial progress
in the region. For Argentina, it was a policy priority to tie democracy to
economic development. Alfonsín and other Argentine officials took that
message to U.S. universities, scientific groups, unions, human rights
organizations, Jewish organizations, and Argentine centers. In 1985,
Alfonsín visited Columbia University, the University of New Mexico,
the American Association for the Advancement of Science, the Jewish
Theological Seminary, and Lane Kirkland, head of the AFL-CIO. For all,
the message was the same. Argentina was now democratic, but that democracy would remain fragile without solutions to crippling debt and
associated social progress. At Columbia, Alfonsín received the university's Presidential Citation. The University of New Mexico awarded
him a doctor honoris causa.[31]

Menem and the Consolidation
of a U.S.-Argentine Alliance

With the election of Peronist Carlos Menem to the presidency in 1989, Argentina did a shocking about-turn to align itself as an ally of the United States in all regards. There was no immediate sign of change. Menem had campaigned as a traditional Peronist, emphasizing strong protectionism and a foreign policy independent of the United States. More so than Alfonsín, Menem did seem to understand immediately how to do business in Washington. Shortly after Menem's swearing-in ceremony, the Argentine government signed on with the Washington law firm of Williams & Connolly to represent Argentina's interests in the United States. The firm charged an annual $60,000 retainer and $260 an hour for the time of firm partners.[32] Despite the perceived need for a powerful Washington law firm on retainer, a March 1990 internal Foreign Relations Ministry policy document made no mention of radical policy change. It highlighted the continued expansion of bilateral relations in all areas, cooperation in the international drug war, and joint U.S.-Argentine support for democracy in the Americas. The tenor of early Menem administration policy toward the United States was less combative than that of Alfonsín on debt and development issues, but by and large, areas targeted for bilateral cooperation were the same as those highlighted by the previous president.[33]

In August 1989, the U.S. ambassador in Buenos Aires, Terrence Todman, outlined the U.S. view of bilateral relations. The George Bush administration wanted an end to the Cóndor missile program. The new foreign minister, Domingo Cavallo, was noncommittal. He did accept an American request not to have dealings with Libya. Six months later, Argentina would join other Latin American countries in criticizing the U.S. invasion of Panama as a breach of the principle of nonintervention in the Americas. But at the meeting with Todman, Cavallo approved of American policy in trying to oust General Manuel Noriega from the presidency. At the time of the Todman-Cavallo meeting, there was no Argentine ambassador in Panama. Cavallo committed Argentina to not appointing a new ambassador until Noriega left office. Where the

Argentine foreign minister departed notably from previous policy was in regard to the nonaligned movement. Cavallo promised Todman that Argentina would work with moderates in the nonaligned movement to try to marginalize the more extreme opponents of the United States within the group.[34]

By April 1990, Menem had decided to discard decades of Peronist anti-American rhetoric and to align his nation's economic, financial, and strategic policies with the United States. On 6 and 7 April 1990, Cavallo met in Paris with Argentina's ambassadors in Europe to explain the sea change that was now taking place in Argentine policy. "There has been no policy zigzag," Cavallo began, referring to reports in the Argentine press by incredulous journalists who accused Menem of abandoning his Peronist roots. President Menem, Cavallo argued, was simply striving for fiscal and political responsibility. But there had, in fact, been a zigzag. The changes Cavallo outlined were revolutionary, and his assembling of diplomats to outline the changes was unprecedented. There would be massive privatizations of public sector companies. Argentina would be opened entirely to direct foreign investment.[35] The Menem administration explained the realignment of policy toward support of American positions in the context of the end of the cold war. But Argentine policymakers expected that U.S. military and economic policy would decline during the 1990s. In a world where strategic alliances and economic change would be increasingly charted through regional alliances, rather than as a function of great power conflict, Argentina saw alliance with the United States as both a necessity for economic growth and an opportunity for Argentine regional leadership. This was precisely the opposite tack to that taken by Perón at the end of World War II and Hipólito Yrigoyen during World War I, both of whom had sought regional Argentine leadership by distancing themselves from the United States.[36]

By June 1990, Argentina had thrown open the doors to foreign investment and trade. It had aligned its foreign policy with that of the United States. Foreign Minister Cavallo told the Bill Clinton administration trade representative Carla Hills that Menem had changed an "old vision" in Argentina. "Before, we thought that it was not advantageous for our country to trade with the rest of the world. Now, many of us think that the globalization of our economy will offer a formidable opportunity for growth. For that reason, Argentina is moving toward accepting the international rules of commerce."[37]

Cavallo's statement echoed other Argentine policymakers for its born-again quality of Argentina as having seen the light in following a U.S. policy line. Here and elsewhere, the Menem administration justified its policy shift by casting Argentina as something just short of a rogue state during the 1980s—unwilling to play by the rules of civilized societies on nuclear power and commerce and in other areas. Cavallo cited the recent reform of the Argentine Patent Law that afforded greater opportunity to foreign multinationals. He informed Carla Hills that Argentine participation in the current General Agreement on Tariffs and Trade (GATT) round of negotiations was due in part to the U.S. government's interest in the Argentines doing so. There would be an Argentine liberalization in the agriculture, services, textiles, and intellectual property sectors in keeping with the coming global liberalization. Argentine policy was in step with a neoliberal shift more generally in Latin America, and Cavallo cast the changes in this context. Argentina was taking necessary steps for change in light of global transformations in conditions of trade and finance.

In July 1990, U.S. government officials arrived in Buenos Aires to try to press Argentine nuclear officials toward a policy shift in keeping with Cavallo's foreign policy revolution. At the urging of the United States, the Alfonsín administration had initiated a series of talks with Brazilian officials about ending competition in the nuclear sector. Now the Americans wanted more. They pressed the Argentines to make their nuclear research program more transparent in anticipation of President George Bush's upcoming visit to Argentina, the prospect of stronger U.S.-Argentine nuclear ties, and what the Americans termed a natural development for a country intending to augment its foreign nuclear commerce.[38]

The Americans also urged the Argentines to adhere to the Tlatelolco Treaty and the Nuclear Non-proliferation Treaty. The Argentines present countered with Argentina's long-standing defense of its position on safeguards. Neither the Tlatelolco nor the nonproliferation agreements protected Argentina's right to the peaceful development of nuclear technologies. Yet despite CNEA's stand, Argentina had already begun to change its nuclear policies, marking both another area of alignment with the United States and the declining importance of CNEA in the setting of Argentine nuclear policy. As part of Menem's plan to align Argentine foreign policy with that of the United States, Argentina simply dropped its decades-old distinction between peaceful and nonpeaceful nuclear explosions. The Agreement for the Exclusively Peaceful Use of Nuclear Energy was signed by Menem and Brazilian president Fernando Collor de Mello on 18 July 1991 (and then quickly ratified by the congress in both countries). The accord confirmed that there was, in fact, no distinction between peaceful and nonpeaceful nuclear explosions. That statement was precisely the position the United States had sought from Argentina for a quarter century. Throughout that time, Argentine nuclear policy had been founded on the premise that there was a clear distinction between peaceful and nonpeaceful nuclear tests.[39] Menem's nuclear zigzag was now in place. In December 1991, Argentina and Brazil reached a nuclear safeguards accord. The agreement promised verification that nuclear materials in the hands of both states would not be used in nuclear detonations of any sort. There was no point even mentioning peaceful or nonpeaceful explosions in the document.[40]

The Alfonsín administration had made the sale of nuclear sector hardware and know-how to poor countries a hallmark of Dante Caputo's Sur-Sur foreign policy and the country's plan to assume a leadership role within the nonaligned movement. Argentina's expanding nuclear ties in the 1980s with Algeria and other countries that the United States regarded as ill equipped to manage reactors had galled Washington. Now, the Argentine government went much further than what Cavallo had promised Todman in August 1989. Argentina abruptly exited the nonaligned movement and, in keeping with its pro-U.S. foreign policy line, curtailed its nuclear foreign relations with Iran, among other nations. Since the early 1970s, through military and democratic governments and through the period of the Iran-Iraq War,

Argentina had fostered nuclear cooperation with Iran. CNEA had built an experimental reactor outside Tehran in the late 1970s and had maintained extensive nuclear ties with Iran in many areas including nuclear medicine.[41] In April 1992, the U.S. government warned the Argentine government that its nuclear shipments to Iran were being used for weapons production. Not only would there be no heavy water plant, but at a cost of eighteen million dollars in lost revenue, Argentina suspended shipments of nuclear equipment to Iran and ended a series of bilateral cooperative agreements with the Iranians. An approving U.S. State Department issued a statement that the revenue loss was unfortunate but necessary in limiting the access of unreliable regimes to the capacity to produce nuclear weapons.[42]

Like its Canadian equivalent, the Argentine nuclear sector was never so profitable so as to offset the millions of dollars invested by the Argentine government in nuclear projects. Both as a cost-cutting measure and as a pro-U.S. policy zigzag, the Menem government decided that this net loss could no longer be supported. Funding to CNEA was slashed dramatically. Morale plummeted in the government nuclear agency during the 1990s. At the same time, private firms took advantage of the nuclear thaw with the United States. In early 1992, representatives of INVAP, Argentina's producer of experimental reactors for export, met with their equivalents at General Atomics in the United States. In March, the two companies signed a memorandum of understanding that identified unprecedented areas for future cooperation between Argentine and U.S. firms. The two companies began working toward an agreement by which they would export experimental reactors jointly. Countries identified as potential markets included Uruguay, Saudi Arabia, and Indonesia. By June INVAP learned that as a result of Menem administration nuclear policy shifts, the U.S. State and Energy departments had signed off on INVAP commercial activity in the United States. INVAP also negotiated contracts with the U.S. Department of Energy to decontaminate and clean nuclear sites in the United States.[43]

There were other immediate improvements to bilateral relations as a result of Argentina's nuclear policy shift. In April 1992 a high-level delegation of American policymakers traveled to Argentina for secret conversations on improved U.S.-Argentine trade in strategic goods and technologies. The delegation included Deputy Assistant Secretary of State for South America J. Philip McLean, Deputy Assistant Director of the Bureau of Nonproliferation Policy (State Department) Vincent F. Decain, and Deputy Director of the Office of Weapons, Proliferation Policy, and Politico-Military Affairs (State Department) Bain Cowell. The Americans told their Argentine counterparts that they viewed Argentine-Brazilian nuclear cooperation as a model for regional cooperation the United States had used in discussions with India and Pakistan. They also told Argentine officials that they believed Brazil's agreement with Argentina to maintain jointly nuclear safeguards in the region might serve as the basis for a similar U.S.-Argentine agreement. And with that agreement in place, the United States would approve the sale of a supercomputer to the Argentine government. Argentine policy objectives were producing important dividends. Argentines found that the United States had begun to treat Argentina as an ally.[44]

Argentina transformed its policy toward Cuba to dovetail with Washington's position. As early as 1990, Argentine diplomats at the United Nations were instructed to begin criticizing Fidel Castro's human rights record and calling for democratization in Cuba. In October, Menem met with anti-Castro Cuban American leader Jorge Más Canosa in New York. The Argentine president promised to work for Castro's ouster. In September 1990, Argentina allied itself militarily with the United States for the first time in history. The Menem administration sent two warships to the Persian Gulf in support of the American effort in the Gulf War. Not only did the Radical Party react critically to the decision but so too did Saúl Ubaldini, president of the CGT, and many Peronist Party deputies in Congress. Nonetheless, the Argentine Senate backed the president's decision in a vote of confidence. President Bush sent Menem a note of warm appreciation for the dramatic policy reversal.

In January 1991, Menem faced congressional opposition from within his own party to a continued Argentine military presence in the Middle East. There was ongoing criticism that by supporting the U.S. war effort, the president was abandoning Peronist nationalist ideals. Menem countered that Argentine participation in the Gulf War responded to UN resolutions. It was not a slavish adherence to U.S. demands. Moreover, Argentine foreign policy reflected a return to traditional Peronist pragmatism. Menem cited Perón's reasoning almost half a century before to explain Argentina's decision in 1945 to join the Allied cause in the final weeks of the Second World War. By entering the war at the end, Argentina had integrated itself into the world community and generated enormous commercial opportunities. Menem argued that his decision to join the Gulf War would have a similar effect. Despite that some Peronist deputies opposed the motion, Menem won the congressional vote, and the warships remained in the Gulf through the war. Throughout the 1990s, Argentina supported U.S. policy toward Iraq, announcing in 1998 that if the United States were to go to war again against Saddam Hussein, Argentina would send troops in support of the American war effort. The Gulf War initiated a decade of extensive bilateral military cooperation that included the increased American sale of many classes of weapons to Argentina and cooperative naval and military exercises. Most important as far as the U.S. government was concerned was the high-level Argentine military cooperation with the United States in the international drug war.[45]

Menem's decision to cancel the Cóndor missile program not only further tied Argentine foreign policy to that of the United States, but it also marked one of several measures the new president took to severely curtail the influence of the Argentine military in national politics. Unlike the about-face on nuclear policy, the decision on the Cóndor came in three stages, each responding to a new level of American pressures from July 1989 through September 1993. Between July 1989 and mid-1990, Menem responded to overtures from Washington by expressing his government's sympathy for the American request that the program be ended. A second stage began with the Defense Ministry's announcement in April 1990 that the missile project would be placed on hold. Between that date and May 1991, when a presidential decree put an end to the missile program, there were intense debates within the Menem administration over Cóndor. A number of high-ranking government members resisted American pressures while others resented air force intransigence over losing "their" program. In January 1991, American military technicians arrived in Argentina to inspect Cóndor facilities in several locations in anticipation of their destruction. With an eye on the stakes, Menem administration sympathy toward U.S. government stands in other areas, and how close Argentina seemed to ending their missile program, American policymakers pulled out all the stops in pressing Argentina on Cóndor. At a February 1991 meeting in Washington, National Security Council Director Brent Scowcroft and Secretary of State James Baker told Argentine foreign secretary Guido Di Tella that they had no contact with the Argentine Air Force on Cóndor. Moreover, the United States was in no way backing that service's continued opposition to bringing the program to an end. In a final stage of the missile program's destruction, it took until September 1993 for all bureaucratic and physical remnants of Cóndor to be dismantled.[46] As important as the missile decision itself was the unprecedented degree to which the Argentine government capitulated to American intervention in the missile dismantling process between 1991 and 1993.[47]

The Argentines acquiesced to U.S. pressures for changes in economic policy. Alfonsín had taken steps toward neoliberal reform in his Austral Plan and in the Primavera Plan (1988) that followed. Menem followed his lead by accepting key tenets of U.S. policy toward Latin America. For the first time in decades Argentina's international economic and strategic policies were aligned with those of the United States. The Menem government privatized whatever state enterprises it could, from the national airline to the military's industrial enterprises. New laws made foreign investment as easy as domestic investment. And in 1991, Domingo Cavallo, now as economy minister, launched his Convertibility Plan. Not a complete "dollarization" of the economy, the plan nevertheless pegged the Argentine peso to the U.S. dollar by law at a one-to-one ratio. The plan remained in place for a decade. For the first time in twenty years inflation came down to zero in 1993. In addition, with the economy stabilized after the rampant inflation of the 1980s, foreign investment poured into the country.[48]

In November 1991, Menem visited Washington to sign a treaty "Concerning the Reciprocal Encouragement and Protection of Investment." The first bilateral investment treaty with a Latin American country that the United States had signed since President George Bush launched his Enterprise for the Americas Initiative in June 1990, the accord protected investors from either country who were interested in investing in the partner nation. It also gave some protection to investors against potential nationalizations or expropriations of private business. American foreign direct investment in Argentina rose from $367 million in 1991 to $1.8 billion in 1997. Bilateral commerce rose even more quickly, increasing 154 percent between 1989 and 1994.[49] Argentine authorities viewed the new North American Free Trade Agreement (NAFTA) with alarm, anticipating the loss of millions of dollars in sales to the United States.[50] They were determined to foster trade with the United States to offset the economic losses attributed to NAFTA. But one important consequence of neoliberal reform was that in Argentina's dollarized economy of the 1990s the cost of labor made many Argentine exports prohibitively expensive. At the same time, the downturn in Argentine industrial production meant that Argentina was forced to import huge quantities of capital goods. The result was a dramatic increase in the country's trade deficit with the United States, which by 1998 had reached four billion dollars.

In multilateral organizations, Argentina also adapted policy to improve relations with the United States. Though one of the first nations to participate in UN peacekeeping missions three decades before, during the 1990s Argentine peacekeeping activity skyrocketed. In 1990 there were sixty Argentine soldiers on missions. That figure reached seventeen hundred in 1994. In the OAS, Argentina supported American diplomatic initiatives to improve inter-American cooperation on fighting the international drug trade and on combating terrorism. Two terrorist attacks in Buenos Aires during the Menem presidency generated a flurry of interest in the United States, but in the end the FBI and other U.S. agencies that tried to help Argentine authorities solve the crimes were unable to achieve results. On 17 March 1992, a bomb ripped through the Israeli embassy in Buenos Aires. And on 18 July 1994, a bomb exploded in front of an Argentine Jewish center, the AMIA building, killing eighty-six people. The United States immediately suspected Iran in the second bombing. James Cheek, the U.S. ambassador in

Buenos Aires, told Argentine authorities that if they broke ties with Iran, his government would support the move.

But the Argentine government maintained good relations with Iran through the late 1990s, despite mounting evidence (some supplied by the United States) that Iranian authorities had, in fact, sponsored the AMIA building bombing. Furthermore, it became increasingly clear to many Argentines that not only had the Menem government and its allies in the judiciary ignored vital evidence on the bombing but also the government had orchestrated a cover-up of the crime. In September 1995, the American rabbi Avi Weiss openly accused Menem of suppressing evidence in the AMIA case before a hearing of the U.S. Congress Foreign Affairs Committee. From that point forward, Jewish groups in the United States took a strong interest in the case. They pressured Congress to demand answers of Menem and kept AMIA in the public eye. The politicization of the AMIA case in the United States was never as significant in American public policy as anti-Semitism under the dictatorship, but the former was reminiscent of the latter both for role of Jewish Americans in raising the profile of an issue in bilateral relations and for the explicit and implicit accusation that the Argentine government, if not anti-Semitic itself, seemed insensitive to the issue.[51]

In 1997, the *New York Times* reported on the Argentine cover-up of the AMIA bombing. At the same time, the FBI became aware of the "triple frontera" border region—where Argentina, Brazil, and Paraguay shared a frontier—as a security threat. For years, there had been rumors in both Argentina and the United States of the triple frontier as porous. On all sides of the borders there, criminals found a haven in a "Wild West" atmosphere of violence and lawlessness. Drugs moved freely across the borders, as did illicit profits from the drug trade and other forms of organized crime. More serious, there was growing evidence that Islamic terrorist groups with links to the Shiite Muslim organization Hezbollah were operating out of the triple border region. The FBI believed that those groups might have had a hand in the AMIA bombing. The U.S. government reacted to the threat by promising funds and training to Argentine police and migration officers. In May 1998, FBI director Louis Freeh traveled to Argentina to promise American intelligence support and funding for Argentine security services.[52] But the AMIA investigation languished. The Menem administration ended without a resolution to the crime.

For Washington, the AMIA case proved relatively insignificant compared to a host of other incidents that exposed the Menem government as a haven for criminality. Sadly for Argentina, Menem's experiment in strong economic alliance with the United States through neoliberal economic policies went badly wrong for Argentina in many regards. Despite some growth in the early 1990s fueled in large measure by the generous privatizations of state-owned corporations, the Argentine economy stagnated in the late 1990s. In the face of unrestricted imports, many industrial sectors, including textile production, almost disappeared entirely. For many the story of Alfredo Yabrán underscored the dramatic failure of dollarization and open trade and investment. A political crony of Menem, Yabrán had first generated capital through mysterious contacts with the military during the dictatorship. In the early stages of the Menem economic transformation, Yabrán founded the largest private courier service in Argentina, Oka. The business thrived. But Yabrán used his vast transportation network to ship cocaine south from Bolivia and out of Argentina through the port of Buenos Aires to European and other markets. For many Argentines, the increasingly fine line in late 1990s Argentina between mafia-like businesses and the liberalized legitimate economy was highlighted by Yabrán's enormously profitable business activities. Yabrán's illicit business activities proved a bitter irony for American policymakers who had celebrated Argentine support for the American war on drugs. Though no evidence ever tied the Menem administration to Yabrán's drug dealings, most Argentines believed it impossible that the president would not have known that Yabrán was using his private courier company to run cocaine through Argentina.

There were a string of other scandals linking Menem's government to organized crime. In each case, there were ties to Argentina's pro-U.S. economic policies and indications of how those policies were implemented recklessly and in many cases criminally. In anticipation of a 1997 visit by President Bill Clinton to Argentina, the Menem administration addressed repeated U.S. government criticisms that the Argentine government allowed and even promoted extensive money laundering. It promised a legislative crackdown. But Clinton came and went, and the legislation languished without ever winning congressional approval.[53] In 1996, U.S. and Argentine investigators exposed a massive bribery scandal. The IBM corporation had made payoffs to dozens of Argentine officials to win a contract to supply computers to Argentina's Central Bank.

In 1994, the Menem administration summed up its foreign policy accomplishments by describing Argentina's about-turn as having given the nation credibility. "We have improved our international image to unimaginable levels and have reinserted ourselves clearly into the first world. . . . Today the principal countries of the universe are our friends, our allies, and our partners." Argentine officials celebrated their having resolved outstanding border conflicts with Chile. More important, they felt that their strong relations with the Bush and Clinton administrations represented a foreign relations triumph. The Menem administration viewed its new "security policy" as an important accomplishment. In addition to supporting nuclear nonproliferation, Argentina signed an agreement proscribing chemical weapons and ended the Condor missile program.[54]

But in the end, Menem's greatest triumph also represented the nation's most important late-twentieth-century failing. Menem opened the economy to foreign investment and trade and dollarized the economy. Although these projects stimulated growth in some areas, they also helped destroy industrial production in many sectors. They also helped generate unprecedented levels of corruption in the Argentine economy, much of which was inextricably linked to Menem-era privatization policies. One of the most striking examples of how privatization policies led to corruption was in the activities of Citibank. The New York–based bank had established branches in Argentina more than seventy years before Menem's election. With Menem's economic and financial policy alignments with the United States, Citibank was one of the first foreign banks to take advantage of new Argentine opportunities. By mid-1991 Citibank held an interest in dozens of Argentine companies. Through its subsidiary Citicorp Venture Capital, it acquired 12 percent of Telefónica, one of two private telephone companies that had taken over the government-run phone system, 10 percent of Frigorífico Santa Elena, and 10 percent of the luxury hotel Llao Llao in the resort of Bariloche. But as foreign investment flowed into Argentina, the Menem administration had neither the interest nor the ability to control illicit banking and investment practices. Citibank began to operate in Argentina in a manner that would have been impossible in the United States. In March 1992, Citicorp Venture Capital had backed the establishment of the Bahamas-based Federal Bank to conceal illicit Argentine financial dealings. With Citibank's financial support, Federal Bank financed the activities of the Grupo Moneta, one of the most corrupt money laundering operations of 1990s Argentina.[55]

In October 1993, the Argentine consul in Atlanta, Juan Carlos Vignaud, reported bad news to Argentine foreign minister Guido Di Tella. For the most part, Vignaud found that Americans viewed Argentina as just one more Latin American country. Nations that held some specific identity for Americans included Mexico, Cuba, Colombia, Nicaragua, and Panama. To a lesser extent, Brazil could be included in this group. And to a still lesser extent, Argentina held some name recognition and national identity in the minds of Americans. But for the most part, Americans confused Argentina with the rest of Latin America and simply assumed that problems afflicting Cuba and Mexico also defined Argentine life. Vignaud argued that American ambivalence toward Argentina was aversely affecting Argentine business prospects in the United States. He noted further that during the 1980s Argentine exports to the United States had declined. Moreover, while in 1981 Argentine exports had represented 0.43 percent of total imports to the United States, that figure had declined to 0.32 percent in 1990. There was urgent need for Argentines to increase their North American profile.[56]

Although under Menem, Argentines had not registered much of an impact in the United States, the reverse was true for U.S. influence in Argentina. Menem's policy zigzag represented a remarkable late-twentieth-century triumph for American foreign policy. After 1987, U.S.–Latin American relations were reshaped dramatically. Cold war imperatives that had guided U.S. policy in the Americas—fears of revolutionary violence, ideologies of economic nationalism, and anti-Communism—no longer drove decision making. U.S. leaders returned to an updated dollar diplomacy. Dollar diplomacy and its successor twentieth-century policies emphasizing open trade and investment in the Americas had failed in the past to transform U.S.–Latin American relations. But several factors made it work after 1987 in Argentina and other hemispheric nations. The Latin American debt crisis, and the 1982–83 Mexican debt moratorium in particular, prompted dismay among U.S. policymakers who came to see the need for radical economic reform in the region as urgent. The collapse of the Soviet Union and the end of leftist insurgencies in Central America eliminated the principal U.S. motivation for military intervention. In addition, the political center in Argentina, Brazil, and a number of other countries shifted to the right. By 1990, Argentina and other countries in the region were governed by presidential administrations more sympathetic to profound neoliberal economic reform than any of their predecessors' governments. Argentina adopted neoliberal economic models lock, stock, and barrel.

Epilogue: The Crash of 2001 and Beyond

During the 1990s, President Carlos Menem dominated Argentine politics. His political control of the judicial, executive, and congressional branches of government allowed for an unchecked implementation of domestic economic, social, and monetary policies that dovetailed with U.S. government and IMF goals for Argentina and the Americas. Menem's government was a Latin American leader in the promulgation of neoliberal policies that included widespread privatizations of large state-run corporations, the dismantling of expensive federal government programs, hostile confrontations with organized labor that helped decimate union membership, and the elimination of barriers on foreign trade and investment. Most important, Argentina legislated "convertibility," the one-to-one exchange rate for the Argentine peso to the U.S. dollar. Although Menem's policies contributed to a period of unprecedented strength in U.S.-Argentine relations, the results of neoliberal policy shifts were mixed. Supporters pointed to relatively consistent economic growth in the 1990s. Opponents highlighted the decline of industrial production and real wages.

By early 2000, there was mounting evidence of severe economic trouble on the horizon. Argentina was still wealthy by Latin American standards, boasting the second largest percentage of population above the poverty line (80.4). But unemployment had reached unprecedented (and some felt dangerous) levels; fully 25 percent of twenty- to twenty-four-year-olds were without work.[1] Provincial government spending had exploded in the face of mounting poverty, taking an enormous leap in 1999, the year Carlos Menem left office. Unlike in the United States, where states are constitutionally prohibited from running a debt, no such constraints bind Argentine provinces. By mid-2001, the combined debt of the Argentine provinces reached twenty-one billion dollars, the

209

vast majority of which was held by foreign creditors. Many in the international financial community came to feel that, combined with a rapidly declining Argentine economy and the weak presidency of Radical Party chief Fernando de la Rua, the extent and rapid rise of Argentina's debt posed a risk of major financial collapse. In July, the *Economist* magazine speculated on whether a possible Argentine default on scheduled foreign loan repayments might have an international impact equivalent to the Asian crisis of 1997 and the Russian crisis of 1998.[2]

Through most of 2001, Argentine officials answered speculation regarding a currency devaluation by promising repeatedly that, come what may, the government would neither end convertibility nor stop foreign debt repayments. As the crisis escalated, however, U.S. treasury secretary Paul O'Neill emerged as Argentina's most prominent foreign critic. Indeed, for the first time since Jimmy Carter's attention to human rights, Argentina became a nation around which a substantial U.S. foreign policy shift was being shaped. Like President George W. Bush, O'Neill was impatient with the international status quo on debt crises. Both viewed countries like Argentina, with ballooning foreign debt, as financially irresponsible and politically reckless. More important, they believed that the IMF, the World Bank, and private international lenders and bondholders were contributing to financial instability by helping corrupt governments in poor countries bloat their debt loads to the point of crisis. Bush had begun to extend long-standing U.S. government disdain for UN "multilateralism" to the IMF. The president rejected the long-standing assumption that the United States would bankroll the IMF but would share decision making on the disbursement of those funds with other wealthy nations. He had also decided that the Bill Clinton–era bailouts of U.S. creditors caught in third-world debt crises were over. International creditors would have to pay the consequences of extending credit to high-risk countries. Argentina now became a policy test case.

In July 2001, O'Neill shocked Argentines and many others by calling Argentina financially irresponsible and by insisting that such unreliability had been a long-standing problem in Argentine history. According to O'Neill, Argentine leaders had been mismanaging their nation's economy for almost a century; corruption and ineptitude were in their nature. Many saw O'Neill's comments as brash, offensive, and provocative. But there was method in the provocation. In lambasting Argentine officials the treasury secretary was, in fact, trying to calm fears that a possible Argentine monetary crash might "infect" world markets in the manner of the Asian crisis four years earlier. O'Neill was making the case that Argentina's problems were exclusively of Argentina's making. As such, no larger risk to the international financial community existed. All the same, foreign investors remained edgy, and the Buenos Aires stock market continued a long decline.

What Argentines called the "crack" came in December 2001. Facing what seemed the menace of economic collapse, the Argentine government did the unthinkable: It abruptly ended convertibility and froze bank accounts to prevent a run on financial institutions. Argentines reacted with violent protests that toppled de la Rua and ushered in a period of political and economic instability. During street protests in December, one of the most prominent targets of angry crowds was the century-old Bank Boston building in the Buenos Aires financial district: The building's stately oversized doors were battered, and its exterior walls were repeatedly defaced with anti-American and anti-IMF slogans. Even in mid-2005, long after the protests were over, the Bank Boston building remained defaced with graffiti. But while middle-class Argentines directed their fury against foreign banks, authorized by their government to freeze their devalued savings, in the months that followed there was as much anger toward the Spanish-owned Banco de Galicia and the Canadian-capitalized Scotiabank as toward U.S. financial institutions. Popular anti-Americanism was not an end product of the Argentine crash.

As Argentina suffered through hard times in early 2002, two revolutionary shifts occurred in U.S.-Argentine relations. Argentina had defaulted on loan repayments in the past, but this was the first time that Argentina defaulted (in this case on a $103 billion debt) without making the usual promises to Washington and the international banking community that payments would start again as soon as the economy was in order. The Argentine government announced that until the economy showed signs of recovery, there would be a moratorium on all foreign debt repayments. Argentine officials anticipated an inevitable clash with Washington. It never came. More remarkable than the moratorium itself was the blasé response of the Bush administration. As it became evident that there would be no "tango effect" (no larger regional or international crisis as a result of the Argentine collapse), the Bush administration put into practice O'Neill's stand on the IMF and the international banking community. There would be no U.S. government multibillion-dollar creditor bailout as there had been at the time of the Mexican crisis in 1994. As such, American officials saw the Argentine debt payment moratorium as an opportunity both to contain the influence of the IMF (widely perceived as having contributed to the Argentine collapse) and to discipline international creditors whom they regarded as reckless lenders. The U.S. government encouraged Argentina to renegotiate its debt with the IMF and private debt holders but did not make the debt issue a burning problem in bilateral relations. On the contrary, American officials tried to be helpful in advising the Argentine government on its negotiating position as, for example, in November 2003 when IMF negotiator John Thornton arrived in Buenos Aires to look over Argentine government spending in the preceding trimester.[3]

In 2002, there was some modest recovery. Argentina's currency plunged to about 25 percent of its convertibility-era value, making Argentine goods, particularly in the agricultural sector, more attractive to foreign buyers. Popular frustration with the legacy of the Menem era focused particularly on rampant corruption. In the aftermath of the December crash, the government adopted a series of reforms, many promoted by the United States, to end illicit practices and corruption in government and beyond. One result was a spike in tax revenues that also helped brighten the country's economic picture. Despite this progress, though, the nation's outlook remained grim. Although in 2000 just under 20 percent of Argentines lived in poverty, that figure reached a staggering 60 percent in 2003. Just as jarring was the ongoing shrinking of the middle class, now representing only 15 percent of the population as compared with 35 percent in 1974. At the same time, the upper middle class and upper class constituted 15 percent of the population, the same figure as in 1974. The economists Robert Barro and Eduardo Pompei argued that the growing gap between rich and poor in Argentina was contributing to economic instability, urban decay, and growing violence.[4]

Although all these issues were a source of concern in Washington, they were far less important than equivalent worries about poverty, economic crisis, and underdevelopment in Latin American during the 1960s. In part, Washington's calm response likely related to the relative significance of American credit in Argentina in 2001. Unlike the 1970s, for example, when American bankers and bondholders had held the lion's share of the escalating Argentine debt, in December 2001, American creditors held only 5 percent of Argentina's debt (compared to 16 percent for Italian creditors and fully 38 percent for Argentines). Moreover, American foreign policy was now firmly focused on Iraq and the war on terror. Growing poverty in Argentina, Peru, Brazil, and elsewhere in the Americas did not prompt U.S. policymakers to shift their preoccupation from national security to the nations south of the border.

The U.S. response to Uruguay's financial crisis in mid-2002 reflected Washington's measured attention to Argentina's recovery from the December 2001 collapse. At the time of the Argentine crisis, Paul O'Neill had remarked to the press that it would not be fair for American plumbers and carpenters to be burdened with Argentina's financial woes. The treasury secretary was stating unequivocally that although the United States would be willing to help Argentina sort out its financial problems, there would be no bailout on the backs of American taxpayers. But in early August 2002, with the Uruguayan banking sector in a crisis very similar to that experienced in Argentina six months earlier, O'Neill approved what he had refused Argentine authorities. On Sunday, 4 August, at a press conference in Montevideo, U.S. ambassador Martin Silverstein confirmed with a two-thumbs-up sign that a $1.5 billion bridge loan had been flown in cash to Uruguay that morning. The money had come from the U.S. Treasury Department's Exchange Stabilization Fund and had not gone through the IMF, as some had speculated it would in the days leading up to the bailout. Though much smaller, the transaction was similar to that undertaken by the Clinton administration to lift Mexico out of its crisis in 1995. In fact, by one measure, the Uruguay bailout was more generous than the Mexican equivalent. Mexican authorities had had to guarantee their $20 billion U.S. government emergency loan in 1995 with oil sales revenues deposited in the Federal Reserve Bank of New York. Uruguay was asked for no such guarantees. Some Argentines grumbled that American plumbers and carpenters had been called on to bail out Uruguay.[5]

Why did O'Neill take a softer stand on Uruguay than he had on Argentina? It seems clear that the Treasury Secretary distinguished between what he viewed as incorrigible Argentines and Uruguayan officials who, according to Washington, were apparently less complicit in bringing about their crisis. On 4 August, in stark contrast to his views on how Argentina's crisis had unfolded, O'Neill insisted in a press release that the current crisis was not caused by the Uruguayan government. Unlike Argentina, Uruguay had not entered into default. The bridge loan was meant in part by O'Neill to reward purported Uruguayan level headedness in the face of a worsening economy and to underline Washington's version of events—that the Uruguayan crisis, unlike its Argentine equivalent, was being caused by "foreign pressures" (primarily fallout from Argentina's economic slump). "For some time now," according to O'Neill, "Uruguay has implemented serious policies and has upheld the free market, trade liberalization, and the maintenance of a low inflation rate." The treasury secretary also pointed out that Uruguayan president Jorge Batlle had acted "courageously" in preceding months by closing Uruguayan banks at financial risk. There was no mistaking the unstated criticism of successive Argentine governments that for over a decade had refused to act in curtailing the activities of more than a dozen shaky Argentine banks, like Banco Patricios, that had collapsed and, in the end, contributed significantly to the country's financial breakdown.[6]

Uruguay's size was also a factor in explaining the American bailout. Initially, Washington had read Argentina's crisis as equivalent to the 1994 Mexican crisis—potentially damaging on a large international scale and outside the immediate influence of U.S. policy decisions. Uruguay's problems, on the other hand, seemed manageable. Treasury

Department Undersecretary John Taylor explained that the bridge loan was sent primarily to ensure that the banks would open on Monday morning in Montevideo (the following day), which they did. Washington expected the loan to be repaid as soon as Uruguay could secure emergency funds from the IMF, the World Bank, and the International Development Bank. Moreover, while in extending the emergency loan O'Neill was clearly interested in telling the international community not to be like Argentina, Washington was also taking the position that a relatively small bailout would quickly stabilize Uruguay. This would avoid larger-scale problems in a still weak Argentina, whose economy was closely tied to that of its neighbor across the Río de la Plata. Despite Washington's criticisms of Argentina's role in its own financial collapse, U.S. policy in Uruguay was directed in significant measure at shoring up Argentina's economic position and potential recovery.

One result of the December 2001 collapse was the revival of a long-standing sense among Argentines that the Radical Party was incapable of managing the economy. Partially as a result, voters gave Peronist Néstor Kirchner a presidential mandate in 2003 (though without a majority of the popular vote). In many respects, and as a political strategy designed to appeal to widespread disenchantment with the neoliberal 1990s, Kirchner positioned himself to the left of Carlos Menem. He extended the debt repayment moratorium, blamed the IMF for having pushed fifteen million Argentines into poverty,[7] and moved quickly to improve trade relations with left-of-center governments in Latin America, including those of Cuba, Venezuela, and Brazil. Despite Kirchner's effort to distance himself from Menem and de la Rua, there were few substantial economic policy changes past the debt repayment moratorium. While casting itself publicly as an antagonist to the IMF, the Kirchner administration, clearly concerned about securing new credits and investments, became quickly absorbed with day-to-day debt-related negotiations with the IMF and private bankers. There was no effort to dismantle the Menem legacy of corporate privatizations, free trade, or the open door to foreign capital flows. Even so, foreign investment remained minimal while relations with the United States remained sound.

A 2003 survey by the Argentine Centro de Estudios de Opinión Pública (CEOP) showed that Argentines continued to hold American or heavily U.S.-capitalized companies in very high regard.. For product quality, service, honesty, ethical integrity, and commercial creativity, Coca-Cola, Microsoft, American Express, Daimler Chrysler, Unilever, and Ford Motors all ranked among the top fifteen foreign and domestic corporations. All but Daimler Chrysler (at seventeenth) ranked in the top fifteen for capacity to adapt to the Argentine economic crisis. Even though the public's regard for banks had declined sharply since 2001, by 2004 Argentines had placed more funds into savings accounts since the crisis than they had held in such accounts at the time of the crack. Moreover, among all banks, survey results showed that Argentines had the most confidence in Bank Boston and Citibank, the two American banks that had first established branches in Buenos Aires ninety years earlier.[8]

In the aftermath of the Twin Towers bombings in September 2001, the Argentine government did not join the United States in the invasion of Afghanistan or Iraq. Even so, Argentina was generally supportive of the Bush administration's antiterrorist measures. In 2004, Argentines were surprised to learn that a U.S.-supervised antiterrorism course for Argentine soldiers had been established two years earlier at a military base in northern Argentina under the auspices of the Inter-American Defense College and the Inter-American Defense Board. This under-lined the ongoing strong (and for some Argentines, disturbing) ties be-tween the two nations' armed forces. In a 2004 visit to Argentina, Deputy Secretary of State for Economic Affairs Alan Larson termed Ar-gentina "a friend, an ally and a valued partner" of the United States. He dismissed notions that Washington viewed Argentina critically over ongoing tensions with the IMF.[9]

Larson was particularly pleased that Argentina had sided with Washington over conflicting versions of Jean Bertrand Aristide's fall from power in Haiti and had supported the United States by sending peacekeeping troops to the island nation. Larson also credited Argentina for having played a crucial mediation role in Bolivia's 2003 political crisis that had led to the resignation of President Gonzálo

Sánchez de Losada and a national referendum that confirmed the presidency of Carlos Mesa. Ironically, perhaps, in light of U.S. criticisms of Argentine leadership efforts in Latin America, after 2001 the United States viewed that leadership positively. In what was seen in Argentina as a statement of support for Kirchner's negotiating position with the IMF, Larson urged international creditors to bear in mind that Argentina's capacity for debt repayment was less now than what had been expected when the credits were initially extended. "We're not mediators," Larson added when questioned about the U.S. role in Argentine debt payment negotiations, "we're friends."[10]

Washington's response to the Argentine crisis and its aftermath reflects the declining importance of the Americas in U.S. foreign policy in the aftermath of 9/11. Although the 2001 collapse was Argentina's worst financial crisis in over a century, the U.S. government responded with almost uncanny calm. Even though the debt repayment moratorium was as radical a measure as anything Juan Perón had undertaken, the American response fifty years after Perón was, in Alan Larson's words, friendly. Moreover, without the imminent threat of a Cuba-like revolution and the backdrop of severe cold war tensions as had been the case in the early 1960s, despite Argentina's troubles in 2001 and 2002 there was no thought in Washington of the implementation of anything equivalent to the Alliance for Progress. As serious as Argentina's problems were, in the face of al-Qaeda, Hezbollah, and other international terrorist menaces from around the world, once it looked like Argentina would avoid a financial crisis such as Asia experienced in 1997–98, U.S. policy was directed toward a thoughtful and unhurried support for Argentina's predicament.

Argentina's economic uncertainty will likely persist indefinitely. There is no prospect for significant economic growth or foreign investment. Though with American cooperation, Argentina has taken steps to end corruption, evidence of poor government spending practices remains. Despite a still bleak economic picture, among the Argentine Congress's 2004 budget line items were $4.5 million in subsidies for the Catholic Church (a 26 percent rise), $4 million for a new congressional office building, and $100 million for the SIDE, beleaguered by accusations of mismanagement and massive corruption. With the waning of U.S. interest in a free trade zone for all the Americas, Argentina under Kirchner has pushed for a stronger Mercosur economic regional free trade zone in the Southern Cone of South America. Where in the 1990s, talk of Mercosur was frequently perceived in Washington as animosity toward the U.S. plan for free trade throughout the hemisphere, U.S. policy has since become generally supportive of regional free trade as a step toward an eventual free trade zone for the hemisphere.[11]

Early in 2005, after almost two years of negotiations, Kirchner scored a major victory by reaching agreement with a majority of Argentina's creditors for a restructured debt repayment scheme. Though lenders will have three options depending on how quickly they want to be paid, in each case they will accept much lower interest payments and as little as a thirty-cent return on each dollar loaned. As of September 2005, there was still no agreement between the IMF and the Argentine government on thirteen billion dollars in outstanding loans. Despite this political triumph for Kirchner, as well as some early success among South American governments in finding ways to work together to renegotiate debt repayments, there is no evidence that Argentina has arrested its long-standing economic slide.[12]

Some observers consider Kirchner part of the "pink revolution" in Latin America—the shift of the political power center to the left in many countries including Bolivia, Chile, Venezuela, and Brazil. In keeping with historical interpretations of U.S.-Argentine relations that have analyzed the twentieth century as one of bilateral conflict, some have predicted a "return" to hostile relations between the two countries as a consequence of Kirchner's leftward shift, his friendly relations with Venezuela's president Hugo Chavez, and his anti-IMF rhetoric. But, just as the history of bilateral conflict has frequently been exaggerated in a larger context of strong bilateral ties, relations between the United States and Argentina are not likely to sour in coming years. Political, economic, military, and cultural relations will continue to grow stronger.

Notes

Abbreviations

AC	Archives Canada
ACLU	American Civil Liberties Union
AGD	Argentine government documents
ARG	Argentina
CDF	Central Decimal File
CERIR	Centro de Estudios Internacionales de Rosario
CIDH	Comisión Interamericana de Derechos Humanos
DEF	Defense
FRUS	Foreign Relations of the United States
GEL	Grupo Editor Latinoamericano
HHPL	Herbert Hoover Presidential Library
LA	Latin America
LAB	Labor
MRE	Ministerio de Relaciones Exteriores, Argentina
NA	National Archives, Washington, D.C.
OEA	Organización de Estados Americanos
OIEA	Organización Internacional de Energía Atómica
PET	Petroleum
POL	Politics
RG	Record Group
SOC	Society
USIS	United States Information Service

Introduction

1. Luis Verdesoto and Gloria Ardaya Salinas, *Entre la presión y el consenso: Escenarios y previsiones para la relación Bolivia–Estados Unidos* (La Paz: ILDIS/UDAPEX, 1993), 74–75.

2. "Documento secreto del Ejército: 'Con la democracia avanza la subversión,'" *El Periodista* 5, no. 225 (13–19 January 1989): 10–11; *XIV Conferencia Bilateral de Inteligencia: Bolivia-Argentina* (Buenos Aires: Ejercito Argentino, 1988).

3. Marisol Saavedra, *La Argentina no alineada: Desde la tercera posición justicialista hasta el menemismo (1973–1991)* (Buenos Aires: Editorial Biblos, 2004), 94–98.

1. Trade, Progress, and Nation Building, 1800–1880

1. Lester D. Langley, *The Americas in the Age of Revolution, 1750–1850* (New Haven: Yale University Press, 1996), 200–201; Natalio R. Botana, *La libertad política y su historia* (Buenos Aires: Editorial Sudamericana, 1991), 67–72.

2. Langley, *Americas in the Age of Revolution*, 4.

3. Langley, *Americas in the Age of Revolution*, 24–25; Sean Wilentz, *Chants Democratic: New York City and the Rise of the American Working Class, 1788–1850* (New York: Oxford University Press, 1984), 63–66; Susan Migden Socolow, *The Merchants of Buenos Aires, 1778–1810* (New York: Cambridge University Press, 1978); Waldo Ansaldi, "Notas sobre la formación de la burguesía argentina, 1780–1880," in Enrique Florescano, coord., *Orígenes y desarrollo de la burguesía en América Latina, 1700–1955* (Mexico City: Editorial Nueva Imagen, 1985), 520–28.

4. Hernán Asdrúbal Silva, "The United States and the River Plate: Interrelations and Influences between the Two Revolutions," in Joseph S. Tulchin, ed., *Hemispheric Perspectives on the United States: Perspectives from the New World Conference* (Westport, Conn.: Greenwood Press, 1978), 22–36; Jacques A. Barbier, "Silver, North American Penetration and the Spanish Imperial Economy, 1760–1800," in Jacques A. Barbier and Allan J. Kuethe, eds., *The North American Role in the Spanish Imperial Economy, 1760–1819* (Manchester: Manchester University Press, 1984), 6–12.

5. Harold F. Peterson, *Argentina and the United States* (Albany: State University of New York Press, 1964), 84, 144.

6. Asdrúbal Silva, "United States and the River Plate," 23–28; Earl C. Tanner, "South American Ports in the Foreign Commerce of Providence, 1800–1803," *Rhode Island History* 16, no. 3 (July 1957): 68; Jerry W. Cooney,

"Oceanic Commerce and Platine Merchants, 1796–1806: The Challenge of War," *Americas* 45, no. 4 (April 1989): 509–10.

7. Hernán Asdrúbal Silva and Marcela V. Tejerina, "De las Georgias del Sur a Canton: Los norteamericanos en la explotación y tráfico de pieles a fines del siglo XVIII y princípios del siglo XIX," *Investigaciones y Ensayos* 41 (1991): 315–27; Eugene W. Ridings, "Foreign Predominance among Overseas Traders in Nineteenth-Century Latin America," *Latin American Research Review* 20, no. 2 (1985): 3–28.

8. Asdrúbal Silva, "United States and the River Plate," 26; Harry Bernstein, *Origins of Inter-American Interest, 1700–1812* (New York: Russell and Russell, 1965), 33–51.

9. Juan Carlos Nicolau, "El comercio ultramar por el puerto de Buenos Aires," *Investigaciones y Ensayos* 44 (1994): 305–6; Peterson, *Argentina and the United States*, 18–20, 40–72.

10. John Herd Thompson and Stephen J. Randall, *Canada and the United States: Ambivalent Allies*, 3rd ed. (Athens: University of Georgia Press, 2002), 11–13.

11. Asdrúbal Silva, "United States and the River Plate," 32; Manuel Belgrano, *Introducción a la despedida de Washington al pueblo de los Estados Unidos* (Buenos Aires: Tipógrafo Dalmazia, 1902), 6; "Address Delivered by Dr. Felipe Espil at the Dedication of the Argentine Pavilion," the Sesquicentennial Exposition, Philadelphia, 30 October 1926, file 27, box 2404, Commercial Division (Com), Argentine Foreign Relations Ministry Archive, Buenos Aires (MRE); John T. Reid, *Spanish American Images of the United States, 1790–1960* (Gainesville: University Presses of Florida, 1977), 15–34; Silvia Fridman, "Los Estados Unidos en el periodismo del Río de la Plata, 1812–1819," in *Estados Unidos y Argentina: Relaciones interculturales* (Buenos Aires: Publicaciones de la Asociación Argentina de Estudios Americanas, 1988), 64–72.

12. Reid, *Spanish American Images*, 24; Walter Licht, *Industrializing America* (Baltimore: Johns Hopkins University Press, 1995), 18–19; Richard D. Brown, *The Strength of a People: The Idea of an Informed Citizenry, 1650–1870* (Chapel Hill: University of North Carolina Press, 1996), 63–68; Langley, *Americas in the Age of Revolution*, 54; John Charles Chasteen, *Heroes on Horseback* (Albuquerque: University of New Mexico Press, 1995), 4–5; M. D. Bordo and C. A. Vegh, "What If Alexander Hamilton Had Been Argentinean? A Comparison of the Early Monetary Experiences of Argentina and the United States," *Journal of Monetary Economics* 49, no. 3 (April 2002): 472–75.

13. Kristine L. Jones, "Indian-Creole Negotiations in the Southern Frontier," in Mark D. Szuchman and Jonathan C. Brown, eds. *Revolution and Restoration: The Rearrangement of Power in Argentina, 1776–1860* (Lincoln: University of Nebraska Press, 1994), 109–10, 116; John Lynch, *Argentine Caudillo* (Wilmington, Del.: SR Books, 2001), 44–49.

14. Joyce Appleby, "Commercial Farming and the 'Agrarian Myth' in the Early Republic," *Journal of American History* 68, no. 4 (March 1982): 848–49.

15. Jeremy Adelman, *Republic of Capital* (Stanford, Calif.: Stanford University Press, 1999); Charles Sellers, *The Market Revolution: Jacksonian America, 1815–1846* (New York: Oxford University Press, 1991), 44–54; Peter Way, *Common Labor: Workers and the Digging of North American Canals, 1780–1860* (Baltimore: Johns Hopkins University Press, 1993), 267; Carlos Mayo, *Terratenientes, soldados y cautivos: La Frontera (1737–1815)* (Mar del Plata: Universidad Nacional de Mar del Plata, 1993), 15–33.

16. Carlos Ibarguren (h.), "La misión diplomática de Manuel Hermenegildo de Aguirre en los Estados Unidos de Norteamerica," *Investigaciones y Ensayos* 30 (Jan.–June 1981): 356–57.

17. Peterson, *Argentina and the United States*, 64–70.

18. Joseph S. Tulchin, *Argentina and the United States: A Conflicted Relationship* (Boston: Twayne, 1990), 7–8; Miguel Angel Scenna, *Argentina-Brasil: Cuatro siglos de rivalidad* (Buenos Aires: Ediciones La Bastilla, 1975), 90–96, 101–4; René Orsi, *James Monroe contra la independencia argentina* (Buenos Aires: A. Peña Lillo Editor, S.A., 1983), 119–21.

19. Clement Eaton, *Henry Clay and the Art of American Politics* (Boston: Little, Brown, 1957), 58–59.

20. Tulchin, *Argentina and the United States*, 10–11; Jorge Mayer, *De Monroe a las Malvinas* (Buenos Aires: Biblioteca de la Académia Nacional de Derecho y Ciencias Sociales de Buenos Aires, 1983), 38; Manuel J. García, minister of foreign relations, to George W. Slacum, U.S. consul general, Buenos Aires, 14 February 1832; No. 70, Statement of Luis Vernet, 9 February 1832; No. 132, Francis Baylies, U.S. chargé d'affaires, Buenos Aires, to Manuel V. Maza, acting minister of foreign relations, 10 July 1832, in Ernesto J. Fitte, ed., *La agresión norteamericana a las islas malvinas* (Buenos Aires: Emecé Editores, 1966), 135–36, 130–31, 229–42.

21. Oscar Abadie-Aicardi and Raúl Abadie-Aicardi, "La política rioplatense entre 1829 y 1843 vista por dos comerciantes," *Nuestra Historia* (Buenos Aires), year 16, no. 31–32 (December 1983): 40–41.

22. Peterson, *Argentina and the United States*, 144; Carlos A. Goñi Demarchi, José Nicolás Scala, and Germán Winox Berraondo, "Los Estados Unidos y la Confederación Argentina: El restablecimiento de sus relaciones diplomáticas," *Nuestra Historia* (Buenos Aires), year 10, no. 20 (1977): 101–11.

23. Samuel Amaral, *The Rise of Capitalism on the Pampas: The Estancias of Buenos Aires, 1785–1870* (New York: Cambridge University Press, 1998), 2–4, 170–71, 261–63; Tulio Halperin Donghi, "La apertura mercantil en el Río de la Plata: Impacto global y desigualdades regionales, 1800–1850," in Reinhard Liehr, ed. *América Latina en la época de Simón Bolívar* (Berlin: Colloquium Verlag, 1989), 131.

24. Horacio Juan Cuccorese, "Proteccionismo y liberalismo en tiempo histórico de la confederación argentina," *Nuestra Historia* (Buenos Aires), year 18, no. 35–36 (December 1990): 267–86.

25. Felix Luna, *Breve historia de los Argentinos* (Buenos Aires: Planeta, 1993), 106, 109, 122.

26. William H. Katra, *The Argentine Generation of 1837* (Madison, N.J.: Fairleigh Dickinson University Press, 1996), 159–61, 168–71, 195–96; Celina Lacay, *Sarmiento y la formación de la ideología de la clase dominante* (Buenos Aires: Editorial Contrapunto, 1986), 129–38; Adelman, *Republic of Capital*, 140.

27. Peterson, *Argentina and the United States*, 153–59; U.S. Congress, House, *Reports of the Commission Appointed Under An Act of Congress Approved July 7, 1884, "To Ascertain and Report upon the Best Modes of Securing More Intimate Relations Between the United States and the Several Countries of Central and South America,"* 49th Cong., 1st sess., Executive Document no. 50 (Washington: 1886), 389–99, 400–401, 429–30, 433–36; Joseph Smith, "The Latin American Trade Commission of 1884–5," *Inter-American Economic Affairs* 24, no. 4 (Spring 1971): 3–24.

28. Sellers, *Market Revolution*, 17–19; Harry L. Watson, *Liberty and Power: The Politics of Jacksonian America* (New York: Hill and Wang, 1990), 27–28.

29. Ezequiel Gallo, *La pampa gringa: La colonización agrícola en Santa Fe (1870–1895)* (Buenos Aires: Editorial Sudamericana, 1983), 287–95.

30. Halperin Donghi, "La apertura mercantil," 133–35.

31. Pilar González Bernaldo, "Social Imagery and Its Political Implications in Rural Conflict: The Uprising of 1828–1829," in Szuchman and Brown, *Revolution and Restoration*, 185.

32. Kristine L. Jones, "Civilization and Barbarism and Sarmiento's Indian Policy," in Joseph T. Criscenti, ed., *Sarmiento and His Argentina* (Boulder, Colo.:

Lynne Rienner, 1993), 35–41; William H. Katra, "Rereading Viajes: Race, Identity, and National Destiny," in Tulio Halperín Donghi, Iván Jaksic, Gwen Kirkpatrick, and Francine Masiello, eds., *Sarmiento: Author of a Nation* (Berkeley: University of California Press, 1994), 76.

33. Roberto Cortes Conde, "Sarmiento and Economic Progress: From *Facundo* to the Presidency," in Tulio Halperín Donghi, Iván Jaksic, Gwen Kirkpatrick, and Francine Masiello, eds., *Sarmiento: Author of a Nation* (Berkeley: University of California Press, 1994), 115–18; Pablo A. Pozzi, "Hostos, el panamericanismo y la sociedad política argentina, 1873–1874," *Cuadernos Americanos* (Mexico City) 4, no. 16 (July–August 1989): 119–22.

34. J. Valerie Fifer, *United States Perceptions of Latin America, 1850–1930: A 'New West' South of Capricorn?* (Manchester: Manchester University Press, 1991), 1–6, 12–14; E. L. Ortiz, "Army and Science in Argentina, 1850–1950," *Boston Studies in the Philosophy of Science* 180 (1996): 153–84.

35. Fifer, *United States Perceptions*, 32–45.

36. Fifer, *United States Perceptions*, 50–60; Vicente Gesualdo, "Primitivos ferrocarriles en América," *Historia* (Buenos Aires) 14, no. 54 (June–Aug. 1994): 43–46.

37. Graciela Silvestri, "La ciudad y el río," in Jorge F. Liernur and Graciela Silvestri, eds., *El umbral de la metrópolis: Transformaciones técnicas y cultura en la modernización de Buenos Aires (1870–1930)* (Buenos Aires: Editorial Sudamericana, 1993), 116.

38. Peterson, *Argentina and the United States*, 159; Thomas F. McGann, *Argentina, the United States, and the Inter-American System, 1880–1914* (Cambridge, Mass.: Harvard University Press, 1957), 93, 110, 123; Mark A. Smith, *The Tariff on Wool* (New York: Macmillan, 1926), 108–14; U.S. Congress, Senate, *Reprint of an Extract from Report No. 13, May 1866 by the United States Revenue Commission on Wool and Manufacturers of Wool*, 61st Cong., 2nd sess., Doc. no. 458 (Washington: Government Printing Office, 1910); U.S. Congress, *Tariff Acts Passed by the Congress of the United States from 1789–1909*, 61st Cong., 2nd sess., H. Doc. no. 671 (Washington: Government Printing Office, 1909), 258–62; H. Doc. no. 93, Hanna to Bayard, 19 November 1887, *Foreign Relations of the United States (FRUS), 1888*, pt. 1, 1–2; Jorge F. Sábato, *La clase dominante en la Argentina moderna* (Buenos Aires: CISEA, 1991), 24–26.

39. Ada Latuca de Chede and María Frutos de Prieto, "La República Argentina en la exposición de Filadelfia," in *Estados Unidos y Argentina: Relaciones interculturales* (Buenos Aires: Publicaiones de la Asociación Argentina de Estudios Americanas, 1988), 263–71.

40. Latuca de Chede and Frutos de Prieto, "La República Argentina en la exposición de Filadelfia," 263–71; Chile, Oficina de Estadística Comercial, *Apuntes Estadísticas sobre la República de Chile* (Valparaiso: Imprenta del Universo de G. Helfmann, 1876); German Burmeister, *Los caballos fósiles de la pampa argentina* (Buenos Aires: Imprenta "La Tribuna," 1875), v–viii; J. S. Ingram, *The Centennial Exposition* (Philadelphia: Hubbard Bros., 1876), 495–98.

2. Pan-Americanism, World War, and the Bolshevik Menace, 1880–1923

1. Jeremy Adelman, *Republic of Capital: Buenos Aires and the Legal Transformation of the Atlantic World* (Stanford, Calif.: Stanford University Press, 1999), 240–46, 283.
2. Drago to García Merou, 29 December 1902; Edward Winslow Ames, U.S. chargé d'affaires in Buenos Aires, to John Hay, secretary of state, 5 May 1903, *FRUS, 1903*, 1–6. In part, the significance of Drago's statement rests in its timing; issued on the eve of three decades of heated American military activity in the Caribbean basin, Drago's suggestions were bound for American rejection. Drago had calculated poorly, but understandably. He had expected U.S. backing for his invocation of Monroe but failed to see U.S. ambitions in the use of military force for filibuster operations. At the same time, those who later ascribed to Drago an anti-interventionist stand focused on the United States were mistaken. Drago meant no criticism of U.S. authority in the Caribbean basin. Moreover, the Drago Doctrine certainly was not taken as a criticism in Washington; a short time later the United States nominated Drago to a term on the International Court of Justice.
3. Peter H. Smith, *Politics and Beef in Argentina: Patterns of Conflict and Change* (New York: Columbia University Press, 1969), 58–60; Rodolfo Puiggrós, *Libre empresa o nacionalización en la industria de la carne* (Buenos Aires: Editorial Argumentos, 1957), 15–31; Roger Gravil, *The Anglo-Argentine Connection* (Boulder, Colo.: Westview Press, 1985), 111–43.
4. A. G. Snyder, U.S. consul general, Buenos Aires, "Details from the Consul-General"; T. B. Van Horne, U.S. consul general, Rosario, "Rosario," *Commercial Relations of the United States, 1906*, 159–63, 163–65; "Ocean Freight Rates and Argentine Trade," *Monthly Consular Reports*, no. 224 (May 1899), 141–43.

5. Lincoln Hutchinson, *Report on Trade Conditions in Argentina, Paraguay, and Uruguay* (Washington: Government Printing Office, 1906), 41; Michael J. Hogan, "Corporatism," *Journal of American History* 77, no. 1 (June 1990): 154.

6. Alicia Vidaurreta, "Vicente Gregorio Quesada," *Investigaciones y Ensayos* 41 (1991): 483–87; Rodolfo S. Follari, "Aspectos de la política de los Estados Unidos en la correspondencia diplomática de Vicente G. Quesada," *Nuestra Historia* (Buenos Aires) 41–42, year 21 (December 1994): 342, 345.

7. "Instrucciones a que deberar ajustarse en el desempeo de su misión los Plenipotenciarios Drs. Vicente G. Quesada, Don Manuel Quintana y Don Roque Saenz Peña nombrados para representar a la República Argentina en el Congreso Internacional Americano que se reunir en Washington el 2 de Octubre del año corriente de 1889," 24 July 1889; Manuel Quintana and Saenz Peña to Estanislao Zeballos, 20 January 1890, file 9/888, box 1, First Pan-American Conference, Pol, MRE; Steven C. Topik, *Trade and Gunboats: The United States and Brazil in the Age of Empire* (Stanford, Calif.: Stanford University Press, 1997), 44–57; Jack Child, "The 1889–1890 Washington Conference through Cuban Eyes: José Martí and the First International American Conference," *Inter-American Review of Bibliography* 20, no. 2 (1989): 443–56.

8. No. 93, Portela to Foreign Minister, 21 November 1905, file 1, box 1, Third Pan-American Conference, Pol, MRE; Antonio Bermejo, Lorenzo Anadon, and Martín García Merou, *Informe que la delegación de la República Argentina presenta a la Segunda Conferencia Pan-Americana* (Mexico City: Oficina Impresora de Estampillas, Palacio Nacional, 1902); Joaquim Nabuco, "El acercamiento de las dos Américas," September 1908, Manuscripts, Subject Files, OAS Archive, Columbus Memorial Library, Washington (OAS); República Argentina, *Delegación a la Tercera Conferencia Interamericana, Memoria de la Delegación de la República Argentina* (Buenos Aires: Imprenta Nacional, 1906), 17–21.

9. "Instrucciones a los delegados que concurieron a la tercera conferencia Panamericana," July 1906, box 2, Fifth Pan-American Conference, Pol, MRE.

10. José C. Moya, *Cousins and Strangers: Spanish Immigrants in Buenos Aires, 1850–1930* (Berkeley: University of California Press, 1998), 347–49; Hugo Biagini, *Intelectuales y políticos españoles a comienzos de la inmigración masiva* (Buenos Aires: Centro Editor de América Latina, 1995), 57, 71.

11. "Cuba and the United States," *Buenos Aires Herald*, 6 April 1898; "The Triumph of Passion," *Buenos Aires Herald*, 15 April 1898; Vicente G. Quesada, "El arbitraje hispanoamericano," *La Enciclopedia Jurídica*, año 1, no. 22 (1 December 1900): 257.

12. Louis A. Pérez Jr., "Politics, Peasants, and People of Color: The 1912 Race War in Cuba Reconsidered," *Hispanic American Historical Review* 56 (August 1986): 509–39; Aline Helg, "Race in Argentina and Cuba, 1880–1930," in Richard Graham, ed., *The Idea of Race in Latin America, 1870–1940* (Austin: University of Texas Press, 1990), 37–69; Eduardo A. Zimmermann, "Racial Ideas and Social Reform: Argentina, 1890–1916," *Hispanic American Historical Review* 72 (February 1992): 23–46.

13. Reyes to Argentine Foreign Minister, 12 March 1912; file 5, box 4, United States, Pol, MRE.

14. Carlos A. Becú, *El "A.B.C." y su concepto político y jurídico* (Buenos Aires: Librería "La Facultad" de Juan Roldán, 1915), 13, 19.

15. Federico M. Moreno Quintana, *La diplomácia de Yrigoyen* (La Plata: Editorial Inca, 1928), 395–458.

16. Henry Robertson, "Bankruptcy Laws of Argentina as Affecting American Trade," 19 August 1916, 835.0445; No. 12, Boaz M. Long, American minister to El Salvador, to Bryan, 11 December 1914, 810.51/30; McAdoo to Bryan, 11 May 1915, 810.51/233, RG 59, NA; "Commercial Dishonesty, Inefficient Bankruptcy Procedure," *Buenos Aires Herald*, 7 October 1915.

17. Mark T. Gilderhus, *Pan American Visions: Woodrow Wilson in the Western Hemisphere, 1913–1921* (Tucson: University of Arizona Press, 1986), 60–61; Bryan to American Embassy, Buenos Aires, 12 March 1915, 810.51/53; Lansing to the Diplomatic Officers of the United States of America in Latin America, 10 July 1915, 810.51/309b, RG 59, NA; William G. McAdoo, *Pan American Financial Conference* (Washington: Government Printing Office, 1915).

18. Charles H. Sherrill, *Modernizing the Monroe Doctrine* (Boston: Houghton Mifflin, 1916), 7–9.

19. Marta E. Savigliano, *Tango and the Political Economy of Passion* (Boulder, Colo.: Westview Press, 1995), 128–34; Jorge Novati and Inés Cuello, "Aspectos histórico-musicales," in *Antología del tango rioplatense: Desde sus comiensos hasta 1920* (Buenos Aires: Instituto Nacional de Musicología 'Carlos Vega', 1980), 37.

20. Charles Lyon Chandler, "Study of the Exports of the United States to the Argentine Republic, during the Fiscal Year Ended June 30, 1910," 30 June 1910, 635.11/-, RG 59, NA; David Sheinin, *Searching for Authority: Pan Americanism, Diplomacy and Politics in United States–Argentine Relations, 1910–1930* (New Orleans: University Press of the South, 1998), chapter 1; Tulchin, *Argentina and the United States.*

21. Varun Sahni, "Not Quite British: A Study of External Influences on the Argentine Navy," *Journal of Latin American Studies* 25, pt. 3 (October 1993): 501.

22. "Foreign Shipbuilding Programs," 6 November 1909, 09–690, A-2-C; D. McD. LeBreton, ensign, U.S. Navy, and H. E. Kummel, ensign, U.S. Navy, USS *Georgia*, to Commander-in-Chief, United States Atlantic Fleet, 20 January 1908, 08–187, 0-4-a; Lieutenant Commander Rodney McLean, "Intelligence Report—The Brazilian Navy," 20 February 1908, 08–187, 0-4-a, RG 38, NA; Roberto Etchepareborda, "Los armamentos navales de 1908," *Investigaciones y ensayos* 13 (July–December 1972): 179–209; "Biggest Battleship," *Buenos Aires Standard*, 7 July 1914.

23. Etchepareborda, "Los armamentos navales de 1908," 179–209; Clive Trebilcock, *The Vickers Brothers: Armaments and Enterprise, 1854–1914* (London: Europa Publications Limited, 1977), 119–20; No. 49, A. C. Niblack, commander, U.S. Naval Attaché, in Buenos Aires, to Office of Naval Intelligence, 27 April 1911, 09–443, 0-4-a, RG 38, NA; Townley, "Argentine Republic, Annual Report, 1910," 28 February 1911, 11122, 1045, FO 371, Public Record Office, London (PRO).

24. Spencer Eddy to Root, 17 December 1908, case 1070, no. 23, vol. 139; Department of State to Whitelaw Reid, 11 February 1909, case 1070, nos. 16, 38, 39, vol. 139; Philander Knox, U.S. secretary of state, to U.S. Legation, Buenos Aires, 7 December 1909, case 1070, no. 125, vol. 140, RG 59, NA; Charles S. Wilson, U.S. chargé d'affaires, Buenos Aires, to De la Plaza, 11 June 1909, "Propuesta de Gobierno de Estados Unidos para que se le encargue las construcciones navales argentinas," file 14, United States, Pol, MRE; Peterson, *Argentina and the United States*, 294.

25. Knox to Secretary of the Navy, 14 July 1909, 4793:38:7, RG 80, NA; Wilson to de la Plaza, 18 June 1909; "Propuesta del Gobierno de los Estados Unidos para que se encargue las construcciones navales argentinas," n.d., file 14, United States, Pol, MRE.

26. Charles S. Wilson to Argentine Minister of Foreign Relations, 11 June 1909; De la Plaza to Charles S. Wilson, 15 June 1909, "Propuesta de Gobierno de Estados Unidos para que se le encargue las construcciones navales argentinas," file 14, United States, Pol, MRE.

27. Taft to President of Argentina, 7 April 1909, case 18551, no. 2, vol. 1039; Sherrill to Knox, 8 July 1909, case 1070, no. 72, vol. 139; Knox to Taft, 30 March 1911, 835.34/270, RG 59, NA; Peterson, *Argentina and the United*

States, 295; De la Plaza to Argentine Minister, Washington, 21 January 1910; "Propuesta del gobierno de los Estados Unidos para que se le encargue las construcciones navales argentinas," n.d., file 14, Pol, MRE.

28. Roberto Etcheparoborda, "Estanislao S. Zeballos y los debates secretos de 1914 en la Cámara de Diputados," *Historia* (Buenos Aires) 1, no. 3 (September–November 1981): 36.

29. "Address of President William Howard Taft at the Banquet Given in his honor by the American Club, Pittsburgh," 2 May 1910, *Congressional Record,* 12 July 1910, 9777.

30. "The Achievements of Dollar Diplomacy," *Saturday Evening Post,* 9 March 1912.

31. Paul V. N. Henderson, "Woodrow Wilson, Victoriano Huerta, and the Recognition Issue in Mexico," *Americas* 41, no. 2 (October 1984): 151–76.

32. Alan Knight, *The Mexican Revolution* (Cambridge: Cambridge University Press, 1986), 2:164–65; Memorandum, American Legation in Buenos Aires, 16 April 1914, file 13, box 5, Niagara Falls Conference, Mexico, Pol, MRE; "Villa Backs Up U.S.," *Washington Post,* 27 April 1914.

33. Etcheparoborda, "Estanislao S. Zeballos y los debates," 25–44.

34. "No Enthusiasm over Mediation," *Washington Star,* 26 April 1914; "A Tender of Good Offices," *New York Times,* 26 April 1914; "Argentina, Brazil and Chili Offer Their Good Offices to Prevent War—President Gives Qualified Acceptance to the Proposal," *New York Press,* 26 April 1914.

35. No. 205, Spring-Rice to Grey, 1 June 1914, 24419, 2029, FO 371, PRO; Romulo S. Naón, "Apuntes sobre el desarrollo de las gestiones," 26 May 1914, file 7, box 3, Niagara Falls Conference, Mexico, Pol, MRE.

36. U.S. Congress, Senate, Committee on Foreign Relations, *Investigation of Mexican Affairs,* 66th Cong., 2nd sess., 2 vols., Testimony of William F. Buckley, 6 December 1919 (Washington, 1921), 794–95; Special Commissioners to Secretary of State, 21 May 1914, 812.00/12631, RG 59, NA.

37. Sheinin, *Searching for Authority,* chapter 4.

38. No. 344, Lorillard to Secretary of State, 1 September 1914, 835.50/6, RG 59, NA.

39. "Hon. Frederick J. Stimson of Dedham, United States Ambassador to Argentina, Speaks before the Dedham Board of Trade," *Dedham Transcript,* 21 October 1916.

40. U.S. Senate, *The Rights of Neutrals: Address by Rómulo S. Naón,* 63rd Cong., 3rd sess., document 801 (Washington: 1915).

41. No. 264, Stimson to Secretary of State, 15 July 1916, 711.35/24, RG 59, NA.

42. W. Henry Robertson, "Important Economic Changes in Argentina during the War," 13 June 1918, 10670–45, RG 165; "Treasury Department Memorandum," 635.119/77, 28 December 1917; No. 1091, Robertson to Secretary of State, 22 June 1918, 611.356/31, RG 59, NA.

43. Lansing to American missions in Central and South America, except Argentina, Mexico, Panama, Cuba, Brazil, and Santo Domingo, 25 May 1917, 763.72110/608, RG 59, NA; Peterson, *Argentina and the United States*, 333–34; Regelio García Lupo, *La Argentina en la selva mundial* (Buenos Aires: Ediciones Corregidor, 1973), 74.

44. "Relations between United States and Other Countries Regarding Important Materials," n.d., Allied Maritime Transport Council, 084.08 materials, Division of Planning and Statistics, Records Relating to Planning and Statistical Work; "Report on Quebracho," 1918, Statistical Division, American Shipping Mission, London, 337.7 report, entry 36, RG 32, NA.

45. Naón to WTB, 23 July 1918, 1724149; Naón to WTB, 24 July 1918, 1731524; Naón to WTB, 27 July 1918, 1724175; Naón to WTB, 29 July 1918, 1736999; Octavio M. Figueroa to M. M. Harper, WTB, 19 July 1918, 1724242, Records of the Bureau of Exports, RG 182, NA.

46. Letcher to Lay, 6 July 1917, 600.359/19, RG 59, NA.

47. Hoover to Lansing, 27 August 1917, file 4156, box 91, RG 32, NA; Memorandum from Hoover to House, 27 October 1917, House Papers, Sterling Library.

48. Hurley to Hoover, 27 August 1917, file 4156, RG 32, NA; Department of Commerce, "The Economic Position of Argentina during the War"; Lansing to American Embassy, London, 23 November 1917, entry 11, RG 182, NA; "Possible matters concerning Latin-America which may be brought up in the coming conference of the associated Governments and later at the Peace Conference," 701.11/380–1/2, RG 59, NA; Hurley to Newton D. Baker, U.S. secretary of war, 17 October 1917, House Papers, Sterling Library.

49. Warren D. Robbins, "Quarterly Report No. 1," 26 August 1918, 835.00/155, RG 59, NA.

50. Stabler, "Memorandum," Division of Latin-American Affairs, 17 April 1918, 635.119/459; Stimson to Lansing, 8 May 1918, 701.3511/139; Barrett, "Appointment of Argentine Financial Commissioner to the United States," 22 May 1918, 701.3511/149, RG 59, NA.

51. Sheinin, *Searching for Authority*, chapter 5.

52. "Enemy Activities: Partial Resume of Names of German Agents," 29 May 1918, WX-7, RG 45, NA; No. 1120, "Report on German Propaganda in Argentina: Reported intensification," 22 April 1918, 10987-200, RG 165, NA;

Juan Ricardo Couyoumdjian, *Chile y Gran Bretaña durante la primera guerra mundial y la postguerra, 1914–1921* (Santiago, Chile: Editorial Andres Bello, 1986), 209–26.

53. No. 1451, "Americans and Germans in Argentina—Number of, property values, etc.," 8 November 1918, 2048–86; No. 1479, "Americans and Germans in Argentina—Number of, Property Values,, etc.," 26 November 1918, 2048–98, RG 165, NA.

54. No. 863, "Comodoro Rivadavia Oilfields; Commerce, Enemy Influence," 13 September 1918, 2896E, H-3-d, RG 165, NA; Ronald C. Newton, *German Buenos Aires, 1900–1933* (Austin: University of Texas Press, 1977), 32–51; Pedro de Córdoba, *Nuestra Guerra: La coalición contra la Argentina* (Buenos Aries: Publicaciones "La Gaceta de España," 1917), 3.

55. No. 1110, "Future Enemy Activity in the Argentine," 23 January 1919, 10987–462:1, RG 165, NA.

56. No. 115433, "Special Report on Effect of Peace Prospects on the Market of Argentina," U.S. Postal Censorship, 10670–55:1; No. 124951, "Special Report on Argentine—Expansion of Trade in Argentina," New York Office of Postal Censorship, 17 December 1918, 10987–427, RG 165, NA; Joseph Smith, *Unequal Giants: Diplomatic Relations between the United States and Brazil* (Pittsburgh: University of Pittsburgh Press, 1991), 120–21.

57. Adee to Benson, 25 March 1920, 618–2, RG 32, NA; Bruce Nelson,s *Workers on the Waterfront: Seamen, Longshoremen, and Unionism in the 1930s* (Urbana: University of Illinois Press, 1988), 7–34.

58. No. 1926, "Lopez, José," 11 February 1920, 10987–627:6, RG 165, NA.

59. No. 1518, "Anarchists in Argentina," 11 December 1918, 10987–461:1; No. 1684, "Copies of Anarchist Newspaper—Bandera Roja," 9 April 1919, 10987–476:7, RG 165, NA.

60. No. 1547, "Anarchistic Meetings in Buenos Aires, and Utterances," 10 January 1919, 10987–477:1, RG 165, NA.

61. "Extracts from *La Razón* newspaper published in Buenos Aires," 30 October 1917, 6370–565:2, RG 165, NA.

62. No. 134, "The Anarchistic-Maximalist Outbreak of January 8 to 12, 1919," 10987–461:23, RG 165, NA.

63. "Conditions in Argentine," 4 June 1917, WX-7, RG 45, NA; Richard J. Walter, *The Province of Buenos Aires and Argentine Politics, 1912–1943* (Cambridge: Cambridge University Press, 1985), 43–45.

64. "Lingering Agony of Bolshevism," *The Standard*, 14 January 1919; "Notes on News," *Review of the River Plate*, 20 January 1919.

65. "Memorandum," British Embassy in Washington, 7 March 1919; Polk to American Embassy, Buenos Aires, 8 March 1919, 835.5045/99, RG 59, NA.

66. No. 1358, Robertson to Secretary of State, 835.5045/112; W. F. Taylor, assistant director of operations, United States Shipping Board, 29 March 1919, 835.5045/119; Robertson to Secretary of State, 12 May 1919, 835.5045/144, RG 59, NA.

67. Sergio González Miranda, Carlos Maldonado Prieto, and Sandra McGee Deutsch, "Las Ligas Patrióticas: Un caso de nacionalismo, xenofobia y lucha social en Chile," *Canadian Review of Studies in Nationalism* 21, no. 1–2 (1994): 57–69.

68. No. 1460, Robertson to Secretary of State, 23 May 1919, 10987–537:9, RG 165, NA.

69. No. 1673, "General Luis J. Dellepiane (General de Division) Argentine Army," 2 April 1919, 10987–461:22, RG 165, NA.

70. Harold Edwin Peters, *The Foreign Debt of the Argentine Republic* (Baltimore: Johns Hopkins University Press, 1934), 144–46; Edward F. Feely, "Translation of a proposed law introduced in the Argentine Senate by Senator Llanos on July 19th, to regulate the establishment and operation of foreign banks in the Argentine," 21 July 1921, box 2, 814, RG 43, NA; "Argentine Credit Is Based on Production," *Wall Street Journal*, 28 December 1921.

71. Sherwood Harvey, U.S. vice consul, Montevideo, "Second Pan American Financial Conference," 8 September 1920, 810.51a/278, RG 59, NA.

72. Argentine Foreign Relations Minister, "Instrucciones a Delegados," n.d., Fifth Pan-American Conference, 1923, file 12, box 4, Fifth Pan-American Conference, Pol, MRE; Argentine Foreign Relations Ministry, "Instrucciones Relativas al Derecho Internacional Privado," file 4, box 2, Fifth Pan-American Conference, Pol, MRE.

73. "Instrucciones: Quinta Conferencia Internacional Americana," box 23, Fifth Pan-American Conference, MRE; "Motions for the Program of the Fifth Pan American Conference," 710.E1a/14, RG 59, NA.

74. "Memorandum for use of American Delegation to Fifth International Conference of American States, to be held at Santiago, Chile, March 25, 1923," 25 January 1923, 710.E1a/52, RG 59, NA; Kenneth J. Grieb, "The United States and the Fifth Pan American Conference," *Inter-American Review of Bibliography* 20, no. 2 (April–June 1970): 157–68; Edwin C. Wilson, Division of Latin American Affairs, to Francis White, acting chief, Division of Latin American Affairs, 10 October 1922, 710.E1a/15, RG 59, NA; Klein to Hoover, 13 July

1922, box 293, Hoover Papers (Commerce), Herbert Hoover Presidential Library, West Branch, Iowa (HHPL).

75. "El programa de la conferencia de Santiago," *La Prensa*, 8 November 1922.

76. Argentine Delegation, Santiago Conference, "Informe presentado al S.E. el Senor Ministro de Relaciones Exteriores por la Delegación Argentina," annex to file 10, box 2, Fifth Pan-American Conference, Pol, MRE.

77. Enrique Gil, *Evolución del panamericanismo* (Buenos Aires: Librería y Casa Editora de Jesus Menendez, 1933), 98; No. 101, Le Breton to Pueyrredón, 11 May 1922; No. 129, Espil to Pueyrredón, 17 June 1922; No. 132, Espil to Pueyrredón, 17 June 1922, file 2, box 19, Fifth Pan-American Conference, Pol, MRE.

3. Sanitary Embargo, Cultural Connections, and Wartime Neutrality, 1924–1946

1. Tulchin, *Argentina and the United States*, 49; Sheinin, *Searching for Authority*, chapter 7.

2. No. 142, Bliss to Secretary of State, 817.00/5350; No. 333–G, Cable to Secretary of State, 29 June 1927, 835.00/399, RG 59, NA.

3. Kellogg to Delegates of the United States of America to the Sixth International Conference of American States, Havana, Cuba, 5 January 1928, box 16, entry 145, RG 43, NA.

4. For example, "La Conférence Panaméricaine s'est terminé hier sur l'équivoque," *Le Matin* (Paris), 21 February 1928; "Le nouvel empire," *L'Information* (Paris), 21 February 1928; "O Brasil e os Estados Unidos na conferencia de Havana," *O Jornal* (Rio de Janeiro), 25 February 1928.

5. No. 15, Olascoaga to Minister of Foreign Relations, 16 February 1928, file 5, Sixth Pan-American Conference, Pol, MRE.

6. Peterson, *Argentina and the United States*, 347.

7. Peterson, *Argentina and the United States*, 384–85; José Joaquín Caicedo Castilla, *El panamericanismo* (Buenos Aires: R. Depalma, 1961), 130–32.

8. White to Secretary of State, 15 September 1930, Francis White Papers, HHPL; Division of Latin American Affairs, Department of State, "Review of Questions of Major Interest in the Relations of the United States with the Latin American Countries, 1929–1933," n.d., Latin American Affairs, Department of State, HHPL; No. 1509, Lindsay to Henderson, 26 September 1930, A6474,

14195, FO 371, PRO; C. A. Mayo, O. R. Andino, and F. García Molina, *La diplomacia del petróleo (1916–1930)* (Buenos Aires: Centro Editor de América Latina, 1976), 154–58.

9. Oscar E. Vázquez Lucio, *Historia del humor gráfico y escrito en la Argentina, 1801–1939* (Buenos Aires: Editorial Universitaria de Buenos Aires, 1985), 1:358–407; Manuel Kantor, *De Munich a Nuremberg* (Buenos Aires: Standard, 1946), 58.

10. Carl E. Solberg, *Oil and Nationalism in Argentina: A History* (Stanford, Calif.: Stanford University Press, 1979), 61–63; Emily S. Rosenberg, *Financial Missionaries to the World* (Cambridge, Mass.: Harvard University Press, 1999), 99.

11. Peter H. Smith, *Politics and Beef in Argentina: Patterns of Conflict and Change* (New York: Columbia University Press, 1969), 57–72.

12. Great Britain, Ministry of Agriculture and Fisheries (MAF), *Report of Proceedings under the Diseases of Animals Acts for the Year 1937* (London: MAF, 1938), 18–19.

13. "La defensa de la producción nacional," *La Nación*, 2 February 1929; "A Plea for Common Sense," *Buenos Aires Herald*, 1 February 1929; No. 354, Robert Woods Bliss, U.S. ambassador, Buenos Aires, to Secretary of State, 7 August 1928, 611.35 Corn/1; "Investigation by Tariff Commission into Cost of Production of Corn and Linseed in Argentina and Adhesion by Argentina to Multilateral Treaty," Memorandum of Conversation between Manuel Malbrán and Frank B. Kellogg, 4 October 1928, RG 59, NA.

14. George S. Messersmith, U.S. consul general, Buenos Aires, "The British Campaign against American Trade and Capital in the Argentine," 29 May 1929, 635.4117/37, RG 59, NA.

15. See Carlos Pueyrredón, "The Meat Problem: It Is to the Advantage of the United States to Look After the Prosperity of the Argentine Market" (New York, 1929); Honório Pueyrredón, *Problemas de la actualidad económica* (Buenos Aires: Impresa Ferrari Hermanos, 1930), 27.

16. Fladness to Minister of Agriculture, 15 June 1927; Fladness to Chief of BAI, 25 July 1927, 528.5-Argentina, RG 17, NA; "The Aftosa Situation," *Review of the River Plate*, 30 December 1927; Frood to Jackson, 7 October 1929, 208, MAF35, PRO; Fladness to Chief of BAI, 15 June 1927; Fladness to Chief of BAI, 30 June 1927, 528.5-Argentina, RG 17, NA.

17. Peter Smith, "Los Radicales argentinos y la defensa de los intereses ganaderos," *Desarrollo Económico* 7 (April–June, 1967): 795–829.

18. Susana M. Flores, *Construcción del espacio urbano* (Buenos Aires: Centro Editor de América Latina, 1993), 18; Adrián Gorelik, *La grilla y el parque: Espacio público y cultura urbana en Buenos Aires, 1887–1936* (Quilmes: Universidad Nacional de Quilmes, 1998), 64, 322–31.

19. Antonio Elio Brailovsky, *Memoria verde: Historia ecológica de la Argentina* (Buenos Aires: Editorial Sudamericana, 1991), 196; S. T. Davis, "Forestry in the Argentine Republic," 5 February 1908, box 92, Research Compilation Files, 1897–1935, Forest Research Divisions, Department of Agriculture, RG 95, NA; David Sheinin, "Its Most Destructive Agents: Pan American Environmentalism in the Early Twentieth Century," in David Sheinin, ed., *Beyond the Ideal: Pan Americanism in Inter-American Affairs* (Westport, Conn.: Greenwood, 2000), 115–32.

20. John King, "The Social and Cultural Context," in John King and Nissa Torrents, eds., *The Garden of the Forking Paths: Argentine Cinema* (London: British Film Institute, 1988), 6.

21. Octavio Getino, *Cine argentino: Entre lo posible y lo deseable* (Buenos Aires: Ediciones Ciccus, 1998), 28.

22. Simon Collier, "Carlos Gardel and the Cinema," in John King and Nissa Torrents, eds., *The Garden of Forking Paths: Argentine Cinema* (London: British Film Institute, 1988), 15–18.

23. Irene Rostagno, *Searching for Recognition: The Promotion of Latin American Literature in the United States* (Westport, Conn.: Greenwood, 1997), 1–2; Rosalie Sitman, *Victoria Ocampo y Sur entre Europa y América* (Buenos Aires: Lumiere, 2005).

24. Ernesto Montenegro, "Virgin Spain," *Literary Review of the New York Evening Post*, 20 March 1962.

25. Rostagno, *Searching for Recognition*, 11; Juan José Sebreli, *Martínez Estrada: Una rebelión inútil* (Buenos Aires: Editorial Palestra, 1960); Alan Trachtenberg, ed., *Memoirs of Waldo Frank* (Amherst: University of Massachusetts Press, 1973), 163–65.

26. Waldo Frank, *Tales from the Argentine* (New York: Farrar & Rinehart, 1930), xv.

27. Waldo Frank, introduction to Ricardo Guiraldes, *Don Segundo Sombra: Shadows in the Pampas* (New York: Farrar & Rhinehart, 1935), ix–x.

28. Michael A. Ogorzaly, *Waldo Frank: Prophet of Hispanic Regeneration* (London: Associated University Presses, 1994), 116–18.

29. Ricardo Fernández Borchardt, *Waldo Frank: Un puente entre las dos Américas* (Madrid: Universidade da Coruña, 1997), 138–41.

30. Waldo Frank, "Argentina—Unwilling Enemy," *Collier's*, 26 September 1942, 67–68.

31. Waldo Frank, *South American Journey* (New York: Duell, Sloan and Pearce, 1943).

32. Tulchin, *Argentina and the United States*, 52.

33. Luna, *Breve Historia* (Buenos Aires: Planeta, 1993), 195–97; Mario Rapoport, *Gran Bretaña, Estados Unidos y las clases dirigentes argentinas, 1940–1945* (Buenos Aires: Editorial Belgrano, 1980), 31.

34. Frank S. Boice, president, Arizona Cattle Growers' Association, to Carl Hayden, U.S. Senate, 2 January 1937, 711.359 Sanitary/246, RG 59, NA; "La convención sanitaria con los Estados Unidos," *La Nación*, 20 December 1936; "El temor de Mr. Carey," *Noticias Gráficas*, 12 December 1936.

35. Andrés Cisneros and Carlos Escudé, *Historia general de las relaciones exteriores de la República Argentina* (Buenos Aires: Nuevohacer, 1998–2003), pt. 2, 9:31; Peterson, *Argentina and the United States*, 388–89.

36. Peterson, *Argentina and the United States*, 391–92; No. 1425, Alexander W. Wedell to Secretary of State, 11 December 1936, 811.001-Roosevelt Visit, 285, RG 59, NA.

37. Peterson, *Argentina and the United States*, 392–93.

38. Tulchin, *Argentina and the United States*, 64.

39. No. 122, Armour to Cantilo, 28 December 1939, 611.3531/1445; No. 379, Armour to Secretary of State, 29 December 1939, 611.3531/1446; No. 3, Armour to Secretary of State, 2 January 1940, 611.3531/1441; No. 1, Hull to American Embassy, Buenos Aires, 2 January 1940, 611.3531/1441, RG 59, NA; "Expónese hasta que extremo habría sido desventajoso al país el pacto con la unión," *La Nación*, 14 January 1940.

40. No. 437, Armour to Secretary of State, 29 January 1940, 611.3531/1496, RG 59, NA; Felix Luna, *Ortiz: Reportaje a la Argentina opulenta* (Buenos Aires: Editorial Sudamericana, 1978), 312.

41. "American Consulate General's Statement of Argentine Exports to the United States," 5 April 1940, 611.35/28; "Statement by the United States Embassy Regarding Argentine Exports to the United States," 4 December 1940, 611.35/35, RG 59, NA.

42. No. 229, Armour to Secretary of State, 17 June 1940, 611.3531/1533, RG 59, NA.

43. No. 231, Armour to Secretary of State, 24 June 1940, 611.3531/1533, RG 59, NA.

44. Susana Pereira, *En tiempos de la república agropecuaria (1930–1943)* (Buenos Aires: Centro Editor de América Latina, 1983), 118–20; Tulchin, *Argentina*

and the United States, 67; J. Edgar Hoover, director, Federal Bureau of Investigation, to Adolf A. Berle, Jr., assistant secretary of state, 4 September 1943, 835.00B/160, RG 59, NA; No. 226, Espil to Cantilo, 27 April 1940; Ministry of Foreign Relations, Memorandum, 6 May 1940; No. 190, Cantilo to Espil, 7 May 1940, file 185, European War, MRE.

45. Ministerio de Marina, "Cuestionario para el examen de la situación," n.d. [1941], file 192, European War, MRE.

46. Ministerio de Marina, "Defensa Continental Americana," 2 December 1941, file 192, European War, MRE.

47. Guido Di Tella and Manuel Zymelman, *Las etapas del desarrollo económico argentino* (Buenos Aires: EUDEBA, 1967), 472–85.

48. Division of the American Republics, Department of State, "The Pinedo Plan to Stimulate the Exports of New Articles from Argentina," 29 November 1940, 611.3515/6, RG 59, NA; Rapoport, *Clases dirigentes argentinas,* 77–80; Roberto Azaretto, *Federico Pinedo: Político y economista* (Buenos Aires: Emecé, 1998), 154–56.

49. Department of State, Memorandum, "Situation with Regard to Trade Agreement Negotiations," 23 May 1939, Lot Files, RG 59, NA; Tulchin, *Argentina and the United States,* 69–72; "Toughest Nut," *Baltimore Evening Sun,* 8 January 1940.

50. No. 450, Vicente Olivera, Argentine ambassador to Germany, to Argentine Foreign Minister, 15 May 1940; No. 249, Cantilo to Argentine Embassy, Berlin, 15 May 1940; "Memorandum para la Dirección de Asuntos Políticos," 24 January 1942, file 186, European War, MRE.

51. Tulchin, *Argentina and the United States,* 73; Leonardo Senkman, "La Argentina neutral de 1940 ante los refugiados españoles y judíos," *Ciclos* 5, no. 9 (1997): 53–76.

52. Isidoro Ruiz Moreno, "Aide Memoire," file 192, European War, MRE; Division of the American Republics, Department of State, "Press Reception of the Argentine Trade Promotion Corporation," 9 August 1941, 611.3515/21, RG 59, NA.

53. Ronald C. Newton, *The "Nazi Menace" in Argentina, 1931–1947* (Stanford, Calif.: Stanford University Press, 1992), xiv; "Entrevista del Embajador de Alemania con el Señor Presidente de la Nación," 31 May 1940, file 186, European War, MRE. Among those works that suggest a strong Nazi influence on Argentine life and politics are Pablo J. Reid, Patricia A. Toni, and Rafael H. Bolasell, *La infiltración nazi en la Patagonia* (Buenos Aires: Centro Editor

de América Latina, 1992); Uki Goñi, *Perón y los Alemanes: La verdad sobre el espionaje nazi y los fugitivos del Reich* (Buenos Aires: Sudamericana, 1999); Ignacio Klich, "La contratación de nazis y colaboracionistas por la Fuerza Aérea Argentina," *Ciclos* 10, no. 19 (2000): 177–216.

54. Department of State, Memorandum, 27 June 1941; No. 2651, S. Pinkney Tuck, U.S. chargé d'affaires, Argentina, to Secretary of State, 27 June 1941, 711.35/133, RG 59, NA.

55. Randall B. Woods, *The Roosevelt Foreign-Policy Establishment and the "Good Neighbor": The United States and Argentina, 1941–1945* (Lawrence: Regents Press of Kansas, 1979), 72–73; Ministerio de Marina, "Cooperación Militar con Estados Unidos," 2 December 1941, file 192, European War, MRE.

56. Woods, *Roosevelt Foreign-Policy Establishment*, 21–42; Cisneros and Escudé, *Historia general*, pt. 2, 10:290; Peterson, *Argentina and the United States*, 410–12; Rapoport, *Clases dirigentes argentinas*, 104–7; Tulio Halperín Donghi, *Argentina en el callejón* (Buenos Aires: Ariel, 1995), 130–31.

57. Tulchin, *Argentina and the United States*, 84.

58. Cisneros and Escudé, *Historia general*, pt. 2, 9:75–77; Tulchin, *Argentina and the United States*, 87; Department of External Affairs (Canada), "Memorandum for the Prime Minister re: Mr. Hull's charges against Argentine good faith," 4 October 1943, 3134–40C, vol. 2954, RG 25, AC.

59. García Lupo, *La Argentina en la selva mundial*, 101; Daniel Lewis, "Internal and External Convergence: The Collapse of Argentine Grain Farming," in David Rock, ed., *Latin America in the 1940s: War and Postwar Transitions* (Berkeley: University of California Press, 1994), 218–19.

60. Daniel Rodríguez Lamas, *Rawson/Ramírez/Farrell* (Buenos Aires: Centro Editor de América Latina, 1983), 33–34; O. Edmund Smith, *Yankee Diplomacy: U.S. Intervention in Argentina* (Westport, Conn.: Greenwood Press, 1980), 92–93; Woods, *Roosevelt Foreign-Policy Establishment*, 147–49, 155; Department of External Affairs (Canada), "The United States, United Kingdom and Argentina," 15 August 1944, 1607–40C (pt. 6), vol. 2856, RG 25, AC.

61. Woods, *Roosevelt Foreign-Policy Establishment*, 184–87; Tulchin, *Argentina and the United States*, 90–91; Peterson, *Argentina and the United States*, 437–39; Marisol Saavedra, "Argentina dentro de sistema interamericano entre 1945 y 1955," Serie de Investigaciones del IDISCO (Buenos Aires: Instituto de Investigación en Ciencias Sociales, Universidad Del Salvador): 4; No. 30,

K. P. Kirkwood to Secretary of State for External Affairs, 28 March 1945, 3135–40c, vol. 2955, RG 25, AC.

62. O. Edmund Smith, *Yankee Diplomacy*, 154–60; Tulchin, *Argentina and the United States*, 92; Leonardo Paso, *Del golpe de Estado de 1943 al de 1955/1* (Buenos Aires: Centro Editor de América Latina, 1987), 62–64.

63. Tulchin, *Argentina and the United States*, 94; Juan Archibaldo Lanús, *De Chapultepec al Beagle: Política exterior argentina 1945–1980* (Buenos Aires: Emecé Editores, 1984), 36–37; Roger Gravil, "El Foreign Office vs. el Departamento de Estado: Reacciones británicas frente al *Libro Azul*," *Ciclos* 5, no. 9 (1995): 77–88; No. 3758, Department of External Affairs (Canada), "Argentina—War and Elections," 16 March 1945, 1607–40c (pt. 6), vol. 2856, RG 25, AC.

64. Carlos Escudé, *La Argentina vs. las grandes potencias* (Buenos Aires: Editorial Belgrano, 1986), 20, 29; Glenn J. Dorn, "'Bruce Plan' and Marshall Plan: The United States's Disguised Intervention against Peronism in Argentina, 1947–1950," *International History Review* 21, no. 2 (June 1999): 331–51.

65. "United States Long-Range Policy towards Argentina," 27 April 1944, box 10, Office of Intelligence Research, Division of Research for the American Republics, Lot Files, RG 59, NA; No. 133, K. P. Kirkwood to Secretary of State for External Affairs, 7 July 1944, 3134–40c (pt. 3), vol. 2954, RG 25, AC.

66. Lila Caimari and Mariano Ben Plotkin, *Pueblo contra antipueblo: La politización de identidades nopolíticas en la Argentina peronista (1943–1955)* (Buenos Aires: Instituto de Investigación en Ciencias Políticas, 1997), 20.

67. Cámara de Senadores de la Nación, *Diario de Sesiones, 1949* (Buenos Aires, 1949), 1:37; Noemí M. Girbal-Blacha, "Dichos y hechos del gobierno peronista (1946–55): Lo fíctico y lo simbólico en el análisis histórico," *Entrepasados*, Year 6, No. 13 (1977): 66–68; Mariano Plotkin, *Mañana es San Perón: Propaganda, rituales políticos y educación en el régimen peronista (1946–1955)* (Buenos Aires: Ariel, 1993), 128, 139–40.

68. Advertisements from *Para Tí*, 30 September 1941.

69. "La colección de Ann Miller," *Leoplán* (4 October 1944): 28; "Las rodillas de Rita Hayworth," *Leoplán* (4 October 1944): 29; "Joan Crawford ama la actividad," *Leoplán* (1 March 1944); Edward Green, "Campo abierto para Luis Bromfield," *Leoplán* (5 June 1946): 8–10, 107; Alfonso S. Betancourt, "Fenimore Cooper: Novelista de la juventud," *Leoplán* (5 June 1946): 14–15; "Ingenua . . . y vampiresa," *Leoplán* (21 August 1946): 21; "Las piernas mas bellas de Hollywood," *Leoplán* (21 August 1946): 20.

4. Cold War and the End of Argentine Democracy, 1947–1961

1. Hugo Gambini, *La primera presidencia de Perón* (Buenos Aires: Centro Editor de América Latina, 1983), 68–72.
2. Stephen G. Rabe, *The Most Dangerous Area in the World: John F. Kennedy Confronts Communist Revolution in Latin America* (Chapel Hill: University of North Carolina Press, 1999), 61.
3. Carlos Castro Madero and Esteban A. Takacs, *Política nuclear argentina: Avance o retroceso?* (Buenos Aires: Libreria "El Ateneo" Editorial, 1991), 28–29.
4. Julio César Carasales, *El desarme de los desarmados* (Buenos Aires: Editorial Pleamar, 1987), 22, 107–9; "Venture of the Atomic Age," *Times* (London), 13 June 1955; Melvyn P. Leffler, *A Preponderance of Power: National Security, the Truman Administration, and the Cold War* (Stanford, Calif.: Stanford University Press, 1992), 114–16; Leonard Weiss, "Atoms for Peace and Nuclear Proliferation," in *Atoms for Peace: An Analysis after Thirty Years*, ed. Joseph F. Pilat, Robert E. Pendley, and Charles K. Ebinger (Boulder, Colo.: Westview Press, 1985), 131–41.
5. Fernando E. Barrera Oro, *Logística Conjunta* (Buenos Aires: Círculo Militar, 1963), 107.
6. Fernando A. Milia, *Estrategia y poder militar* (Buenos Aires: Instituto de Pubilcaciones Navales, 1965), 129.
7. Raúl A. Boix-Amat, interview with author, 26 May 1999.
8. Zulema del Valle Marzoratti, "Análisis de *Mundo Atómico:* Revista de divulgación científica," *Saber y Tiempo* (July–December 1998): 88; Mario Mariscotti, *El secreto atómico de Huemul: Crónica del origen de la energía atómica en la Argentina* (Buenos Aires: Sudamericana-Planeta, 1987), 96–108.
9. Mariscotti, *El secreto atómico de Huemul,* 22–23.
10. Ibid., 27; "Sensacional anuncio de Perón: La Argentina ha logrado el dominio de la energía atómica," *Democracia,* 25 March 1951.
11. Sergio Ceron, Jorge Bertoni, Mario Orsollini, and Pedro Stipanicic, "O programa nuclear argentino," *Política e Estrategia* 2, no. 4 (October–December 1984): 185.
12. "U.S. Financier's Plans in Argentina," *Times* (London), 7 September 1954.
13. Argentine Foreign Relations Ministry, "Instrucciones para la delegación argentina que actuara en la reunión de la junta de gobernadores del or-

ganismo internacional de energía atómica que se reunira en Viena, el martes 11 de junio de 1963," n.d., file 480, Junta de Gobernadores OIEA, 1963, MRE.

14. No. 103, Department of International Organizations and Treaties to Subsecretary of Foreign Relations, 5 May 1961, "Acuerdo con Euratom—Creación de una Embajada," file 807, Euratom, MRE; "En Chamical, La Rioja, hubo otros lanzamientos de cohetes," *La Prensa,* 28 August 1963.

15. Tulchin, *Argentina and the United States,* 104–8; "Probable Developments in Argentina," 9 March 1954, NIE-91-54, FRUS, 1952–54, 4:463; Laura Ruiz Jiménez, "Peronism and Anti-Imperialism in the Argentine Press: 'Braden or Perón' Was Also 'Perón Is Roosevelt,'" *Journal of Latin American Studies* 30, no. 3 (October 1998): 551–71.

16. Tulchin, *Argentina and the United States,* 107; Bruce to Truman, 17 November 1948, 711.35/111748; Pinedo to Armour, 20 May 1948, 835.50/52048, RG 59, NA.

17. Peterson, *Argentina and the United States,* 476–79; No. 331, U.S. Ambassador in Buenos Aires to Department of State, 28 April 1948, 711.35/4-2848; Department of State, Memorandum, 19 May 1949, 811.503135/5-1949, RG 59, NA; Norma Delia Gonzalez, "U.S.-Argentine Relations in the 1950s," (PhD diss., University of Massachusetts, 1992), 57; Carlos Escudé, *Gran Bretaña, Estados Unidos y la declinación argentina, 1942–1949* (Buenos Aires: Editorial Belgrano, 1983), 322–30.

18. Tulchin, *Argentina and the United States,* 109–10; Mario Rapoport, "Argentina and the Soviet Union: History of Political and Commercial Relations (1917–1955)," *Hispanic American Historical Review* 66, no. 2 (1986): 247–51; Mario Rapoport, "La Argentina y la Guerra Fría: Opciones económicas y estratégicas de la apertura hacia el Este, 1955–1973," *Ciclos* 5, no. 8 (1995): 92–122.

19. Perón to Miller, 28 June 1950, box 1, Records of Assistant Secretary of State for Latin America Edward G. Miller, 1949–53, entry 1130, Lot Files, RG 59, NA; Stephen Rabe, *Eisenhower and Latin America: The Foreign Policy of Anticommunism* (Chapel Hill: University of North Carolina Press, 1988), 20–23; Peterson, *Argentina and the United States,* 480–81.

20. Stanton Griffis, U.S. ambassador in Argentina, to Arthur G. Miller Jr., 19 December 1949; Miller to Griffis, 28 December 1949, box 1, Records of Assistant Secretary of State for Latin America Edward G. Miller, 1949–53, entry 1130, Lot Files, RG 59, NA.

21. U.S. Department of State, "State Department Recommendation to the Ex-

port-Import Bank That It Give Sympathetic Consideration to Argentina's Request for Assistance to Finance Essential Imports from the United States," December 1949, box 1, Records of Assistant Secretary of State for Latin America Edward G. Miller, 1949–53, entry 1130, Lot Files, RG 59, NA.

22. Ibid.; U.S. Department of State, Memorandum of Conversation, "Financial Assistance to Argentina," 2 December 1949; No. 111, L. D. Mallory, U.S. counselor in Argentina, to Secretary of State, 1 March 1950, box 1, Records of Assistant Secretary of State for Latin America Edward G. Miller, 1949–53, entry 1130, Lot Files, RG 59, NA.

23. Miller to Lester D. Mallory, U.S. chargé d'affaires in Argentina, 12 September 1949, box 1, Records of Assistant Secretary of State for Latin America Edward G. Miller, 1949–53, entry 1130, Lot Files, RG 59, NA; Mario Rapoport and Claudio Spiguel, *Estados Unidos y el peronismo: La política norteamericana en la Argentina, 1949–1955* (Buenos Aires: Grupo Editor Latinoamericano, 1994), 55–63.

24. Marta Merkin, Juan José Panno, Gabriela Tijman, and Carlos Ulanovsky, *Días de Radio: Historia de la Radio argentina* (Buenos Aires: Espasa Calpe, 1995), 142, 174; Dóris Fagundes Haussen, *Rádio e política: Tempos de Vargas e Perón* (Porto Alegre: Pontifícia Universidade Católica do Rio Grande do Sul, 1997), 114–17.

25. Walter Thiers, *El jazz criollo y otras yerbas (1945–1998)* (Buenos Aires: Corregidor, 1999), 51–67; Oscar A. Troncoso, "Las nuevas formas del ocio," in *Buenos Aires: Historia de cuatro siglos*, ed. José Luis Romero and Luis Alberto Romero (Buenos Aires: Altamira, 2000), 2:287.

26. Carlos Ulanovsky, Silvia Itkin, and Pablo Sirvén, *Estamos en el aire: Una historia de la televisión en la Argentina* (Buenos Aires: Planeta, 1999), 11, 13, 17; Sylvia Saítta and Luis Alberto Romero, *Grandes entrevistas de la historia Argentina (1879–1988)* (Buenos Aires: Aguilar, 1998), 217.

27. Ulanovsky, Itkin, and Sirvén, *Estamos en el aire*, 78, 85, 93, 95; Donald S. Castro, "The Massification of the Tango: The Electronic Media, the Popular Theatre, and the Cabaret from Contursi to Perón, 1917–1955," *Studies in Latin American Popular Culture* 18 (1999): 93–114.

28. Ulanovsky, Itkin, and Sirvén, *Estamos en el aire*, 162.

29. "Argentine House Passes Bill Imposing Local Dubbing on Foreign Telepix," *Variety*, 24 November 1965, 35; Kerry Seagrave, *American Television Abroad: Hollywood's Attempt to Dominate World Television* (Jefferson, N.C.: McFarland, 1998), 91–92.

30. Rosana Guber, "Occidente desde la Argentina: Realidad y ficción de una oposición constructiva," in *Cuando opinar es actuar: Revistas argentinas del siglo XX*, ed. Noemí Girbal-Blacha and Diana Quatrocchi-Woisson (Buenos Aires: Academia Nacional de la Historia, 1999), 362; Jorge B. Rivera, *El auge de la industria cultural (1930–1955)* (Buenos Aires: Centro Editor de América Latina, 1968), 593.

31. Marilyn S. Kushner, "Exhibiting Art at the American National Exhibition in Moscow," *Journal of Cold War Studies* 4 (2002): 6–26; Tony Shaw, "The Politics of Cold War Culture," *Journal of Cold War Studies* 3 (2001): 59–76.

32. José Gómez Sicre, interview, *Del Arte* (Buenos Aires), no. 4 (October 1961): 1, 3.

33. Andrea Giunta, *Vanguardia, internacionalismo y política: Arte argentino en los años sesenta* (Buenos Aires: Paidós, 2001), 249–50; James P. Brennan, *El Cordobazo* (Buenos Aires: Sudamericana, 1996), 56; Elizabeth A. Cobbs, *The Rich Neighbor Policy: Rockefeller and Kaiser in Brazil* (New Haven: Yale University Press, 1992), 190–234.

34. Stephen M. Streeter, "The Myth of Pan Americanism: U.S. Policy toward Latin America during the Cold War, 1954–1963," in *Beyond the Ideal: Pan Americanism in Inter-American Affairs*, ed. David Sheinin (Westport, Conn.: Praeger Publishers, 2000), 167–69.

35. "La bienal de Córdoba en Washington," *Revista Américas* (Washington) 15, no. 3 (March 1963): 16–17.

36. U.S Department of State, Memorandum, "Conference with President Perón on Monday, February 20, 1950," 20 February 1950; U.S. Department of State, Memorandum, "Argentina," 14 July 1950; Griffis, Memorandum for Reference, 31 August 1950; Griffis to Miller, 1 September 1950; Miller, "Thoughts for your Reply to Questions Regarding Perón's Third Position and His Attacks on Capitalism," n.d. [December 1950], box 1, Records of Assistant Secretary of State for Latin America Edward G. Miller, 1949–53, entry 1130, Lot Files, RG 59, NA.

37. Miller, "Suggestions for Argentine Policy," 11 March 1952, box 1, Records of Assistant Secretary of State for Latin America Edward G. Miller, 1949–53, entry 1130, Lot Files, RG 59, NA; "El fogoso Mr. Miller y 'South America,'" *Democracia*, 23 January 1952.

38. Miller, "Suggestions for Argentine Policy."

39. Andrés Cisneros and Carlos Escudé, *Historia general de las relaciones exteriores de la República Argentina* (Buenos Aires: Nuevohacer, 1998–2003),

13:97–104; Rabe, *Eisenhower and Latin America*, 6–7, 73–75; Thomas Zoumaras, "The Path to Panamericanism: Eisenhower's Foreign Economic Policy toward Latin America" (PhD diss., University of Connecticut, 1987), 20–23; Rapoport and Spiguel, *Estados Unidos y el peronismo*, 151–54.

40. Rabe, *Eisenhower and Latin America*, 66–67; Milton Eisenhower, *The Wine Is Bitter: The United States and Latin America* (Garden City, N.Y.: Doubleday, 1963), 187–95.

41. Gonzalez, "U.S.-Argentine Relations," 130–33; "Improvement in Relations with Argentina," 19 November 1953, 735.00/11–1953, FRUS, 1952–54, 4:451–52; "Memorandum of Conversation, by Henry Dearborn of the Office of South American Affairs," 29 September 1953, 835.10/9–2953, FRUS, 1952–54, 4:448.

42. "Memorandum of Conversation," 4:135–37; Department of State, Memorandum, 22 March 1954, 835.33/3–2254; Department of State, Memorandum, 25 June 1954, 835.2614/6–2554, RG 59, NA; Rapoport and Spiguel, *Estados Unidos y el peronismo*, 175–82.

43. Perón to Milton Eisenhower, 27 June 1954; U.S. Department of State, Memorandum of Conversation, "Argentine Reaction to the Guatemalan Problem," 10 June 1954; Albert F. Nufer, U.S. ambassador in Argentina, to Henry F. Holland, 24 June 1954, box 1, Records of Assistant Secretary of State for Inter-American Affairs Henry F. Holland, 1953–56, entry 1132, Lot Files, RG 59, NA; "Memorandum of Conversation by the Assistant Secretary of State for Inter-American Affairs (Holland)," 19 September 1954, Holland Files, Lot 52 D, 1954–56, FRUS, 1952–54, 4:474–75.

44. Gonzalez, "U.S.-Argentine Relations," 155–67; Department of State, Memorandum, 24 March 1954, 611.35/3–2454, RG 59, NA.

45. Gonzalez, "U.S.-Argentine Relations," 176–82; Rabe, *Eisenhower and Latin America*, 77; Zoumaras, "Path to Panamericanism," 164.

46. Drumm to Holland, 14 April 1955, box 1, Records of Assistant Secretary of State for Inter-American Affairs Henry F. Holland, 1953–56, entry 1132, Lot Files, RG 59, NA.

47. Zoumaras, "Path to Panamericanism," 201–5; Hipólito Paz, *Memorias: Vida pública y privada de un argentino en el siglo XX* (Buenos Aires: Planeta, 1999), 255–59; "Memorandum of a Conversation, Department of State, Washington, June 27, 1955," 735.00/6–2755, FRUS, 1955–57, 7:367–69; Alejandro Horowicz, *Los cuatro peronismos* (Buenos Aires: Editorial Legasa, 1985), 132–33.

48. U.S. Department of State, Memorandum of Conversation, "Consultation on Various Economic and Political Problems," 7 March 1956, box 1, Records of Assistant Secretary of State for Inter-American Affairs Henry F. Holland, 1953–56, entry 1132, Lot Files, RG 59, NA; Rapoport and Spiguel, *Estados Unidos y el peronismo*, 218–19.

49. U.S. Department of State, Memorandum of Conversation, "Developments in Argentina," 25 April 1956, box 1, Records of Assistant Secretary of State for Inter-American Affairs Henry F. Holland, 1953–56, entry 1132, Lot Files, RG 59, NA; James F. Siekmeier, *Aid, Nationalism and Inter-American Relations — Guatemala, Bolivia and the United States, 1945–1961* (Lewiston, N.Y.: Edwin Mellen, 1999), 156–57.

50. Gonzalez, "U.S.-Argentine Relations," 218–24; "Memorandum from the Deputy Assistant Secretary of State for Inter-American Affairs (Lyon) to the Secretary of State," 7 October 1955, 735.00/10–755, FRUS, 1955–57, 7:381–82.

51. Gonzalez, "U.S.-Argentine Relations," 236–39; Peterson, *Argentina and the United States*, 505.

52. Department of State, "U.S. Policy toward Argentina," 27 October 1957, box 1, Subject Files, 1957–59, Records of Assistant Secretary of State for Inter-American Affairs Roy R. Rubottom, entry 1135, Lot Files, RG 59, NA.

53. Willard L. Beaulac, U.S. ambassador to Argentina, to Rubottom, 29 April 1957, box 1, Subject Files, 1957–59, Records of Assistant Secretary of State for Inter-American Affairs Roy R. Rubottom, entry 1135, Lot Files, RG 59, NA.

54. Beaulac to Mark A. May, chairman, U.S. Advisory Commission on Information, 4 November 1957, box 1, Subject Files, 1957–59, Records of Assistant Secretary of State for Inter-American Affairs Roy R. Rubottom, entry 1135, Lot Files, RG 59, NA.

55. Gonzalez, "U.S.-Argentine Relations," 287–88; "Memorandum from the Assistant Secretary of State for Inter-American Affairs (Rubottom) to the Secretary of State," 26 February 1958, 735.00/2/2–2658, FRUS, 1958–60, 5:465–66; "Memorandum of a Conversation between the Ambassador in Argentina (Beaulac) and President-Elect Frondizi, Buenos Aires, March 1958," 611.35/3–658, FRUS, 1958–60, 5:468–72.

56. Marcelo Luis Acuña, *De Frondizi a Alfonsin: La tradición política del radicalismo* (Buenos Aires: Centro Editor de América Latina, 1984), 1:105–14; Celia Szusterman, *Frondizi: La política del desconcierto* (Buenos Aires: Emecé, 1998), 113–46.

57. Szusterman, *Frondizi*, 158–90; Julio E. Nosiglia, *El desarrollismo* (Buenos Aires: Centro Editor de América Latina, 1983), 66–76.

58. Cisneros and Escudé, *Historia general*, 11:93–98; Gonzalez, "U.S.-Argentine Relations," 346–49; Carl E. Solberg, *Oil and Nationalism in Argentina: A History* (Stanford, Calif.: Stanford University Press, 1979), 167–68; George Philip, *Oil and Politics in Latin America* (Cambridge: Cambridge University Press, 1982), 411–14; Jorge Landaburu, *Una alternativa en la historia, Frondizi: Del poder a la política* (Buenos Aires: Grupo Editorial Norma, 1999), 423–33; "Memorandum from Viron P. Vaky of the Office of South American Affairs to the Director of the Office of South American Affairs (Bernbaum)," 22 August 1958, 735.00/8–2258, FRUS, 1958–60, 5:503–7; No. 424, Felipe A. Espil, Argentine ambassador, Rio de Janeiro, to Carlos Alberto Florit, Argentine foreign minister, 30 July 1958, 51, Contratos Petrolíferos, MRE.

59. Gonzalez, "U.S.-Argentine Relations," 352–53.

60. Ibid., 354–57; "Memorandum from Viron P. Vaky of the Office of South American Affairs to the Director of the Office of South American Affairs (Bernbaum)," 8 August 1958, ARA/EST Files: Lot 61 D 34, Export Import Bank Loans, Argentina 1958, FRUS, 1958–60, 5:497–500.

61. Luigi Manzetti, *The International Monetary Fund and Economic Stabilization: The Argentine Case* (Westport, Conn.: Praeger, 1991), 37–52.

62. González, "U.S.-Argentine Relations," 365–71; Arturo Frondizi, *Política económica nacional* (Buenos Aires: Ediciones Arayú, 1963), 149–52; "Memorandum of a Conversation, White House, Washington, 22 January 1959," 735.11/1–2259, FRUS, 1958–60, 5:533–35.

63. "Memorandum of a Conversation, Department of State, Washington, April 7, 1959," 735.5-MSP/4–759, FRUS, 1958–60, 5:552–554. Oscar Camilión, *Memorias políticas: De Frondizi a Menem, 1956–1996* (Buenos Aires: Planeta, 2000), 25–26; Roberto Cortés Conde, *Progreso y declinación de la economía argentina* (Buenos Aires: Fondo de Cultura Económica, 1998), 72–73; Pablo Gerchunoff and Lucas Llach, *El ciclo de la ilusión y el desencanto: Un siglo de políticas económicas argentinas* (Buenos Aires: Ariel, 1998), 278–81.

64. H. F. Propps, "Argentine Desire That the United States Remove Restrictions on the Importation of Argentine Meat," 20 September 1961; R. J. Morris, "Argentine Desire That the United States Intercede with France and Germany on the Subject of Meat and Grain Imports," 20 September 1961, Bureau of Inter-American Affairs, Argentina, 1956–64, box 3, entry 3167, Lot Files, RG 59, NA.

65. Cisneros and Escudé, *Historia general,* 13:260–76; Gonzalez, "U.S.-Argentine Relations," 389–90; "Memorandum of a Conversation, San Carlos de Bariloche, February 28, 1960, 5:30 PM," Conference Files, Lot 64 D 559, CF 1596, FRUS, 1958–60, 5:620–21; Rabe, *Most Dangerous Area,* 60.

66. J. G. Day, "Castro-Communism and OAS Action," 26 September 1961, Bureau of Inter-American Affairs, Argentina, 1956–64, box 3, entry 3167, Lot Files, RG 59, NA; Camilión, *Memorias políticas,* 53–59.

67. Rabe, *Most Dangerous Area,* 148–53; W. Michael Weis, "The Twilight of Pan-Americanism: The Alliance for Progress, Neo-Colonialism, and Non-Alignment in Brazil, 1961–1964," *International History Review* 23, no. 2 (June 2001): 324–29. See also Edwin McCammon Martin, *Kennedy and Latin America* (Lanham, Md.: University Press of America, 1994) and Jerome Levinson and Juan de Onís, *The Alliance That Lost Its Way* (Chicago: Quadrangle Books, 1970).

68. J. G. Day, "Argentine Relations with the United States and the West," 26 September 1961, Bureau of Inter-American Affairs, Argentina, 1956–64, box 3, entry 3167, Lot Files, RG 59, NA; Jorge C. Carrettoni, *De Frondizi a Alfonsin: El BID, Yacyretá, la Constituyente* (Buenos Aires: Catálogos, 1998), 83–98; "Memorandum from Viron P. Vaky of the Office of South American Affairs to the Assistant Secretary of State for Inter-American Affairs (Rubottom)," FRUS, 1955–57, 7:499–507.

69. Robert A. Potash, *The Army and Politics in Argentina, 1945–1962* (Stanford, Calif.: Stanford University Press, 1980), 329; Nosiglia, *El desarrollismo,* 150–52.

5. The Sixties: Military Ties, Economic Uncertainties

1. María Seoane and Vicente Muleiro, *El dictador: La historia secreta y pública de Jorge Rafael Videla* (Buenos Aires: Sudamericana, 2001), 188; Raúl Jassen, *Seineldín: El ejercito traicionado, la patria vencida* (Buenos Aires: Editorial Verum y Militia, 1989), 180–92.

2. Michael T. Klare and Peter Kornbluh, "The New Interventionism: Low-Intensity Warfare in the 1980s and Beyond," in *Low Intensity Warfare: Counterinsurgency, Proinsurgency, and Antiterrorism in the Eighties,* ed. Michael T. Klare and Peter Kornbluh (New York: Pantheon, 1988), 10–12; Saul Landau, *The Dangerous Doctrine: National Security and U.S. Foreign Policy* (Boulder, Colo.: Westview Press, 1988).

3. Argentine Armed Forces, "Sintesis de la exposición sobre la subversión en la Argentina," 1976, AGD; Daniel H. Mazzei, *Medios de comunicación y golpismo* (Buenos Aires: Grupo Editor Universitario, 1997), 23–26; Alain Rouquié, *Poder militar y sociedad política en la Argentina* (Buenos Aires: Emecé, 1984), 154–55; Horacio L. Veroni, *Estados Unidos y las fuerzas armadas en América Latina* (Buenos Aires: Editorial Periferia, 1971); "Guerrilleros: Los problemas de la seguridad nacional," *Primera Plana*, 5 May 1964, 8–10.

4. "Misión criolla en Vietnam," *La Nación*, 2 September 2001; No. 67, William H. Rodgers, acting public affairs officer, USIS, Buenos Aires, to USIA, 25 March 1968, "Vietnam Poll by A&C Investigación," AR-I-68, box 1, Office of Research, Field Research Reports, 1953–82, entry 1007B, RG 306, NA; A659, John David Lodge, U.S. ambassador, Buenos Aires, to Department of State, 20 March 1968, POL 23-8 ARG, CDF 1967–69, RG 59, NA.

5. Villegas, "Estudio de Estado Mayor," Cartas de Situación, 1969, AGD.

6. Fernando A. Milia, *Estrategia y poder militar* (Buenos Aires: Instituto de Publicaciones Navales, 1965), 128–29; Oscar Enrique Jardel, *Algunas nociones sobre aviación de ejercito* (Buenos Aires: Circulo Militar, 1960).

7. Rabe, *Most Dangerous Area*, 127.

8. Ibid., 129; Joint Chiefs to Kennedy, 30 November 1961, FRUS 1961–63, 12:214–17.

9. Seoane and Muleiro, *El dictador*, 37–38, 43, 165; Rabe, *Most Dangerous Area*, 106.

10. Seoane and Muleiro, *El dictador*, 188–89; Robert A. Potash, *The Army and Politics in Argentina, 1962–1973* (Stanford, Calif.: Stanford University Press, 1996), 46–58.

11. Seoane and Muleiro, *El dictador*, 194; Eduardo S. Bustelo, *El Período político argentino, 1966–1970* (Mendoza: Universidad Nacional de Cuyo, 1974), 31–32.

12. Paul G. Buchanan, "State Corporativism in Argentina: Labor Administration under Perón and Onganía," *Latin American Research Review* 20, no. 1 (1985): 61–95; Potash, *Army and Politics*, 205–7; Gerardo Bra, *El gobierno de Onganía* (Buenos Aires: Centro Editor de América Latina, 1985), 14–17.

13. Escude and Cisneros, *Historia general*, 13:932; A-1111, McClintock to State Department, 25 April 1964, PET 10-2 ARG; No. 1267, Rusk to U.S. Embassy, Buenos Aires, 23 June 1964; No. 1259, Rusk to U.S. Embassy, Buenos Aires, 20 June 1964, PET 15 ARG, CDF 1964–66, RG 59, NA.

14. Ellwood M. Rabenold Jr., counselor, political affairs, U.S. Embassy, Buenos Aires, "Military Assistance Program," 6 February 1965, DEF 19, CDF 1964–66, RG 59, NA.

15. U.S. Department of State, "Notes on the Tacuara Movement in Argentina," 13 November 1961; Martin to John Slawson, executive vice president, American Jewish Committee, 18 July 1962, entry 3167, Argentina, Bureau of Inter-American Affairs, Lot Files; A-59, Rusk to U.S. Embassy, Buenos Aires, 21 November 1961, 835.411/11-2161; Slawson to Martin, 16 April 1962, 835.411/4-1662, RG 59, NA; "Por que, Para que y por quienes," *Informativo FUCE*, 21 November 1962, 1; Raanan Rein, *Argentina, Israel y los judíos* (Buenos Aires: Ediciones Lumiere, 2001), 248–55.

16. A-452, McClintock to Department of State, 25 September 1962, 835.062/ 9-2562, CDF 1960–63, RG 59, NA.

17. U.S. Department of State, Memorandum of Conversation, 7 May 1964, LAB 3-2 ARG, CDF 1964–66; U.S. Department of State, Meeting with Argentine Trade Union Group, 28 August 1962, entry 3167, Argentina, Bureau of Inter-American Affairs, Lot Files, RG 59, NA.

18. U.S. Department of State, "Progress Report on Free Labor Development in Latin America and Evaluation of Supporting U.S. and Other Programs," 16 December 1964, LAB 2 LA; A154, Martin to USAID, 18 September 1964, LAB 3-2, ARG, CDF 1964–66, RG 59, NA.

19. Streeter, "The Myth of Pan Americanism," in Sheinin, *Beyond the Ideal*, 167–73.

20. Comisión Preparatoria para la Desnuclearización en América Latina (COPREDAL), Discurso del delegado argentino, Embajador Luis Santiago Sanz, acta de la 19a. sesión, 19 de abril de 1966, in Secretaria de Relaciones Exteriores de México, *Desnuclearización militar de América Latina— Documentos (1964–1967)* (México: Secretaria de Relaciones Exteriores, 1967), 4:182.

21. Julio César Carasales, "Las explosiones nucleares pacíficas y la actitud argentina," Colección Documentos de Trabajo, No. 20 (Buenos Aires: Consejo Argentino para las Relaciones Internacionales, 1997), 18–19; Tercer Informe del Grupo de Trabajo 1, Documento COPREDAL/GT. 1/3, 3 de febrero de 1967, in Secretaría de Relaciones Exteriores de México, *Desnuclearización*, 5:197–98; Argentine Foreign Relations Ministry, "Desnuclearización de América Latina," 30 October 1963, AGD; "Adhesión," *Clarín*, 30 April 1963, 7; "Las armas nucleares en América Latina," *La Nación*, 7 May 1963, 4.

22. Asamblea General de las Naciones Unidas, 22 Período de Sesiones, Primera Comisión, sesión 1572a, 22 de mayo de 1968, Documento A/C. 1/PV. 1572, 8–9; "Intervención del representate permanente de la República Argentina, Embajador José María Ruda, ante la primera comisión sobre el tema 28a.

'No-Proliferación de Armas Nucleares,'" 22 May 1968, *Discursos y De-claraciones*, 709, AGD.

23. José María Ruda, "La posición argentina en cuanto al Tratado sobre la No Proliferación de las armas nucleares," *Estrategia*, no. 9 (January–February 1971): 77–79; Carlos Escudé, *El realismo de los Estados débiles: La política exterior del primer Gobierno Menem frente a la teoría de las relaciones internacionales* (Buenos Aires: GEL, 1995), 11–17; "Proscribió Latinoamérica el armamento nuclear," *La Prensa*, 14 February 1967, 2; "Veda nuclear: Objeciones argentinas," *Clarín*, 22 May 1968, 11.

24. "Proyecto innecesario; derrota inevitable," *Clarín*, 23 February 1967, p. 12; Natalio R. Botana, Rafael Braun, and Carlos A. Floria, *El régimen militar, 1966–1973* (Buenos Aires: Ediciones La Bastilla, 1973), 481–84.

25. No. 2, Raúl Quijano, Argentine ambassador to the division, Argentine Foreign Relations Ministry, to F. J. Figuerola, 23 June 1970; Enrique Martinez Paz, Argentine ambassador, Mexico, to Juan B. Martín, Argentine foreign minister, 14 May 1970; No. 62, Julio César Carasales, "Proyecto argentino sobre terrorismo y secuestro en el ámbito de la O.E.A," n.d. [1970], AGD; Potash, *Army and Politics*, 292–95; Pablo Pozzi and Alejandro Schneider, *Los Setentistas: Izquierda y clase obrera, 1969–1976* (Buenos Aires: Editorial de la Universidad de Buenos Aires, 2000), 49–58.

26. "Programa de Política Exterior Justicialista," 12 October 1973, 400, AGD.

27. No. 314, Amadeo to Múgica, 3 June 1961; "Discurso del Dr. Mario Amadeo en la reunión annual del World Affairs Council of Northern California el 7 de mayo 1961," 12, United Nations, AGD.

28. W. Michael Weis, *Cold Warriors and Coups d'État: Brazilian-American Relations, 1945–1964* (Albuquerque: University of New Mexico Press, 1993), 113–27; W. Michael Weis, "Pan American Shift: Oswaldo Aranha and the Demise of the Brazilian-American Alliance," in Sheinin, *Beyond the Ideal*, 147–49.

29. No. 223, Argentine Foreign Minister to Argentine Ambassador in Lima, 22 July 1958, AGD.

30. Ibid.

31. "Conferencia de Punta del Este," 1965, AGD.

32. Lanús, *Chapultepec*, 239–53.

33. "Conferencia de Punta del Este," 1970, AGD.

34. Escudé and Cisneros, *Historia general*, 13:912; "Mensaje del presidente de la Nación, Dr. Arturo Frondizi, pronunciado desde el Salón Blanco de la Casa de Gobierno el día 21 de agosto de 1961," in Arturo Frondizi, *La Argentina*

ante los problemas mundiales (Buenos Aires: Presidencia de la Nación, 1961), 221; Richard N. Goodwin, "Memorandum for the President," 22 August 1961, cited in Michael Ratner and Michael Steven Smith, eds., *Che Guevara and the FBI: The United States Political Dossier on the Latin American Revolutionary* (New York: Ocean Press, 1997), 76–80; Rosendo Fraga, *El ejército y Frondizi* (Buenos Aires: Emecé, 1992), 209–23.

35. Entrevista Presidencial, 26 September 1961, Operación Panamericana, AGD; Department of State, "Memorandum of Conversation," 26 September 1961, 611.35/2-761, CDF 1960–63, RG 59, NA; Rabe, *Most Dangerous Area*, 58.

36. Ibid; "Temas discutidos entre el presidente Frondizi y el Sr. Dillon," 1961, AGD.

37. "Elementos a ser tenidos en cuenta para discurso," 1961, AGD; Lester D. Langley, *America and the Americas* (Athens: University of Georgia Press, 1989), 200–201.

38. Cisneros and Escudé, *Historia general*, 13:922; Stevenson to Secretary of State, 24 March 1962, 735.00/3-162, CDF 1960–63, RG 59, NA; Memorandum from the Assistant Secretary of State for Inter-American Affairs (Martin) to Secretary of State Rusk, 13 April 1962, FRUS 1961–63, 12:374–79; Memorandum from the President's Special Assistant (Dungan) to President Kennedy, 17 April 1962, FRUS 1961–63, 12:382–83.

39. Cisneros and Escudé, *Historia general*, 13:922; Kennedy to Betancourt, 17 April 1962, 611.35/4-262, box 1221, CDF 1960–63, RG 59, NA; Daniel Rodríguez Lamas, *La presidencia de José María Guido* (Buenos Aires: Centro Editor de América Latina, 1990), 52–59; "Briefing Papers for Mr. Goodwin—Argentina," 26 April 1962, Argentina, Bureau of Inter-American Affairs, entry 3167, Lot Files, RG 59, NA.

40. A-352, McClintock to Department of State, 1 June 1962, 835.10/6-162; Rusk to U.S. Embassy, Buenos Aires, 27 July 1962, 835.00/7-1262, CDF 1960–63; Edwin M. Martin to Secretary of State, 18 July 1962; Roger Hilsman, director of intelligence and research, U.S. Department of State, to Secretary of State, "Prospects for Argentina—Political Repression and Military Rule," 27 April 1962, entry 3167, Argentina, Bureau of Inter-American Affairs, Lot Files, RG 59, NA.

41. Memorandum of Conversation, 6 November 1962, FRUS 1961–63, 12:402–3.

42. No. 1577, Memorandum of Conversation, 13 June 1962, 835.10/6-1462, CDF 1960–63, RG 59, NA.

43. No. 101, Rusk to U.S. Embassy, Buenos Aires, 12 July 1962, 835.00/7-1262; A-352, McClintock to Department of State, 1 June 1962, 835.10/6-162; No. 2533,

Rusk to U.S. Embassy, Buenos Aires, 18 June 1962, 835.10/6-1462, RG 59, NA.

44. "Ofrecimiento de la República Argentina de maestros y escuelas normales," 1963, Latin America Series, AGD; No. 1617, Rusk to U.S. Embassy, Buenos Aires, 835.10/1-2463, RG 59, NA.

45. U.S. Department of State, Memorandum of Conversation, 23 January 1963, 611.35/1-463, CDF 1960–63; No. 1344, Rusk to U.S. Embassy, Buenos Aires, 835.00/12-462, RG 59, NA.

46. Antonio E. Castello, *La democracia inestable* (Buenos Aires: Ediciones La Bastilla, 1986), 116–19, 181; "Relaciones con el FMI," *Clarín*, 3 March 1966, 10; Richard D. Mallon and Juan V. Sourrouille, *La política económica en una sociedad conflictiva: El caso argentino* (Buenos Aires: Amorrortu, 1973), 35–42.

47. Raúl García Heras, "El Fondo Monetario, el Banco Mundial, y la política económica del gobierno de Illia, 1963–1966," unpublished manuscript, 2000, 3; "Situación financiera nacional deudas externas," 1970, AGD.

48. Ricardo Illia, *Arturo Illia: Su vida, principios y doctrina* (Buenos Aires: Corregidor, 2000), 76–86.

49. "EEUU: Reducen 20 millones al fondo de progreso social," *Clarín*, 15 November 1963, 3; "Washington: Aprobó el Senado la Ley de Ayuda al Exterior," *Clarín*, 16 November 1963, 3.

50. U.S. Department of State, "Application of Hickenlooper Amendment with Respect to Oil Contract Question in Argentina," 26 March 1964, PET 15-2 ARG, CDF 1964–66, RG 59, NA.

51. "La Argentina pide tratar a fondo el asunto Panamá," *La Nación*, 5 February 1964, 1, 16; "Irá a Panamá una comisión de la OEA," *La Nación*, 9 February 1964, 1, 2.

52. Argentine Foreign Relations Ministry, "Algunos hechos salientes de la acción subversiva castrista en América," 6 May 1965, Latin America, AGD; Fernando Sabsay, *Frondizi, Illia, Alfonsin* (Buenos Aires: Ciudad Argentina/Universidad del Salvador, 2000), 170–71; Juan Archibaldo Lanús, *De Chapultepec al Beagle*, 208–18.

53. "La posición argentina ante los sucesos dominicanos," *La Nación*, 21 May 1965, 1; "Las FF.AA. están preparadas para ir en misión de paz a la República Dominicana," *Clarín*, 15 May 1965, 7; Escudé and Cisneros, *Historia general*, 13:931.

54. "A la crisis y a la posición argentina se refirió el canciller," *La Nación*, 10 May 1965, 1, 8; Miguel Angel Scenna, *Cómo fueron las relaciones argentino-*

norteamericanos (Buenos Aires: Plus Ultra, 1970), 255–56; Carlos E. Azcoitia, *La guerra olvidada: Argentina en la guerra del Congo* (Buenos Aires: Marymar Ediciones, 1992).

55. "Una adhesión a los Estados Unidos," *La Nación*, 6 May 1965, 18; Potash, *Army and Politics*, 213; "Desórdenes callerejos hubo en Rosario por la crisis del Caribe," *La Nación*, 11 May 1965, 4; Castello, *La democracia*, 215–17.

56. U.S. Organization of the Joint Chiefs of Staff, "The Military Establishment in Latin America," August 1969, U.S.–Latin America Project Files, National Security Archive, Washington, D.C., (NSA).

57. Gerardo Bra, "El derrocamiento de Illia," *Todo es Historia* 10, no. 109 (April 1976): 7–26; Mario Antonio Verone, *La caida de Illia* (Buenos Aires: Editorial Coincidencia, 1985), 73–77; No. 10728, Rusk, Memorandum for the President, 12 July 1966, POL 16 ARG, CDF 1964–66, RG 59, NA.

58. "El Ingeniero Alsogaray," *La Razón*, 28 July 1966, 4; "El Ejército comprará en Europa tanques y obuses," *La Prensa*, 1 March 1968, 7; Potash, *Army and Politics*, 156–73.

59. U.S. Department of State, Memorandum for the President, 5 October 1966, Pol 3 IA, CDF 1964–66, RG 59, NA. In January 1966, 47 percent of Argentines had never heard of the Alliance for Progress, and only 20 percent said they approved of it. Instituto IPSA, S. A. "Omnibus III," January 1966, 65–001, entry 1018, Records of Research Projects, 1964–73, RG 306, NA.

60. A941, Martin to Department of State, 28 June 1967; A859, Saccio to Department of State, 1 June 1968, PET 2 ARG; A969, Martin to Department of State, 30 June 1967; U.S. Department of State, "Esso Investments in Argentina," 23 August 1967, PET 5 ARG, box 1326, CDF 1967–69, RG 59, NA.

61. A490, Ellwood M. Rabenold Jr., counselor for political affairs, U.S. Embassy, Buenos Aires, to Department of State, 21 November 1964, LAB 13 ARG; A690, Rabenold to Department of State, 8 March 1966, LAB 6-1 ARG, box 1278; No. 2009, U.S. Embassy, Buenos Aires, to Secretary of State, 29 June 1966, POL 23-9 ARG, box 1893, CDF 1964–66, RG 59, NA.

62. Rusk to U.S. Embassy, Buenos Aires, 8 May 1967, DEF 6 ARG, box 1520, CDF 1967–69, RG 59, NA. See Luis Fernando Ayerbe, *Los Estados Unidos y la América Latina* (La Habana: Fondo Editorial Casa de las Américas, 2001), 134–35.

63. Eusebio González Breard, *La guerrilla en Tucumán* (Buenos Aires: Círculo Militar, 1999); Guillermo Rojas, *Años de terror y pólvora: El proyecto cubano en la Argentina, 1959–1970* (Buenos Aires: Editorial Santiago Apóstol, 2001), 517–50; U.S. Organization of the Joint Chiefs of Staff, "The Military Estab-

lishment in Latin America," August 1969, United States–Latin America Project Files, NSA.

64. No. 831, Edwin Martin, U.S. Ambassador in Buenos Aires, to State Department, 30 August 1966; No. 302, Rabenold to State Department, 8 September 1965, DEF 9, CDF 1964–66, RG 59, NA; Potash, *Army and Politics*, 297–327.

65. A1017, Saccio to Department of State, 7 August 1968, LAB 2 ARG, box 1213, CDF 1967–69, RG 59, NA.

6. Descent to Dictatorship, 1970–1983

1. Sergio Víctor Palma, interview with author, 20 July 2003.

2. Bersuit, *Libertinaje* (Buenos Aires: Universal Music Argentina S. A., 1998); Bersuit, *Hijos del culo* (Buenos Aires: Universal Music Argentina S. A., 2000).

3. Enrique Mono Villegas, *Obras de Ellington, Porter.* . . . (Buenos Aires: Página 12, 2003).

4. Ed Michel, liner notes, Gato Barbieri, *Latino America* (Impulse! 1973).

5. Nat Hentoff, liner notes, Gato Barbieri, *Bolivia* (RCA Victor, 1973); Laurent Goddet, liner notes, Gato Barbieri, *Bolivia* (RCA Victor reissue, 1975).

6. No. A-653, Lodge to Department of State, 6 December 1971, POL 1 ARG, box 2085, Subject Numeric File, 1970–73, RG 59, NA.

7. CIA, "Intelligence Memorandum: Cooperation among Latin American Terrorist and Insurgent Groups," 21 September 1970, Argentina Project, National Security Archive, Washington, D.C. (NSA).

8. "Report of the Meeting of the Executive Committee of the Embassy Narcotics Control Action Committee," 10 August 1973, SOC 11-5 ARG, box 3050; No. 185715, Department of State to U.S. Embassy, Buenos Aires, 12 November 1970, SOC 11-5 ARG, box 3049, Subject Numeric Files, 1970–73, RG 59, NA.

9. Department of State, Memorandum of Conversation, 24 September 1970, POL 15 ARG, box 2087, Subject Numeric File, 1970–73, RG 59, NA.

10. No. 11011, William Rogers to U.S. Embassy, Buenos Aires, 27 January 1971, POL 15 ARG, box 2087, Subject Numeric File, 1970–73, RG 59, NA.

11. No. A-447, Krebs to Department of State, 15 November 1973, POL 2-3 ARG, box 2086, Subject Numeric File, 1970–73, RG 59, NA.

12. See Raanan Rein, *Argentina, Israel, and the Jews: Peron, the Eichmann Capture and After* (College Park: University Press of Maryland, 2002).

13. No. 76737, Lodge to Secretary of State, 6 May 1971, SOC 14 ARG, box 3050, Subject Numeric File, 1970–73, RG 59, NA.

14. A-201, Lodge to Department of State, 30 April 1971; No. 81313, Department of State to U.S. Embassy, Buenos Aires, 11 May 1971, SOC 14 ARG, box 3050, Subject Numeric File, 1970–73, RG 59, NA.

15. No. A-555, U.S. Embassy, Buenos Aires, "Current Level of Anti-Semitism in Argentina," 25 October 1972, SOC 14 ARG, box 3050, Subject Numeric File, 1970–73, RG 59, NA.

16. No. A-290, U.S. Embassy, Buenos Aires, to Department of State, 1 June 1971; No. A-648, U.S. Embassy, Buenos Aires, to Department of State, 6 December 1972; No. A-480, U.S. Embassy, Buenos Aires, to Department of State, 14 December 1973, E2-4 ARG, box 717; U.S. Department of State, Intelligence Note, "Argentina: Inflation and Economic Nationalism Ahead," 19 February 1971, E1 ARG, box 3050, Subject Numeric Files, 1970–73, RG 59, NA.

17. Burns, "Argentine Financial Markets," n.d. [1972], box 105, Arthur Burns Papers, Gerald R. Ford Presidential Library, Ann Arbor, Michigan.

18. No. 71-12, Richard Nixon, "Determination under Section 33(c) of the Foreign Military Sales Act, as Amended," 9 April 1971, DEF 12-5 LA, box 1763, Subject Numeric Files, 1970–73, RG 59, NA.

19. Rogers, Memorandum for the President, 5 March 1971, DEF 12-5 LA, box 1763, Subject Numeric File, 1970–73, RG 59, NA.

20. Marshall Wright, assistant secretary for congressional relations, to Carl Albert, Speaker, House of Representatives, 11 June 1973, DEF 12-5 LA, box 1763, Subject Numeric Files, 1970–73, RG 59, NA.

21. No. A-763, U.S. Embassy, Buenos Aires, to Department of State, LAB 9-1 LA, box 1386, Subject Files, 1970–73, RG 59, NA. See Osvaldo Calello and Daniel Parcero, *De Vandor a Ubaldini/2* (Buenos Aires: Centro Editor de América Latina, 1984), 2:140–50.

22. No. A-025, Lodge to Department of State, 24 January 1972, POL 29 ARG, box 2090, Subject Numeric Files, 1970–73, RG 59, NA.

23. See Peter Kornbluh, *The Pinochet File: A Declassified Dossier on Atrocity and Accountability* (New York: New Press, 2003).

24. No. A-446, Max K. Krebs to Department of State, 19 November 1973; No. A-238, Lodge to Department of State, 14 May 1973; No. 3112, Lodge to Department of State, 4 May 1973, POL 23.8 ARG, box 2090, Subject Numeric File, 1970–73, RG 59, NA.

25. No. 2041, Lodge to Secretary of State, 23 March 1973, POL 14 ARG, box 2092,

Subject Numeric File, 1970–73, RG 59, NA; No. 7322871, Kissinger to President, 20 December 1973, Henry Kissinger Papers, box A2, Ford Library.

26. No. 4021, Lodge to Secretary of State, 6 June 1973, POL ARG-US, box 2092, Subject Numeric File, 1970–73, RG 59, NA.

27. No. 5843, U.S. Embassy, Buenos Aires, to Secretary of State, 8 September 1976, Argentina Project, NSA; "Cuba and Argentina: Latin Odd Couple," *Miami Herald,* 14 July 1981.

28. CIA, 17 January 1974; U.S. Embassy, Buenos Aires, to Director, Federal Bureau of Investigation (FBI), 12 September 1974; U.S. Embassy, Buenos Aires, to Director, FBI, 17 September 1974; U.S. Department of State, General Debriefing of Robert Hill, ambassador to Argentina, 27 November 1974, Argentina Project, NSA; Diego Felipe Medus, chief, North American Department, Argentine Foreign Relations Ministry, "Plan terrorista contra funcionarios oficiales de los Estados Unidos residentes en el país," 23 April 1974, 5(3), AGD; Office of the Vice President, Memorandum of Conversation, 16 January 1974, box 65, Gerald R. Ford Vice Presidential Papers, Ford Library.

29. Calello and Parcero, *De Vandor a Ubaldini,* 160–61; José Pablo Feinmann, *López Rega: La cara oscura de Perón* (Buenos Aires: Legasa, 1987); Ignacio González Janzen, *La triple A* (Buenos Aires: Contrapunto, 1987); White House, Meeting with Robert C. Hill, 3 April 1975, White House Central File, box 3, Ford Library.

30. Diego Felipe Medus, chief, North American Department, Argentine Foreign Relations Ministry, "Plan terrorista contra funcionarios oficiales de los Estados Unidos residentes en el país," 23 April 1974, 5(3), AGD; U.S. Department of State, General Debriefing of Robert Hill, ambassador to Argentina, 27 November 1974, Argentina Project, NSA; A377, U.S. Embassy, Buenos Aires, to Department of State, 16 July 1971, POL 23-8 URG, Anderson Files; Fearey, Memorandum, 5 September 1975, Argentina Project, NSA.

31. CIA, "Latin American Trends," 23 June 1976; No. 178852, Secretary of State to All American Republic Diplomatic Posts, 20 July 1976. See John Dinges, *The Condor Years* (New York: New Press, 2004); Alfredo Boccia Paz, *En los sótanos de los generales* (Asunción: Expolibro, 2002).

32. Graciela Mochkofsky, *Timerman: El periodista que quiso ser parte del poder, 1923–1999* (Buenos Aires: Sudamericana, 2003), 220–29; No. 7691, U.S. Embassy, Buenos Aires, to Department of State, 21 December 1975; Harold H. Saunders, Department of State, to Secretary of State, 10 February 1976, State Argentina Declassification Project (1975–84) (AGD).

33. María Seoane and Vicente Muleiro, *El dictador: La historia secreta y pública de Jorge Rafael Videla* (Buenos Aires: Sudamericana, 2001), 38.
34. No. 209192, Secretary of State to U.S. Embassy, Buenos Aires, 23 August 1976; Joint Chiefs of Staff, Department of Defense, Memorandum, 20 September 1976; No. 6804033476, CIA, "Special Operations Forces (Argentina)," 1 October 1976, Argentina Project, NSA.
35. White House, "Meeting with Foreign Minister César Augusto Guzzetti," 6 October 1976, White House Central File, box 7, Ford Library; "Papers Show No Protest by Kissinger," *New York Times*, 27 August 2004; "Kissinger Cool to Criticizing Juntas in '76," *New York Times*, 1 October 2004.
36. MRE, "Intercambio Comercial Argentino–Estados Unidos," 1983, AGD.
37. Warren Christopher, deputy secretary of state, "Presidential Review Memorandum/NSC-28: Human Rights," 8 July 1977, box 19, Papers of Robert Lipschutz, White House chief counsel, Presidential Papers of Jimmy Carter, Jimmy Carter Library, Atlanta; Kenneth Cmiel, "The Emergence of Human Rights Politics in the United States," *Journal of American History* 86 (December 1999): 1248; Victor S. Kaufman, "The Bureau of Human Rights during the Carter Administration," *Historian* 61 (Fall 1998): 51–66.
38. Robert A. Strong, *Working in the World: Jimmy Carter and the Making of American Foreign Policy* (Baton Rouge: Louisiana State University Press, 2000).
39. Henry A. Kissinger to Edward M. Levi, attorney general, 21 July 1976; Bobbie Greene Kilberg, counsel to the president, Memorandum, 28 September 1976, box 7, Bobbie Greene Kilberg Papers, 1974–77, Ford Library.
40. "Discurso pronunciado por la Señora Elizabeth María Sigel de Semper, Ministra de Educación y Cultura de la Provincia de Corrientes," n.d. [1978]; "Intervención en sesión de la tercera comisión de la Asamblea General del 26 de noviembre de 1980 al tratarse el tema 12 del programa (derechos humanos)," Informe Final, XXXV Período Ordinario de Sesión, Asamblea General, ONU, AGD.
41. "Soviet Pushing to Expand Role in Latin America," *Los Angeles Times*, 27 February 1980; W. Graham Claytor, Deputy Secretary of Defense, "U.S. Policy toward Argentina," 27 October 1980, box 1, National Security Affairs Staff Material, Carter Library.
42. Ezequiel F. Pereyra, director of external politics, Argentine Foreign Relations Ministry, "Entrevista del Director General de Política Exterior con S.E. el Embajador de Cuba," 24 April 1976, AGD.
43. No. 2583, U.S. Embassy, Buenos Aires, to Department of State, 4 April 1977, Argentina Project, NSA.

44. "Actitud de los Estados Unidos de América con respecto a Chile," 1978, AGD; Samuel Blixen, *Operación Cóndor: Del archivo del terror y el asesinato de Letelier al caso Berríos* (Barcelona: Virus Crónica, 1998).

45. Servicio de Inteligencia Naval, "Chile: R/Secretario Ejecutivo de la CDHA," 7 September 1979, AGD; Tom J. Farer, *The Grand Strategy of the United States in Latin America* (New Brunswick, N.J.: Transaction Books, 1988), 110–14; Viron P. Vaky, "U.S. Initiatives to Effect Human Rights Improvements in Argentina," 16 March 1979, AGD.

46. CIDH, *Informe, 1976* (doc. OEA, Ser. L/V/II 40 doc. 5 del 11 de febrero 1977).

47. Ministry of the Interior, "Aspectos básicos para la visita de la Comisión Interamericana para los Derechos Humanos," August 1979, AGD; Elizabeth Jelin, "The Politics of Memory: The Human Rights Movement and the Construction of Democracy in Argentina," *Latin American Perspectives* 21 (1994): 38–58.

48. "Argentine Military Shaken by Rights Report," *Washington Post*, 23 January 1980; Argentine Foreign Minister to Secretary of State, 20 April 1980, AGD.

49. Ministry of the Interior, Memorandum, 1980, AGD; Jessica Tuchman, member of the National Security Council, "Human Rights," 27 January 1977; Zbigniew Brzezinski, "Human Rights Improvements," 16 May 1977, box HU-1, White House Central Files, Carter Library; Mark T. Gilderhus, *The Second Century: U.S.–Latin American Relations since 1889* (Wilmington, Del.: SR Books, 2000), 207.

50. No. 30278, Vance to U.S. Embassy, Buenos Aires, 2 February 1977, Argentina Project, NSA; Raul Castro, U.S. ambassador, Buenos Aires, to Rosenthal, 29 November 1979; Rosenthal to Richard Fairbanks, assistant secretary of state for congressional affairs, 30 April 1982, AGD.

51. Daniel Barberis et al., *Los derechos humanos en el "otro país"* (Buenos Aires: Puntosur, 1987), 42; Marguerite Feitlowitz, *A Lexicon of Terror: Argentina and the Legacies of Torture* (New York: Oxford University Press, 1998), 90; Jacobo Timerman, *Prisoner without a Name, Cell without a Number* (New York: Knopf, 1981), 55, 78.

52. "Testimony of Burton S. Levinson," 28 September 1976, box 1, Domestic Policy Staff Special Projects, Carter Presidential Papers, Carter Library; Feitlowitz, *Lexicon*, 98; Ignacio Klich, "Política comunitaria durante las juntas militares argentines: La DAIA durante el proceso de reorganización nacional," in *El antisemitismo en la Argentina*, compiled by Leonardo Senkman (Buenos Aires: Centro Editor de América Latina, 1989), 278–79.

53. Morton M. Rosenthal, "Headlines and Footnotes: Free Timerman!" *National Jewish Monthly,* April 1979, 1–3; Foxman to President Roberto Eduardo Viola, 18 November 1981, AGD; Joel Barromi, "Israeli Policies toward Argentina and Argentinean Jewry during the Military Junta, 1977–1983," *Israel Affairs* 5 (Autumn 1998): 27–44; Camilión to Liendo, 5 May 1981, AGD.

54. Poder Judicial de la Nación, Suprema Corte, 7 September 1979; Enrique Lopez, Ministerio de Relaciones Exteriores, 2 October 1979; SIDE doc. 205, 16 January 1979, AGD; No. 4811, U.S. Embassy, Buenos Aires, to Department of State, 29 June 1981, AGD.

55. Centra Nacional de Inteligencia, Secretaria General, "Informe sobre la campaña que utiliza los derechos humanos (período del 21 dic al 30 abr 82)," AGD.

56. Argentina sent at least two hundred soldiers to Bolivia in support of the plotters. MRE, "Apreciación Introductoria," 1982, AGD; James J. Blystone, "Meeting with Argentine Intelligence Service," 19 June 1980, SAPD.

57. See Jeanne J. Kirkpatrick, *Leader and Vanguard in Mass Society: A Study of Peronist Argentina* (Cambridge, Mass.: M.I.T. Press, 1971); Jeanne J. Kirkpatrick, *Dictatorships and Double Standards: Rationalism and Reason in Politics* (New York: Simon and Schuster, 1982).

58. No. 27731, Secretary of State to U.S. Embassy, Buenos Aires, 2 February 1982, AGD.

59. Hernández-Campos, Memorandum, 9 April 1982, AGD.

60. MRE, Misión Permanente de la República Argentina ante la OEA, "Evolución y perspectivas en la OEA de los principales temas en relación con la Argentina," 10 November 1983, AGD.

61. Ariel C. Armony, *Argentina, the United States, and the Anti-Communist Crusade in Central America, 1977–1984* (Athens: Ohio Center for International Studies, 1997), 71; "Expert Views Differ on Falklands' Impact in U.S.–Latin American Relations," *Miami Herald,* 21 July 1982.

62. Armony, *Anti-Communist Crusade,* 23; Claudio Díaz and Antonio Zucco, *La ultraderecha argentina* (Buenos Aires: Contrapunto, 1987), 108–26.

63. No. 14, Presidency, Secretariat of Intelligence, "Informe de Inteligencia Periódico," October–December 1981, AGD; A. Glenn Mower Jr., *Human Rights and American Foreign Policy* (Westport, Conn.: Greenwood Press, 1987), 41–44; Joshua Moravchik, *The Uncertain Crusade: Jimmy Carter and the Dilemmas of Human Rights Policy* (Lanham, Md.: Hamilton Press, 1986), 46–47; No.

9972, U.S. Embassy, Buenos Aires, to Department of State, 22 June 1981, AGD.

64. No. 180, Juan Manuel Fauvety, Argentine ambassador to Nicaragua, to Oscar Montes, foreign minister, Argentina, 26 June 1978, AGD.

65. No. 248, Foreign Relations Ministry to Argentine Embassy, Panama, 16 August 1979, AGD.

66. Armony, *Anti-Communist Crusade*, 25, 76–90.

67. Ibid., 130–31.

68. No. 370, Ballestrin to Foreign Relations Ministry, 11 September 1979; No. 310, Ballestrin to Foreign Relations Ministry, 8 August 1979, AGD.

69. No. 799/78, Fauvety to Montes, 10 July 1978; No. 40346, Ballestrin to Foreign Relations Ministry, 2 July 1979, AGD.

70. No. 955, Bianculli to Foreign Relations Ministry, 11 December 1980, AGD.

71. Deapartamento Organismos Internacionales, Memorandum, MRE, 21 December 1982, AGD.

72. Departamento America Latina y Caribe, MRE, Memorandum, 16 February 1983, AGD.

73. MRE, "America Central y Caribe," 1982, AGD.

74. As late as June 1984, the Argentine government shipped $2.5 million in weapons to the Nicaraguan Contras. "Argentina Sends More Weapons to Central America," *Washington Post*, 10 June 1984.

75. Efraim Zadoff, *A Century of Argentinean Jewry: In Search of a New Model of National Identity* (Jerusalem: Institute of the World Jewish Congress, 2000), 18–19; "For First Time, U.S. Court to Weigh Claim of Rights Abuses in Foreign Land," *New York Times*, September 2, 1996; "ACLU SO California Announces Settlement in Landmark Human Rights Case for 85-year-old Tortured in Argentina's 'Dirty War,'" *ACLU Media Advisory*, September 13, 1996.

7. The Forging of a New Relationship, 1984–1999

1. "Los derechos humanos bajan de las estrellas," *El Periodista*, no. 213 (21–27 October 1988): 5; "Derechos humanos en zapatillas," *El Periodista*, no. 209 (23–29 September 1988): 56.

2. "El tope," *El Periodista*, no. 223 (30 December 1988–5 January 1989): 7.

3. Carlos A. Scolari, *Historietas para sobrevivientes: Comic y cultura de masas en los años 80* (Buenos Aires: Colihue, 1999), 259–78.

4. Ulanovsky, Itkin, and Sirvén, *Estamos en el aire,* 433–46, 506; Adriana Schettini, *Ver para crecer: Televisión y política en la Argentina de los 90* (Buenos Aires: Sudamericana, 2000), 186–88; Pablo Sirven, *Quién te ha visto y quién TV* (Buenos Aires: Ediciones de la Flor, 1998), 219–23.

5. MRE, Memorandum, 12 March 1984, AGD.

6. American Jewish Committee, Press Release, 9 April 1984; Anti-Defamation League, B'nai Brith, Press Release, 5 April 1984.

7. Argentine Foreign Relations Ministry, "Reunión de Trabajo con Subsecretario de Estado Kenneth Dam," 6 November 1984; Argentine Foreign Relations Ministry, "Reunión del Subsecretario de Estado Kenneth Dam con el Ministro del Interior," 7 November 1984, AGD; "El auxilio financiero de los Estados Unidos," *Tiempo Argentino* (Buenos Aires), 8 November 1984; "El subsecretario de Estado norteamericano llegará hoy," *La Nación,* 6 November 1984.

8. Argentine Foreign Relations Ministry, "Visita de los legisladores Stephen Solarz y Robert García," 12 January 1984; "Ayuda Memoría Entrevista Canciller salvadoreño y Canciller argentino," n.d. [1985], AGD; "Alfonsín dialogó con diputados de EE.UU.," *Clarín,* 15 December 1984.

9. Foreign Relations Ministry, "Reuniones mantenidas con funcionarios del Consejo de Planeamiento Político del Departamento de Estado los dias 9 y 10 de mayo del corriente año," May 1985, AGD.

10. See Daniel Santoro, *Operación Cóndor II: La historia secreta del misil que desactivó Menem* (Buenos Aires: Letra Buena, 1992); "La novela del Cóndor," *Somos,* no. 748 (28 January 1991): 4–5; Anabella Busso, *Las relaciones Argentina–Estados Unidos en los noventa: El caso Cóndor II* (Rosario, Argentina: CERIR, 1999).

11. MRE, "El Grupo Contadora y la posición argentina en la situación de América Central," n.d., AGD.

12. MRE, "Entrevista del Embajador de la Unión Soviética Sr. Oleg Kvasov," 13 April 1984, AGD.

13. No. 627, García del Solar to Foreign Relations Ministry, 8 March 1984; No. 644, García del Solar to North American Department, Argentine Foreign Relations Ministry, 8 March 1984; "Reunión celebrada enre el Sr. Richard Holwill, Subsecretario de Estado Adjunto para Asuntos Inter-Americanos del Departamento de Estado (EE.UU.) y el Ministro Adolfo Saracho, Director General de Asuntos Nucleares y Desarme de la Cancillería," 30 July 1985; MRE, Dirección General de Asuntos Nucleares y Desarme, "Solicitar

audiencia de Señor Canciller para ex-presidente EE.UU., Señor James Carter," 8 October 1984, AGD.

14. "Reactor atómico a Argelia," *La Razón*, 11 June 1985; "Asistencia nuclear argentina a Argelia," *Clarín*, 28 May 1985.

15. Jorge Coll and Renato Radicella, interview with author, 20 July 2000.

16. MRE, "Argelia," 19 September 1985, AGD.

17. "Argentina Confirms Its Plans for Deeper Nuclear Ties with Cuba," *Nucleonics Weekly*, 11 February 1986; "La conexión cubana," *La Prensa*, 11 December 1987; Alberto H. Costantini, president, CNEA, to Sábato, 18 February 1986; SIDE, "El régimen cubano se halla abocado a la fabricación, en un futuro cercano, de su propia bomba atómica," n.d. [1985]; MRE, Dirección General de Asuntos Nucleares y Desarme, "Cooperación nuclear con Argelia: Provisión de un reactor RA 6," December 1994, AGD.

18. Misión Especial de la República Argentina para Desarme, "Intervención del Jefe de la Delegación Argentina ante la conferencia de desarme Embajador Mário Cámpora en la sesión plenaria del día 9 de febrero 1989"; MRE, Dirección General de Asuntos Nucleares y Desarme, "Ampliar Información Declaración de Nueva Delhi," 27 August 1985; MRE, "Conversaciones con la URSS sobre temas multilaterales," 23 July 1984; MRE, Departamento de Asuntos Nucleares y Desarme, "Militarización del espacio ultraterrestre," 23 November 1984; MRE, "Posiciones de la República Argentina sobre temas nucleares," n.d. [1987], AGD.

19. MRE, "Conversaciones con la URSS sobre temas multilaterales," 23 July 1984, AGD.

20. Cisneros and Escudé, *Historia general* 14:457–58; Roberto Russell, "Un año de política exterior: Las relaciones con Estados Unidos, América Latina y Europa Occidental," in *Argentina en el mundo (1983–1987)*, ed. Rubén M. Perina and Roberto Russell (Buenos Aires: GEL, 1988), 135.

21. Roberto Bouzas and Saúl Keifman, "Las negociaciones financieras externas de la Argentina en el período 1982–1987," in *Entre la heterodoxia y el ajuste: Negociaciones financieras externas de América Latina (1982–1987)*, ed. Roberto Bouzas (Rosario, Argentina: GEL, 1988), 38–40.

22. "Nueva York: La óptica de los bancos," *Somos*, no. 406 (29 June 1984): 57.

23. Argentine Foreign Relations Ministry, "Notas tomadas por el Embajador Lucio García del Solar sobre entrevista presidentes Alfonsín y Reagan, 23.ix.84," n.d., AGD.

24. No. 876, MRE, Dirección de Relaciones Económicas Multilaterales, "Instrucciones para la XVI Asamblea General de la OEA," 27 October 1986, AGD.

25. No. 625, García del Solar, "Visita oficial del Sr. Presidente de la República Raúl Alfonsín a los EE.UU.," 3 June 1985; MRE, "Sanciones econónicas impuestas por E.E.U.U. a Nicaragua," 8 May 1985, AGD.

26. Joseph A. Tulchin, "La política exterior del gobierno democrático y sus relaciones con los Estados Unidos," in *La nueva democracia argentina, 1983–1986*, ed. Ernesto Garzón Valdés, Manfred Mols, and Arnold Spitta (Buenos Aires: Sudamericana, 1988), 293–97; Russell, "Un año," 135–36.

27. Cisneros and Escudé, *Historia general*, 14:460.

28. "Dos para negociar," *El Periodista*, no. 159 (25 September–1 October 1987): 4. In 1988, U.S. president George Bush had pressured the Argentine government to offer a $300 million contract to the Enron Corporation to build an oil pipeline from Neuquén province to Chile. Marcelo Zlotogwiazda and Luis Balaguer, *Citibank vs. Argentina: Historia de un país en bancarrota* (Buenos Aires: Sudamericana, 2003), 239.

29. "Un mito de un ejército nacional," *El Periodista*, no. 145 (19–25 June 1987): 2–3; "Ejército: Asume Caridi y retiran a otros ocho generales," *Clarín*, 21 April 1987.

30. "Nueva Política Militar," *El Periodista*, no. 144 (12–18 June 1987): 2–3; "Sigue la sublevación en Campo de Mayo," *Clarín*, 18 April 1987; "Confusa situación imperaba a medianoche en Campo de Mayo," *La Nación*, 19 April 1987.

31. MRE, Dirección América del Norte, "Evolución de la relación bilateral con los EE.UU. desde la asunción del gobierno constitucional," 23 February 1989, AGD.

32. No. 24, Guido di Tella, Argentine ambassador, Washington, to Domingo Cavallo, Argentine foreign minister, 10 January 1990, AGD; Gregory B. Craig, Williams & Connoly, to Di Tella, 7 January 1990, AGD.

33. Argentine Foreign Relations Ministry, "Objetivos de política exterior con respeto a los EE.UU.," 15 March 1990, AGD.

34. MRE, Dirección América del Norte, "Entrevista del Embajador Todman con el Sr. Canciller," 28 August 1989, AGD.

35. "Transcripción textual de la grabación de la reunión de embajadores, presidida por el Sr. Canciller, que tuvo lugar en Paris los dias 6 y 7 de abril de 1990," AGD.

36. MRE, "Argentina-Brasil," n.d. [1992], AGD.

37. Zothner Meyer, Argentine Foreign Relations Ministry, to Director, North American Division, Argentine Foreign Relations Ministry, 7 June 1990; Argentine Foreign Relations Ministry, "Reunión del Sr. Canciller con la

Representante Comercial de los Estados Unidos, Sra. Carla Hills," 8 June 1990, AGD.

38. No. 115, José Luis Sutera, "Visita del equipo de expertos de los Estados Unidos de América sobre confidencialidad de las salvaguardias nucleares," 30 July 1990; Dirección América del Norte, "Questiones tratadas en la V ronda de consultas bilaterales en materia nuclear entre la Argentina y los EE.UU.," 23 May 1990; Guillermo Jacovella, "Reciente reunión planeamiento político entre representantes diplomáticos de alto nivel del Brasil y de Argentina," 23 August 1991, AGD.

39. See Carlos Escudé, *Realismo periférico: Fundamentos para la nueva política exterior argentina* (Buenos Aires: Planeta, 1992); Roberto Russell, *La política exterior argentina en el nuevo orden mundial* (Buenos Aires: FLACSO, 1992); David H. Martin and David Argue, *Nuclear Sunset: The Economic Costs of the Canadian Nuclear Industry* (Ottawa: Campaign for Nuclear Phaseout, 1996).

40. See Carlos Escudé, *Estado del mundo: Las nuevas reglas de la política internacional vistas desde el Cono Sur* (Buenos Aires: Ariel, 1999), and Carlos Escudé, *Foreign Policy Theory in Menem's Argentina* (Gainesville: University of Florida Press, 1977); Federico Beltrán Villegas, Dirección de Seguridad Internacional y Asuntos Nucleares, Argentine Foreign Relations Ministry, to Argentine Embassy, Washington, 25 April 1993, AGD.

41. MRE, "Reseña de la entrevista mantenida entre la presidente de la Comisión Nacional de Energía Atómica de la República Argentina, Dra. Emma Pérez Ferreira, y el presidente de la Atomic Energy Organization of Iran, Dr. Reza Amrollahi," 20 September 1988, AGD.

42. MRE, "Entrevista Sr. Canciller con Embajador Kennedy," 16 January 1992, AGD; MRE, "Embarque de combustible nuclear a Iran," 10 April 1992, AGD; "Washington cancela una exportación argentina," *Página 12,* 2 February 1992.

43. MRE, "Conversación INVAP S.E.—General Atomics," 16 June 1992, MRE.

44. MRE, "Conversaciones con los Estados Unidos de América sobre comercio de bienes y tecnologias estratégicas," 5 May 1992, AGD.

45. No. 011178/90, Di Tella to Argentine Foreign Relations Ministry, 25 September 1990, AGD; Cisneros and Escude, *Historia general,* vol. 15, electronic edition; "Elogió Bush la determinación del presidente," *La Nación,* 21 September 1990; "La Argentina enviará tropas al Golfo Pérsico," *La Nación,* 13 February 1998; "Menem dijo que la Guerra del Golfo 'va a beneficiar al país,'" *Página 12,* 19 January 1991.

46. MRE, "Informe sobre la visita de la misión expertos del régimen de control de tecnología misilística (MTCR)," 6 May 1992, AGD; Cisneros and Escudé, *Historia general*, vol. 15, electronic edition; "Argentina Gives Missile Parts to U.S. for Disposal," *New York Times*, 7 March 1993; "Todman negociará el final del misil Cóndor," *La Nación*, 15 June 1993; Eduardo Barcelona and Julio Villalonga, *Relaciones carnales: La verdadera historia de la construcción y destrucción del misíl Condor II* (Buenos Aires: Planeta, 1992).

47. MRE, "Discurso del Presidente de la Nación en Davos," 11 December 1992, MRE, "Acontecimientos principales, 1991–1992," 15 December 1992, AGD.

48. Deborah Norden and Roberto Russell, *The United States and Argentina* (New York: Routledge, 2002), 74–75; "Cavalo se sacó un ceero," *Página 12*, 3 September 1993; Carlos Escudé and Andrés Fontana, "Argentina's Security Policies: Their Rationale and Regional Context," in *International Security and Democracy: Latin America and the Caribbean in the Post–Cold War Era*, ed. Jorge I. Domínguez (Pittsburgh: University of Pittsburgh Press, 1998), 55–57.

49. Norden and Russell, *United States and Argentina*, 77.

50. Eugenio Díaz Bonilla, Argentine Embassy, Washington, "El Impacto del NAFTA sobre las exportaciones agropecuarias de la Argentina," 6 January 1993; Díaz Bonilla, "Impacto de NAFTA sobre la Argentina," 14 January 1993, AGD.

51. Cisneros and Escudé, *Historia general*, vol. 15, electronic edition; "AMIA: Quejas ante los Estados Unidos," *La Nación*, 28 September 1995; "Di Tella rechazó las críticas a la Cancillería," *La Nación*, 4 October 1995; Delegación de Asociaciones Israelitas Argentinas (DAIA), *La denuncia: El documento completo presentado al juez Galeano con los hechos y nombres de quienes obstaculizaron la investigación* (Buenos Aires: Planeta, 1997); MRE, "B'nai Brith: Antecedentes y temas que podrían ser de interes para dicha institución," 10 April 1989, AGD.

52. "Argentina Is Pursuing New Lead in Bombing," *New York Times*, 23 November 1997; Norden and Russell, *United States and Argentina*, 82–83.

53. "Apuran la ley contra el lavado de dinero," *La Nación*, 7 February 1998.

54. MRE, "Nueva inserción internacional," n.d. [1994]; MRE, "Reseña del Señor Presidente de la Nación en materia de política exterior entre el 1 de mayo de 1993 y el 1 de mayo de 1994," n.d. [1994], AGD.

55. Zlotogwiazda and Balaguer, *Citibank vs. Argentina*. See also Andrés Oppenheimer, *Ojos vendados: Estados Unidos y el negocio de la corrupción en América Latina* (Buenos Aires: Sudamericana, 2001).

56. No. 86/93, Vignaud to Di Tella, 4 October 1993, AGD.

Epilogue: The Crash of 2001 and Beyond

1. "América Latina, lejos de cifras optimistas," *La Nación*, 19 July 2000; "Los más castigados por el desempleo son los jóvenes," *La Nación*, 19 July 2000.

2. "La resaca de elecciones pasadas pesa en las finanzas provinciales," *Página 12*, 24 July 2001.

3. "El gobierno cumplió tanto que a los del FMI no les quedó qué pedir," *Página 12*, 11 November 2003.

4. "Mejor que pelear es hacer," *Veintitres*, 8 July 2003.

5. "Uruguay: Llegan dólares de EE.UU. y abren los bancos," *Clarín*, 5 August 2002.

6. "Cambio en la estrategia de Bush," *Clarín*, 5 August 2002.

7. "Por la 'unidad' y contra el fondo," *Página 12*, 31 July 2004.

8. "Las 100 empresas más admiradas de la Argentina," *Clarín*, 2 November 2003; "La caída en imagen de los servicios financieros," *Clarín*, 2 November 2003.

9. "No somos mediadores, somos amigos," *Página 12*, 20 July 2004.

10. Ibid.

11. "Crónica de un ajuste no anunciado," *Página 12*, 11 November 2003; "Todos los participantes tuvieron premio," *Página 12*, 9 July 2004.

12. Alejandro Horowicz, "El quinto peronismo," *Veintitres*, 15 July 2005, 24–28; "Economía y política," *Página 12*, 7 August 2005.

Bibliographical Essay

There are a number of works on U.S.-Argentine relations, though relatively few compared to studies on the relations between the United States and the Latin American countries most influenced by Americans in the twentieth century, particularly nations in the Caribbean basin. While there are many more books and articles that address topics relevant to bilateral ties, this chapter is concerned primarily with works that explicitly consider problems in relations between the two countries. The most thorough and comprehensive study of the history of Argentine foreign relations, including U.S.-Argentine ties, is the *Historia general de las relaciones exteriores de la República Argentina* (Buenos Aires, 1998–2003) by Andrés Cisneros and Carlos Escudé. While Cisneros and Escudé wrote a number of chapters in this fifteen-volume study, other authors in the series include the historians Kristin Ruggiero, Francisco Corigliano, and Alejandro Corbacho. Chapters on U.S.-Argentine relations are both more numerous and more significant to the collection as a whole than chapters on other areas of Argentine foreign relations. This is a departure in the tradition of Argentine foreign policy writing, particularly for the pre-1960 period, where authors have tended to emphasize the importance of Argentina's ties to Great Britain.

Funding for this series came about as a result of Escudé's dismissal in 1992 from his position as an adviser to Foreign Minister Guido di Tella. An architect of the Menem-era foreign policy about-face, Escudé was also a vociferous critic of Argentina's position on the Falkland/Malvinas Islands. This latter stand, which questioned Argentine sovereignty over the islands, was too much for the government. It fired him for his outspokenness but quietly rewarded his important work on the withdrawal of Argentina from the nonaligned movement by funding *Historia*. Cisneros was a Menem-era deputy foreign minister. The authors' hostility to Argentina's tradition of diplomatic differences with the United States is palpable and is reflected in the latter chapters of the book.

Harold F. Peterson's *Argentina and the United States, 1810–1960* (Albany, N.Y., 1964) is exceptionally well researched in U.S. diplomatic sources. Joseph S. Tulchin's *Argentina and the United States: A Conflicted Relationship* (Boston, 1990) remains the best synthesis of bilateral relations and a crucial starting point for anyone interested in this topic. Tulchin's bibliographic essay is an important complement to this chapter. There is a valuable collection of treaties by Marita Rosell, *Argentina-Estados Unidos: Acuerdos bilaterales, 1853–2000* (Buenos Aires, 2000). Miguel Angel Scenna's *Cómo fueron las relaciones argentino-norteamericanas* (Buenos Aires, 1970) considers Argentina an important international player in Latin America and beyond, whose interests have been consistently subordinated by the United States to the latter's regional objectives. For their analytical depth, *De Chapultepec al Beagle: Política exterior argentina 1945–1980* (Buenos Aires, 1984) and *Aquel Apogeo* (Buenos Aires, 2002), both by Juan Archibaldo Lanús, are essential reading for those interested in Argentine foreign relations in the twentieth century.

There is very little written on bilateral relations for the period before 1880. René Orsi explicitly frames his *James Monroe contra la independencia argentina* (Buenos Aires, 1983) in the context of the recent Falklands/Malvinas War, arguing in a Marxist theoretical framework that the history of U.S.-Argentine bilateral relations is one of U.S. imperial control with origins in the early nineteenth century. Ernesto J. Fitte's *La agresión norteamericana a las islas malvinas* (Buenos Aires, 1966) is a dense collection of archival documents purporting to show the U.S. role in having denied Argentina sovereignty over the Malvinas/Falkland Islands in the early nineteenth century. Also in this vein is *El mito de Monroe* (Buenos Aires, 1959) by Carlos Pereyra, who explains the Monroe Doctrine as part of an American conspiracy against Argentina and other Latin American countries to facilitate the incursion of British and U.S. capital. To place these works in the context of U.S. diplomacy, readers should see Christian J. Maisch's "The Falkland/Malvinas Islands Clash of 1831–32: U.S. and British Diplomacy in the South Atlantic," *Diplomatic History* 24, no. 2 (2000): 185–209.

Thomas F. McGann's *Argentina, the United States, and the Inter-American System, 1880–1914* (Cambridge, Mass., 1957) and David Sheinin's *Search-*

ing for Authority: Pan Americanism, Diplomacy and Politics in United States–Argentine Relations, 1910–1930 (New Orleans, 1998) stress the place of Pan-American diplomacy in bilateral ties. Sheinin draws on Argentine archival sources, while McGann does not. Luis C. Alén Lascano's *Pueyrredón el mensajero del destino* (Buenos Aires, 1951) is an excellent (albeit excessively celebratory) political biography that concentrates little on the U.S.-Argentine conflict at the Havana Conference in 1928 but provides important historical context for the clash, including Pueyrredón's earlier activity in limiting the influence of foreign multinational corporations in Argentina. Readers will also find useful Alén Lascano's extremely well written *Yrigoyen, Sandino y el panamericanismo* (Buenos Aires, 1986) and *Yrigoyenismo y antipersonalismo* (Buenos Aires, 1986) both of which are indispensable for an understanding of 1920s Argentine government policy toward the United States.

La diplomacia del petróleo (1916–1930) (Buenos Aires, 1976) by C. A. Mayo, O. R. Andino, and F. García Molina and *El general Uriburu y el petróleo* (Buenos Aires, 1985) by F. García Molina and C. A. Mayo remain the strongest analyses of the role of U.S. oil companies in Argentine politics before 1932. Expertly researched in American archival sources, the authors of the first book suggest a possible link between U.S. companies and the architects of the 1930 coup d'état in Argentina, though they stop short of providing evidence of that connection. The second of the two works reaches a stronger conclusion; this was not a coup produced by U.S. corporate interests, but Yrigoyen's fall was clearly precipitated by American oil companies. *Uriburu* was based on primary materials from the Uriburu manuscript collection in the Archivo General de la Nación (Buenos Aires) to which the authors did not have access when they published the first of these works.

There are more studies of bilateral ties during the World War II era than for all remaining chronological periods combined. At the core of this literature are studies on Nazis and Nazism in Argentina during the 1930s and 1940s and the impact of that presence on U.S.-Argentine relations. Ignacio Klich is the author of "La contratación de nazis y colaboracionistas por la Fuerza Aérea Argentina," *Ciclos* 10, no. 19 (2000): 177–216, and *Sobre Nazis y nazismo en la cultura argentina* (Buenos Aires,

2002). He is also the former chair of an Argentine Foreign Relations Ministry committee that was charged, during the 1990s, with uncovering evidence of Nazis and their ill-gotten gains in Argentina during the Second World War. Ronald Newton's masterfully researched *The "Nazi Menace" in Argentina, 1931–1947* (Stanford, Calif., 1992) argues convincingly that the so-called Nazi menace in Argentina was dramatically overestimated by the United States. In *Perón y los Alemanes: La verdad sobre el espionaje nazi y los fugitivos del Reich* (Buenos Aires, 1999), Uki Goñi takes a dramatically different view than Newton, reasoning that, if anything, Americans underestimated the presence and influence of Nazis in Argentina during the 1940s.

Yankee Diplomacy: U.S. Intervention in Argentina (Westport, Conn., 1980) by O. Edmund Smith Jr. is useful for the author's efforts to frame an understanding of U.S.-Argentine relations in the 1940s through a prism of inter-American relations and OAS instruments. Enrique M. Peltzer's *Diez Años de conflicto entre la casa rosada y la casa blanca (1936–1946)* (Buenos Aires, 2002) is interesting in part as the only major monograph on bilateral relations concerning the World War II years that is not organized thematically or methodologically around the war itself. Peltzer highlights failed opportunities in the late 1930s for a conversion of the Monroe Doctrine into a multilateral, Pan-American accord for inter-American cooperation. Deteriorating relations during the war are the result of those failures. Randall Bennett Woods's *The Roosevelt Foreign-Policy Establishment and the "Good Neighbor": The United States and Argentina, 1941–1945* (Lawrence, Kans., 1979) remains the only history of bilateral relations for any period focused on politics, bureaucracy, and power within a U.S. presidential administration. More than twenty-five years after publication, it is still the best study of U.S. diplomacy and decision making with regard to Argentina for any period.

Jack E. Friedman offers a good overview of relations in *Los malos vecinos: Las relaciones entre Estados Unidos y la Argentina durante la Segunda Guerra Mundial* (Córdoba, Argentina, 1999), while Gary Frank interviewed a still bitter Spruille Braden for *Juan Peron vs. Spruille Braden: The Story behind the Blue Book* (Lanham, Md., 1980). Based almost exclusively on published sources, Frank's book is an in-depth account of the 1946

Blue Book debate. Frank understands the conflict as fueled in large measure by the personal animosity that Braden and Perón harbored for one another. Readers should also consult Roger Gravil, "El Foreign Office vs. el Departamento de Estado: Reacciones británicas frente al *Libro Azul*," *Ciclos* 5, no. 9 (1995): 77–88.

Gran Bretaña, Estados Unidos y las clases dirigentes argentinas, 1940–1945 (Buenos Aires, 1981) reflects Mario Rapoport's interest in how Argentine political economy shaped foreign policy. The author explains Braden's pressures on Perón as the U.S. politics of the "garrote." Less important is the author's *Política y diplomacia en la Argentina: Las relaciones con EE.UU. y la URSS* (Buenos Aires, 1986), though the chapters on Argentine-Soviet relations are based on impressive primary research in the United States and are valuable in understanding American attitudes toward a potential Communist menace in Argentina during the early cold war. Carlos Escudé's *Gran Bretaña, Estados Unidos y la declinación argentina, 1942–1949* (Buenos Aires, 1983) is primarily concerned with U.S. economic pressures on Argentina and efforts to isolate it during the 1940s. Glenn J. Dorn's recent scholarship updates Escudé. It expands the context effectively to include problems in U.S. policymaking and inter-American relations. See also "'Bruce Plan' and Marshall Plan: The United States's Disguised Intervention against Peronism in Argentina, 1947–1950," *International History Review* 21, no. 2 (1999): 331–51; "Peron's Gambit: The United States and the Argentine Challenge to the Inter-American Order, 1946–1948," *Diplomatic History* 26, no. 1 (Winter 2002): 1–20; "'Exclusive Domination' or 'Short Term Imperialism': The Peruvian Response to U.S.-Argentine Rivalry, 1946–1950," *The Americas* 61, no. 1 (2004): 81–102; and *Peronistas and New Dealers: U.S.-Argentine Rivalry and the Western Hemisphere, 1946–1950* (New Orleans, 2004).

Estados Unidos y el peronismo: La política norteamericana en la Argentina: 1949–1955 (Buenos Aires, 1994) by Mario Rapoport and Claudio Spiguel picks up where Escudé and Dorn left off. The authors draw on a thorough review of Argentine and U.S. archival sources. They highlight Perón's commercial and diplomatic initiatives in Great Britain and Western Europe as a counterweight to growing U.S. influences in Argentina. They also analyze political and economic change in Argentina that prompted Perón's foreign policy reversals after 1950. Norma Delia Gonzalez's "U.S.-Argentine Relations in the 1950s" (Ph.D. dissertation, University of Massachusetts, 1992) is a thoughtful, original analysis that merits publication as a monograph. Mario Rapoport and Rubén Laufer have written a short study highlighting U.S. military assistance and influence in Argentina and Brazil during the 1960s, *Estados Unidos ante el Brasil y la Argentina: los golpes militares de la década de 1960* (Buenos Aires, 2000).

A rich and growing literature on Argentina's negotiations with the World Bank, the IMF, and other international lenders includes Roberto Frenkel and José Fanelli, "La Argentina y el Fondo en la década pasada," *Trimestre Económico*, no. 213 (1987): 75–131, and Michael Mussa, *Argentina y el FMI: Del triumfo a la tragédia* (Buenos Aires, 2002). Raúl García Heras's *Presiones externas y política económica: El Fondo Monteario y el Banco Mundial en Argentina, 1955–1966* (Buenos Aires, 2003) is outstanding. A handful of useful studies examine U.S. capital investments in Argentina before 1960, including Jaime Fuchs, *La penetración de los trusts yanquis en la Argentina* (Buenos Aires, 1957), and Guillermo Gutierrez, *Penetración imperialista en la Argentina* (Buenos Aires, 1974). Five important analyses of U.S. capital movements and commercial activity in Argentina during the 1960s and 1970s are Naum Minsburg, *Multinacionales en la Argentina* (Buenos Aires, 1976); Jaime Fuchs, *Argentina: Estructura económico-social actual* (Buenos Aires, 1985); Ofelia Marino, "La ley de capitales extranjeros y las protestas de las transnacionales," *Problemas de Economía*, no. 46 (1976): 47–58; Guillermo Martorell, *Las inversiones extranjeras en la Argentina* (Buenos Aires, 1969); and *La presencia y el comportamiento de las empresas extranjeras en el sector industrial argentina* (Buenos Aires, 1978) by Juan V. Sourrouille (an Economy minister during the Alfonsín administration).

Perón-Fidel: Linea directa (Buenos Aires, 2003) by José Bodes and José Andrés López is the intriguing story of Argentina's refusal to support the American blockade of Cuba during the Cámpora and Perón presidencies. Between 1973 and 1976 Bodes was in charge of the Argentine office of the Cuban press agency Prensa Latina. On Argentine-U.S. nuclear relations during the cold war there is very little. Readers should consult Carlos Castro Madero and Esteban A. Takacs, *Política nuclear argentina: Avance o retroceso?* (Buenos Aires, 1991).

María Seoane's *El burgués maldito: La historia secreta de José Ber Gelbard* (Buenos Aires, 1998), María Seoane and Vicente Muleiro's *El dictador: La historia secreta y pública de Jorge Rafael Videla* (Buenos Aires, 2001), and the Asociación Madres de Plaza de Mayo's *Massera: El genocida* (Buenos Aires, 2000) are three remarkable studies documenting in different ways the growing interest of U.S. government agencies in right-wing politics in Argentina in the 1970s. Marcelo Larraquy and Roberto Caballero's *Galimberti: De Perón a Susana, de Montoneros a la CIA* (Buenos Aires, 2000) is eye popping. One of Argentina's most notorious left-wing revolutionaries of the 1970s, Galimberti claims to have been a CIA operative in the 1990s. When Larraquy and Caballero first approached him about cooperating with them on their project, Galimberti calmly offered them a bribe to stop the project. While his testimony should be taken with a grain of salt, the insights into U.S.-Argentine relations by one of Argentina's most prominent political figures of the 1970s are invaluable. On Operación Condor see J. Patrice McSherry, "Tracking the Origins of a State Terror Network: Operation Condor," *Latin American Perspectives* 29, no. 1 (2002): 38–60; John Dinges, *The Condor Years* (New York, 2004); and Samuel Blixen, *El vientre del Cóndor: Del archivo del terror y el asesinato de Letelier al caso Berríos* (Montevideo, Uruguay, 1995).

Ariel C. Armony's fascinating and highly original *Argentina, the United States, and the Anti-Communist Crusade in Central America, 1977–1984* (Athens, Ohio, 1997) charts U.S.-Argentine cooperation in Central America's counterinsurgency warfare. Along with Woods's study of the Second World War period, this work represents the very best in the historical literature of bilateral relations. Like many Argentine Marxist analyses written in the final stages of the *proceso* and in its immediate aftermath, Alejandro Dabat and Luis Lorenzano's *Conflicto malvinense y crisis nacional* (Buenos Aires, 1982) is an overly optimistic period piece. The authors interpret the U.S. failure to avert the British reassertion of control over the Malvinas/Falkland Islands as the end of an era of U.S. imperial domination in Argentina and in South America more generally. J. R. Lallemant's *Malvinas: Norteamérica en guerra contra Argentina*

(Buenos Aires, 1983) is useful as a period-piece document, reflecting the bitterness of many Argentines toward the American unwillingness to back Argentina at the time of the Malvinas/Falklands War. Two excellent analyses of the U.S. place in the war are Richard C. Thornton, *The Falklands Sting: Reagan, Thatcher, and Argentina's Bomb* (Washington, D.C., 1998), and Michael Parsons, "The South Atlantic Conflict of 1982: A Test for Anglo-American Relations," *Revue Francaise de Civilisation Britanique* 12, no. 1 (2002): 85–99.

A number of studies focus on the bilateral ties during the Alfonsín and Menem periods of government. Horacio Verbitsky's *La posguerra sucia* (Buenos Aires, 1985) is a collection of previously published journalistic essays, several of which address Foreign Minister Dante Caputo's foreign policy shifts toward the United States. *Las relaciones Argentina Estados Unidos (1983–1993)* (Buenos Aires, 1993), compiled by Alfredo Rizzo Romano and Artemio Luis Melo, is a thoughtfully assembled collection on a range of factors that prompted changes in bilateral relations in the 1980s and 1990s. This book is particularly rich because of the authors' willingness to step beyond the boundaries of bilateral diplomatic ties in examining the impact of the end of the cold war, the rise of Mercosur, and the debates in Argentine political theory around the questions of realism, neo-idealism, and peripheral realism. *The United States and Argentina: Changing Relations in a Changing World* by Deborah L. Norden and Roberto Russell (New York, 2002) is a dynamic overview of bilateral ties in the 1980s and 1990s, with particular attention paid to foreign policymaking processes and the rising importance of international institutions in U.S.–Latin American relations. A good starting point for understanding the policy shift toward Washington under Menem is the Consejo Argentino para las Relaciones Internacionales's *Argentina y EE.UU.: Fundamentos de una nueva alianza* (Buenos Aires, 1997). This collection of essays by Roberto Russell, Carlos Escudé, Joseph Tulchin, and Raúl Granillo Ocampo, among others, is a mostly favorable assessment of bilateral ties in the 1990s. *Foreign Policy Theory in Menem's Argentina* (Gainesville, Fla., 1997) by Carlos Escudé is a rich analysis of policy shift toward Washington undertaken by Menem (see also Escudé's *Realismo periférico: Fundamentos para la nueva política exterior argentina* [Buenos Aires, 1992]), as is Roberto Russell, *La política exterior argentina en el nuevo orden mundial* (Buenos Aires, 1992).

Carlos Saul Menem's *Estados Unidos, Argentina y Carlos Menem* (Buenos Aires, 1990) is fascinating as a document. Written quickly after the 1989 election, the book lays out Menem's policy strategies toward the United States. While the president signals his interest in Argentina's playing a larger and more cooperative role in the international community, much of what he writes evinces a combative tone in regard to the United States, evoking traditional Peronist stands. On the Argentine nuclear industry, for example, Menem is emphatic in his rejection of U.S. pressures for Argentina to dismantle the sector and his insistence that his government will maintain the nation's nuclear independence. Part of what makes this book particularly striking is how radically the Menem government departed from its nationalist line in the two years that followed, including the decision to radically scale down the nuclear sector.

Based on more than one hundred interviews, Martín Granovsky's *Misión cumplida: La presión norteamericana sobre la Argentina, de Braden a Todman* (Buenos Aires, 1992) reviews the history of U.S. pressures on Argentina, with particular attention to missiles and illicit drugs in the 1980s and 1990s. Rosendo Fraga, Robert Potash, Carlos Ortiz de Rozas, and V. Manuel Rocha reflect the friendly bilateral climate of the 1990s. Their *Argentina–United States of America* (Buenos Aires, 2002) focuses on four presidential meetings that helped advance close bilateral ties— Justo and Roosevelt (1936), Frondizi and Eisenhower, (1960), Menem and Bush senior (1990), and Menem and Clinton (1997). Meetings under more unhappy circumstances, most notably that between Videla and Carter (1976), are not considered.

For strong muckraking examinations of the purported complicity of U.S. investors in the escalating corruption of the Menem era, see Andrés Oppenheimer's *Ojos vendados: Estados Unidos y el negocio de la corrupción en América Latina* (Buenos Aires, 2001) and Marcelo Zlotogwiazda and Luis Balaguer's *Citibank vs. Argentina: Historia de un país en bancarrota* (Buenos Aires, 2003). Paul Blustein's *And the Money Kept Rolling In (and Out): Wall Street, the IMF, and the Bankrupting of Argentina* (New York,

2005) reprises a twenty-five-year-old criticism of the international financial community in regard to third-world debt. Blustein argues that for not having imposed harsh austerity measures on corrupt Argentine governments after 1990, the IMF and Wall Street are directly responsible for the December 2001 crash in Argentina. A less inflammatory and equally informative assessment is Tiziano Vicario's "Argentina y el FMI: Una visión integrada de los factores internos y externos de la crisis," *Ciclos* 14, no. 1 (2004): 49–80.

Several very good studies of the Argentine Condor missile programs originated in the 1970s and were brought to an end in the 1990s. Each makes clear the important roles played by the CIA, the U.S. Armed Forces, the State Department, and other American government agencies in both the origins and collapse of the programs. They include Eduardo Barcelona and Julio Villalonga, *Relaciones carnales: La verdadera historia de la construcción y destrucción del misil Condor II* (Buenos Aires, 1992); Anabella Busso, *Las relaciones Argentina–Estados Unidos en los noventa: El caso Condor II* (Buenos Aires, 1999); and Daniel Santoro, *Operación Cóndor II: La historia secreta del misil que desactivó Menem* (Buenos Aires, 1992).

There is no single study of U.S. cultural impacts on Argentina. Among dozens of valuable works in this area are Osvaldo Soriano, *Rebeldes, soñadores y fugitivos* (Buenos Aires, 1987); Edgardo Cozarinsky, *Borges y el cinematógrafo* (Barcelona, 2002); Laura Podalsky, *Specular City: Transforming Culture, Consumption, and Space in Buenos Aires, 1955–1973* (Philadelphia, 2004) (particularly the section on the advertising boom of the 1960s and 1970s); David Sheinin, "'Its Most Destructive Agents': Pan American Environmentalism in the Early Twentieth Century," in David Sheinin, ed., *Beyond the Ideal: Pan Americanism in Inter-American Affairs* (Westport, Conn., 2000), 115–32; Sergio Pujol, *La década rebelde: Los años 60 en la Argentina* (Buenos Aires, 2002); Carlos A. Scolari, *Historietas para sobrevivientes: Comic y cultura de masas en los años 80* (Buenos Aires, 1999); Adriana Schettini, *Ver para crecer: Televisión y política en la Argentina de los 90* (Buenos Aires, 2000); Pablo Sirven, *Quién te ha visto y quién TV* (Buenos Aires, 1998); Carlos Ulanovsky, Silvia Itkin, and Pablo Sirvén, *Estamos en el aire: Una historia de la televisión en la Argentina*

(Buenos Aires, 1999); Graciela Mochkofsky, *Timerman: El periodista que quiso ser parte del poder, 1923–1999* (Buenos Aires, 2003); Walter Thiers, *El jazz criollo y otras yerbas (1945–1998)* (Buenos Aires, 1999); and Marta Merkin, Juan José Panno, Gabriela Tijman, and Carlos Ulanovsky, *Días de Radio: Historia de la Radio argentina* (Buenos Aires, 1995).

Index